There can be no deep disappointment where there is not deep love.

—Martin Luther King Jr.

Love's a Mystery

Love's a Mystery in Sleepy Hollow, New York
Love's a Mystery in Cape Disappointment, Washington

Love's a Mystery

in

Cape Disappointment
WA

Leslie Gould &
Elizabeth Ludwig

Guideposts

Love's a Mystery is a trademark of Guideposts.

Published by Guideposts Books & Inspirational Media
100 Reserve Road, Suite E200
Danbury, CT 06810
Guideposts.org

Copyright © 2022 by Guideposts. All rights reserved.

This book, or parts thereof, may not be reproduced, stored in a retrieval system, or transmitted in any form or by any means, electronic, mechanical, photocopying, recording, or otherwise, without the written permission of the publisher.

This is a work of fiction. While the setting of Love's a Mystery as presented in this series is fictional, the locations actually exist, and some places and characters may be based on actual places and people whose identities have been used with permission or fictionalized to protect their privacy. Apart from the actual people, events, and locales that figure into the fiction narrative, all other names, characters, businesses, and events are the creation of the author's imagination and any resemblance to actual persons or events is coincidental.

Every attempt has been made to credit the sources of copyrighted material used in this book. If any such acknowledgment has been inadvertently omitted or miscredited, receipt of such information would be appreciated.

Scripture references are from the following sources: *The Holy Bible, King James Version* (KJV). *The Holy Bible, New International Version* (NIV). Copyright ©1973, 1978, 1984, 2011 by Biblica, Inc. Used by permission of Zondervan. All rights reserved worldwide. www.zondervan.com

Cover and interior design by Müllerhaus
Cover illustration by Dan Burr, represented by Illustration Online LLC.
Typeset by Aptara, Inc.

Printed and bound in the United States of America
10 9 8 7 6 5 4 3 2 1

Love's Beacon

by
Leslie Gould

But they that wait upon the L*ORD* shall renew their strength; they shall mount up with wings as eagles; they shall run, and not be weary; and they shall walk, and not faint.

—Isaiah 40:31 (kjv)

Chapter One

Cape Disappointment, Washington
Friday, February 3, 1899

Sitting on her steamer trunk, Julia Warren looked past the wharf to the mighty Columbia River, blaming it for her wobbly knees. It had only been a two-hour boat ride from Astoria, but it felt as if it had been two days.

She seemed to have lost her childhood sea legs, but at least she still had her stomach of steel. She'd never suffered from seasickness in her life—and planned not to, not even in the location deemed the "Graveyard of the Pacific."

The midafternoon sun shone brightly in the clear blue sky. Wind off the river tugged at her curls under her securely pinned hat, but the relentless Northwest rain Uncle Edward had written about was nowhere to be seen.

She turned toward the town of Ilwaco, really no more than a village. Beyond the wharf and cluster of canneries were houses and businesses. A train ran from the docks into the town and, Julia knew from Uncle Edward's letters, on up the Long Beach Peninsula. Evergreen trees covered the hill, most likely Cape Disappointment. She couldn't see the lighthouse, where Uncle Edward was the keeper, from where she stood. But she knew it was up there. Somewhere.

She squinted into the afternoon sun. Clouds formed over the hill. Perhaps the sunny day would be short-lived. What kind of bird flew above the cape? A boy on the wharf pointed to it. "Look at the eagle, Ma!" he called out to the woman next to him.

"It looks just like the one we saw this morning." His mother took his hand and hurried toward town.

Perhaps it was unusual to see eagles in this far southwestern corner of Washington State. Regardless, it was unusual for Julia. Occasionally, she'd see an eagle on the outskirts of Philadelphia but not often. She pivoted around to face the street off the wharf. She'd sent Uncle Edward a telegram from Denver, saying she'd probably be a day later than she expected due to blizzards slowing down the train. But then she'd made her connection in Portland after all. Was he here to meet her on the chance that she'd made it on time? She scanned the crowd of people for her uncle but saw no one with a white beard and hair. No worries. She was sure she could find a driver to take her to the lighthouse.

And on the way, she'd stop by the office of the Ilwaco newspaper. She'd lived frugally in Philadelphia and saved what she could, but living expenses took most of her salary. Then, when she was in Denver, a packet of her money went missing from her bag, most likely taken as she dozed in the train station. She had wanted to find a job out west if she could, but now it was imperative that she did so soon. She didn't want to be dependent on Uncle Edward.

Surely, with a degree from Vassar and seven years of experience at the *Philadelphia Times*, she'd qualify to work as a reporter for a village newspaper.

However, after her disastrous relationship with Jack Turner, she wouldn't grow close to a newspaperman ever again. Jack had taught her everything she knew about the business—and then he broke her heart. She wouldn't let it happen again.

"Need a ride, miss?" A young man wearing a brown coat and a derby hat nodded to a buggy on the street. He had a kind smile and a handsome face. "I can take you anywhere within a few miles. My name is Billy Jones. Everyone knows me here."

"Perfect." Julia grabbed her own hat as a gust of wind whipped against the blue felt as if it were a sail. Perhaps it wasn't secured as tightly as she thought. "I need to stop by the newspaper office while I am here in town. Then, my destination is the lighthouse." She stepped away from her trunk.

"All right." Billy lifted the trunk. "Is Alexander Blake expecting you?"

"I don't know that name."

"He's the owner of the *Cape Dispatch*."

She smiled. "He isn't expecting me. I wanted to speak to someone about a position. Perhaps the publisher or editor would be more inclined to have a spare moment."

"Miss, he's the publisher and editor, along with being the owner."

"I see."

"And the main reporter."

"Well." She stepped quickly to keep up with the driver. "That settles it." She brushed her hands together. "Take me to Mr. Alexander Blake, please."

They passed the Ilwaco Railway train depot, and then Billy stopped in front of a wooden building on Main Street. He jumped down and gave her a hand.

"The office for the *Dispatch* is on the right side of the building. There's a side door." He nodded to the alley between the large white building and a small brick one. The large building had the words WINTHER'S GENERAL STORE painted above the door.

Julia stepped onto the boardwalk and then around the side of the building into the alley. She strode purposefully around several puddles—obviously it had rained recently—not wanting to muddy her button-up boots. When she reached the side door, she turned the knob and walked in.

A large desk, covered with papers, sat in the middle of the room. A large table was pushed against the wall.

"Hello!" Julia called out.

When no one responded, she called a little louder. "Mr. Blake? Are you on the premises?"

She started toward the closed door on the interior wall as it was flung open. A man nearly a head taller than Julia, with broad shoulders, thick dark hair, and lively brown eyes greeted her. "Good afternoon. How may I help you?"

Julia groaned within at the sight of another handsome newspaperman. At least this time, she'd know to guard herself. "I am Julia Warren, recently employed as a reporter with the *Philadelphia Times*. I'm inquiring about a position as a reporter."

He extended his hand, then noticed the ink stains and swiped his hand down his apron as he nodded in greeting instead. "Alexander Blake. Pleased to meet you. Any chance you know how to set type?"

She took a step backward. "No." That was one thing she hadn't learned in Philadelphia.

He sighed. "That's a shame." He led her through the door into the next room.

Inside, reams of paper lined the floor next to a printing press. Mr. Blake started to say something to the man standing beside the press, but a bell from the street began to clang.

Mr. Blake took off his apron and tossed it behind him. "Finish setting the last article and then start running the press," he said to the other man. "The delivery boys will be here soon." Then he stepped past Julia, saying, "Excuse me" as he did, and headed toward the door, where he grabbed an oilcloth coat from the rack.

"Come on," he said to her. "I'm closing shop."

"Don't you have a newspaper to print?"

"It'll get done, one way or the other. It always does." He opened the door and then wiggled into his coat. "I'm in a hurry."

"Goodness." Jack had been a scoundrel but never this rude.

As Julia stepped out into the alley, Mr. Blake bounded through the door after her. Trying to get out of his way and not step in a puddle, she dodged to the right at the same time he did. They collided, and she feared the impact would topple her. But he quickly grabbed her elbow. "My apologies," he said. "I certainly didn't mean to send you tumbling."

She planted her feet and steadied herself. "I'm quite all right."

"Are you sure?"

She nodded.

"I'm sorry," he said. "I got ahead of myself. I can't afford a reporter at this time, but let's talk later. Perhaps on Monday?"

"All right."

The clanging of the bell grew louder. She started toward the street and the buggy. Mr. Blake rushed past her.

Someone shouted. "It's a sailboat, taking on water. The tide is washing it up to the beach."

As she rounded the corner, Mr. Blake was yelling at her driver. "Billy, are you coming?"

Billy hopped down from the buggy. "Maybe later. I'm giving this lady a ride to the lighthouse. I'll stop by on my way back."

As Julia reached the buggy, a man stepped from the boardwalk and offered her his hand. He had blond hair, blue eyes, and a charming smile. Were all the men in these parts so handsome?

As she took his hand and climbed into the buggy, the man said, "I'm Lucien Graham. Welcome to Ilwaco." He gestured to Mr. Blake. "Don't mind our newspaperman. He's always in a hurry."

She smiled. "I'm Julia Warren. From Philadelphia."

"Ahh, Edward Warren's niece?" he said.

She nodded.

"Isn't he expecting you tomorrow?"

"He is," she answered. "But I was able to make my original connection in Portland."

"I'm an assistant lightkeeper on the cape," Mr. Graham said. "Mr. Warren is working tonight. He'd want you to go straight to the lighthouse."

"Thank you." She glanced back at the general store. "Perhaps I should place a telephone call first, to let Uncle Edward know I'll be arriving soon."

Mr. Graham laughed, his voice booming. "You just gave yourself away as a big-city girl. The telephone hasn't made its way to

in Cape Disappointment, Washington

Ilwaco yet. Astoria is the nearest, so far. We're hoping it will arrive here within the decade."

"Oh," Julia said. Nearly every business and many of the homes in Philadelphia, even the boardinghouse she lived in, had telephones. It hadn't occurred to her that Cape Disappointment wouldn't.

As Billy approached the buggy, Mr. Graham said something to him. Billy nodded and then jumped up into the driver's seat. As the buggy began to roll, Julia said, "I take it Mr. Blake is off to report on the sailboat that's sinking."

"Yes, ma'am," Billy said. "And to help save the crew. He's part of the volunteer rescue brigade."

The forest grew dense on the edge of town, and as Billy drove the horse up the plank road, Julia pulled her coat tight. The damp chill in the air, even though it wasn't raining, began to seep into her bones. Through breaks in the trees, she could see clouds billowing over the Pacific, although she didn't have a view of the ocean yet. She expected the rain wouldn't hold off for long.

The light grew dimmer as the trees grew thicker. Finally, the road crested, and two houses appeared.

"Those are the keepers' houses," Billy said.

"They're lovely." Life on Cape Disappointment would be more comfortable than she'd expected. "But where's the lighthouse?"

"Around the corner."

"Can you take me there?"

"Yes, ma'am. Do you want to drop off your trunk first?"

"No, we can do that on the way back." At home in Rhode Island, the keeper's residence had been on the ground floor of the lighthouse, not "around the corner."

When they reached the lighthouse, it was clear that daylight was waning. Julia scrambled down from the buggy before Billy could help her, raised her skirts, ran to the lighthouse, and flung open the door.

"Uncle Edward," she called out. "I'm here!"

"What in the world?" came a husky voice from above.

She hurried to the staircase and started up. But coming down was a man much younger than Uncle Edward.

"You must be looking for Mr. Warren?"

Julia froze, clutching the handrailing. "Yes. Where is he?"

"He's at the Cape Disappointment Lighthouse."

"Isn't this the Cape Disappointment Lighthouse?"

He shook his head. "This is the North Head Lighthouse on Cape Disappointment. I'm John Parker. The keeper here."

"Oh." Uncle Edward hadn't mentioned there were two lighthouses on the cape.

"It's only a short distance away. Two miles or so."

"All right," Julia said, backing down the stairs. "Thank you."

When she reached the buggy, she told Billy about the mix-up.

"I'm sorry, ma'am. I thought you meant this lighthouse."

"No." She hoped she hid her disappointment. "I'm the niece of Edward Warren, the keeper of the Cape Disappointment Lighthouse." She couldn't blame Billy. "I'm sorry. It's not your fault."

The first drops of rain were soft against her hands. But then the wind picked up and the rain began to sting her face. Now an iciness settled deep inside her, colder than the blizzard in Denver.

A few minutes later, darkness fell completely. Billy stopped and lit a lantern and then hung it on the buggy. "It's not much farther," he said. "See." He pointed. "You can see the beacon."

The beam of light flashed.

The lighthouse—and Uncle Edward—weren't far now.

Soon the road turned, and the beacon was out of sight. Julia buried her hands in her coat and tried to ignore the icy rain. She'd soon be in the lighthouse, brewing a cup of tea and telling Uncle Edward about her trip. She smiled at the thought, but then a shout startled her out of her daze.

"It must be the rescuers on the beach," Billy said. "By now they should have any survivors from the sailboat on the shore."

A bell began to clang again—whether it was the same one as before, she didn't know, although this one was more distant, and there were more shouts.

"It's the *Pacific Star*," someone yelled. "It's on the bar."

"Whoa." Billy brought the horse to a stop. "That's much more serious than the sailboat sinking. I need to go down to the beach, to see if they need me to go for help or anything. There's a trail here." He grabbed the lantern. "I'll be right back."

Julia wasn't staying by herself. "I'm going with you." She scrambled down from the bench.

Billy led the way to the trail. "It's steep." He held the lantern up high as he sidestepped down the trail. "Watch out for the tree roots," he said to Julia. And then, "There's a rock here. Don't step on it—it's slick."

The wind snatched at her hat again and Julia held on to it. Until she slipped. Her feet flew out from under her, slamming into Billy and causing the lantern to go flying. Both of them fell, sliding down the trail. Finally, Billy grabbed a branch, stopping both of them.

"I'm sorry," she said.

"Are you all right?" he asked.

"I'm fine." At least she hoped she was.

"Can you stand?"

"Yes."

He helped her up, then scrambled back up the hill for the lantern. The flame had gone out, but he took matches from his coat pocket and relit it. Then he returned, holding the lantern high once again. Julia wiped her muddy gloved hands on her equally muddy skirt.

"Get that rescue boat out there!" someone yelled.

"Let's go," Billy said, taking her hand. "The trail is easier from here."

When the trail flattened, Billy let go of her hand. A dozen lanterns lit up the beach, showing a rescue boat with a rope attached to a wooden cart at the edge of the water. Several men shoved the boat into the waves.

Beyond, a lifeboat bobbed in the ocean, and past it, the waves battered a ship.

"Billy!" Mr. Blake approached. "You missed going out on the rescue boat."

"I only came down to see if you needed me to go get more help."

Mr. Blake's eyes met Julia's. "I didn't expect to see you again so soon."

"Billy is driving me to the lighthouse."

Billy motioned to the ship. "What's happened to the ship?"

"The men are going to try to pull it off with the rope, if it's long enough to reach. I think the vessel may be too big though, even if it is."

A man in a bowler hat approached them. "Is that really the *Pacific Star*?" It appeared he'd run to the beach.

"That's right, Mr. Petersen," Mr. Blake said.

"It's being rescued, right?"

"We don't know yet." Mr. Blake spoke kindly to the man. "Hopefully."

"It's breaking up!" someone on the rescue boat shouted.

Another lifeboat appeared, coming from the ship.

"We need to get the cargo!" Mr. Petersen shouted.

"We need to save the lives!" someone from the rescue boat shouted back.

Julia wondered if Uncle Edward could see from the lighthouse what was happening. She glanced up to the bluff and waited, but the beacon wasn't in view.

Fog began to roll in from the ocean, and she directed her attention to the disappearing boats until Mr. Blake pointed at the bluff. "The beacon is out."

"You should be able to see it from here?" Julia asked.

"Yes," Mr. Blake replied.

Julia swallowed hard. This couldn't be good.

"What's going on?"

A man came bounding onto the beach from the trail. *Mr. Graham.*

"It's the *Pacific Star*," Billy called out. "Stuck on the bar."

Mr. Graham turned toward the lighthouse. "Where's the beacon? It was on a little while ago—I saw it when I came from town." He shook his head. "Something must have happened. Mr. Warren wouldn't let the beacon go out."

Chapter Two

Mr. Blake followed Mr. Graham. Julia picked up her skirt and hurried after the two, followed by Billy. Going up the trail was easier than coming down, although it was still slippery. Several times Julia dug the heel of her boot in to stop herself from sliding. When they reached the top, Mr. Graham and Mr. Blake started sprinting down the road.

"Let's take the buggy," Billy said.

Julia breathed a sigh of relief.

Billy assisted her up to the bench and handed her the lantern. Then he climbed up and urged the poor horse forward. In no time, the horse picked up the pace, probably eager to get out of the rain.

The forest of evergreen trees was as thick on top of the cape as it had been when they left Ilwaco. When they arrived at the lighthouse, the door was open. Julia jumped down from the buggy and ran. When she entered the lighthouse, she noted the kerosene lamp on the table in the sitting area that included a woodstove. Obviously, electricity hadn't reached the cape yet either.

"Uncle Edward?" She expected him to come down the stairs, wrap her in a bear hug, and explain that the lens had malfunctioned.

"He's up here." She wasn't sure if it was Mr. Blake or Mr. Graham who spoke. She lifted her mud-caked skirt and started up the circular stairs, with Billy behind her. Near what seemed to be close to the top stood Mr. Blake. A few steps above him was Mr. Graham. In between them was Uncle Edward, sprawled on the stairs.

Out of breath, Julia slipped past Mr. Blake and knelt next to her uncle's head. He wore his blue US Lighthouse Service uniform, but his cap had fallen off, revealing his full head of white hair. His beard was neatly trimmed, as always.

"Go check the lens," Mr. Blake said.

"Good idea." Mr. Graham hurried up the steps.

Julia brushed a strand of hair from Uncle Edward's brow. He stirred but didn't open his eyes. She sniffed and then sniffed again. Was that alcohol?

Mr. Graham returned with the neck of a bottle in his hands. "The lens is broken."

"What?" Mr. Blake's eyes were wide with disbelief.

Mr. Graham held up what was left of the bottle. "It appears he used this."

"No!" Julia gasped.

Mr. Graham's brows rose. "I can hardly believe it myself."

With a look of disgust on his face, Mr. Blake said, "We'd better move him down to the first level."

Julia agreed. "And then go get the doctor."

Mr. Blake stepped closer to Uncle Edward. "And the law."

"For what?" Julia raised her head.

"Dereliction of duty." Mr. Blake met Julia's gaze. "He reeks of alcohol. He broke the lens. And a ship has wrecked on the bar."

After they carried Uncle Edward down the stairs and laid him on the sofa in the sitting area, Billy and Mr. Blake went to fetch the sheriff and the doctor. Then Mr. Graham left to collect blankets to keep Uncle Edward warm, even though a fire was burning in the woodstove.

Julia sat in a chair beside her uncle. She took his hand. "Uncle Edward? Can you hear me? Can you tell me what happened?"

He didn't stir.

She leaned closer. He definitely smelled of alcohol. She had never, not once in her life, seen him take a drink, let alone become inebriated.

Julia felt ill. The lenses were works of art, besides being lifesavers. She couldn't imagine that Uncle Edward would destroy such a thing. He'd written, when he arrived, that the Cape Disappointment Lighthouse beacon was a Fresnel lens. It rotated with a lamp inside and reflected the light from prisms into beams. It was a masterpiece of a design.

Uncle Edward turned his head away from her. Was that a bump growing on the back of his head? She ran her hand over the bulge showing through his hair.

Julia began to shake, both from the icy coldness that soaked through her and the realization of what had happened. Someone had shattered the lens and attacked Uncle Edward. Who would do such a thing?

Nearly an hour later, Mr. Graham returned with a blanket for Uncle Edward and one for Julia. She tucked the blanket around her uncle and then draped the other one around her shoulders.

"Did you check on how things are going with the ship?" Julia asked. "Is that what took you so long?"

Mr. Graham nodded. "The last of the crew was in a lifeboat. Only the captain remained aboard."

"Why hadn't he left?"

"He was probably making sure no one had been left behind."

"Was the rescue cart able to free the ship?"

"No." Mr. Graham shook his head. "It appears it can't be saved. A barge will tow whatever is left to the dry dock."

When Julia didn't respond, he said, "James Evert is the captain. He's been piloting ships across the bar for over twenty years. He traveled down to San Francisco where the *Pacific Star* was built and piloted it up here as a favor to the investors. He's never lost a ship—until now."

"It's a new ship?"

"Brand-new," Mr. Graham said. "Several businessmen in town invested in it to ship local products to California. Wood. Fish. Cranberries. It's a big loss to the entire area." He sighed. "So is the breaking of the Fresnel lens. If it can't be repaired, a new one will have to be sent. That could take weeks and mean that more ships will be at risk."

"How about oil lamps until the lens can be repaired or replaced? The old-fashioned way."

"I suppose you're right," he said. "We'll need to do something."

Julia shivered again, even as she stood a foot from the stove. The whole town was likely to hold Uncle Edward responsible.

A half hour later, the doctor arrived.

Mr. Graham introduced Julia as Mr. Warren's niece and then said, "This is Dr. Nathan Olsen."

"Everyone calls me Doc," the man said. "Pleased to meet you, although I'm sorry about the circumstances."

"Yes," Julia said.

The doctor gave his attention to Uncle Edward. He pulled the blanket back and shook his shoulder. Uncle Edward stirred but didn't open his eyes. Doc leaned down and placed his hand on Uncle Edward's throat and then sniffed. He turned to Mr. Graham. "Is Mr. Warren a drinker?"

"He's been known to drink," Mr. Graham said.

"To excess?"

"On occasion. He—"

Julia bristled. "I've never seen him take a drink," she said. "Not even one. Not even when he was offered."

"Didn't you just arrive today?" Doc asked.

"Well, yes. But Uncle Edward raised me. I know him better than anyone."

"But you haven't spent any time with him lately, right?"

"No, I haven't, but—"

"People change," Doc said. "Believe me. I see it all the time."

Julia focused on not stamping her foot. Reacting rudely would only draw attention to herself—and away from Uncle Edward. She crossed her arms.

The doctor glanced at her and chuckled. "He was sent to the edge of the world. You can't blame him for doing his best to cope."

Julia retorted, "He's been near the edge of the world his entire working life and never drank before."

"That you know of."

Julia shook her head. "He worked on ships until he was thirty and then took a job as a lightkeeper to raise me." The lighthouse where she grew up in Rhode Island wasn't as remote as this one, but Uncle Edward was isolated simply by the tasks of being a keeper.

"Well." Doc Olsen rubbed his chin. "My assessment is that we have a drunk lightkeeper. Let him sleep it off and have the law deal with him in the morning."

Julia stepped closer to her uncle. "He has a lump on the back of his head."

"No doubt," Doc said. "If one gets drunk and falls down the lighthouse stairs, one is bound to bump one's head."

Julia reached down and took her uncle's hand. "Please examine his head."

The doctor knelt by the settee and ran his hand under Uncle Edward's head. "That's quite a bulge." He stood. "Instead of letting him sleep it off, I think I'd better take him into the hospital and keep an eye on him."

"Can you wait until the law arrives?" Julia pleaded. "The sheriff should see all the evidence possible. Moving my uncle any further will disrupt what happened here tonight. Hopefully Mr. Blake and Billy will arrive with him soon."

Doc Olsen frowned. "I don't have all night."

"How about this," Mr. Graham replied. "Just wait a few more minutes. If they don't arrive, I'll help you carry Mr. Warren to your wagon."

A half hour later, Doc said, "I've waited long enough."

"I'll get the stretcher from the wagon." Mr. Graham started toward the door, and Julia added her blanket to the one on top of Uncle Edward.

A couple of minutes later there was a commotion at the front door and Mr. Blake appeared. He was followed by a man Julia assumed to be the sheriff and then Billy and Mr. Graham, who carried a stretcher.

Mr. Blake introduced the man as Deputy Martin. He appeared to be in his early thirties.

Julia extended her hand and said, "Nice to meet you." She turned to Mr. Blake. "Is the sheriff not available?"

"The sheriff is in South Bend, the county seat," Mr. Blake explained. "It's a distance from here—fifty miles. He'll be notified about what happened."

"Focus on Mr. Warren," Doc Olsen said to Deputy Martin. "I need to get him down to the hospital and then see if any of the sailors from the wrecks need attention."

"All right." The deputy looked at Uncle Edward, sniffed him, and said, "Yep. It appears he's had too much to drink."

"He has a lump on the back of his head," Julia said.

"From falling on the stairs," Doc Olsen added.

"We don't know that for sure." Julia addressed the deputy. "If the lens was broken with a bottle, Uncle Edward could have been hit on the head with the bottle first."

Deputy Martin gave Mr. Blake a knowing look.

"It's not much of an investigation if you don't consider all of the possibilities," Julia said, again to the deputy.

Deputy Martin bristled. "I don't need any advice from you."

"Of course not," Julia said. "I'm sure you're more than capable. But any investigator needs to be open to seeing more than what's obvious." She eyed Mr. Blake. "And journalists need to do the same."

Mr. Blake grimaced. "Yes, you're right."

Deputy Martin ignored both of them. "I'll gather the pertinent information and then make my report."

He addressed Doc Olsen. "You can take Mr. Warren to the hospital. I'll come by to question him once he's conscious."

Mr. Blake, Billy, and Mr. Graham all helped Doc Olsen roll Uncle Edward onto the stretcher and then carried him out. Julia walked beside them. When they reached the wagon, she was grateful to see that it was covered. Once they had Uncle Edward inside, Julia asked where the hospital was.

"Right downtown," Doc Olsen said.

"A block from the newspaper office," Mr. Blake explained. "Near the wharf."

"All right." Julia was anxious to get back inside the lighthouse and see what evidence Deputy Martin was collecting. "I'll come down first thing in the morning."

When Julia reached the tower, she found the deputy holding the broken bottle and standing beside the shattered glass that littered the floor. "So this is what Mr. Warren used to break the beacon," he said.

"The lens," Julia said.

The man's face reddened.

"And we don't know that Uncle Edward broke the lens, not until we know who else was in the lighthouse this evening. I saw the beacon from the road about a half hour before we realized it was out. We know the lens was intact then. What we need to find out is if there was someone else in the lighthouse between that time and when the beacon stopped."

Deputy Martin ignored her as he placed the bottle in a bag. "One broken bourbon bottle used to break the—" He looked at Julia. "Lens."

"Yes, it's a Fresnel lens." She nodded to the stairs. "May I show you where Mr. Graham and Mr. Blake found Uncle Edward?"

"Please do," Deputy Martin said.

Julia walked down the stairs, counting them as she did, and stopped on the one with the blood spot on it, where Uncle Edward's head had rested. "Right here, on the fifty-third step from the top."

"All right. Continue," he said.

She did. As she came around the final curve, she saw Billy, Mr. Graham, and Mr. Blake standing at the bottom of the stairs. She counted two hundred fifty stairs in all.

Concerned about Deputy Martin's investigative skills, she said, "Mr. Graham, will you send a telegram to the custom house in

Ilwaco and ask them to start a full investigation into the breaking of the lens, Uncle Edward's fall, and the shipwreck, please?"

Mr. Graham shook his head. "There is no custom house in Ilwaco. The closest is Astoria. And, yes, I'll send a telegram tonight. I can assure you that a full federal investigation will begin immediately."

Mr. Blake looked at her, an empathetic expression on his face. "We want the truth as much as you do, Miss Warren. Whatever it might be."

Chapter Three

After Deputy Martin left, Mr. Graham asked, "Where do you plan to spend the night?"

"Here," she answered.

"You can't." He glanced at the door. "But you could stay in the keeper's cottage until the custom official gives further direction."

Mr. Blake nodded. "You're right. I suppose it won't hurt for the time being."

"I'll take your trunk there," Billy said. "And give you a ride." He turned to Mr. Blake. "I can give you a ride back into town."

"I need to go check on how things are going on the beach and interview some of the sailors. And the captain, if he's off the ship by now."

"Of course." Billy opened the door. "I'll go with you."

Mr. Graham blew out the lamp on the main floor of the lighthouse and then followed them out. "I'll head straight to town and send the telegram."

"Thank you," Julia said.

Billy had changed horses in town. The new one was a roan mare and larger, but she looked miserable too. It only took a couple of minutes to reach the cottage. Julia carried the lantern, and Mr. Blake and Billy carried her trunk. She held the lantern high as she entered the cottage and spotted the lamp and matches on the kitchen table.

After she lit the lamp, she returned the lantern to Billy. "Thank you," she said. "You've been so kind and caring. You've made a miserable night bearable."

"You're welcome, miss. Let me know if I can be of any more help to you. You can usually find me close to the wharf."

"I'll remember that," she said.

"Good night, Miss Warren," Mr. Blake said.

"Good night." Julia gave him a nod. Not only was Mr. Blake handsome, but he seemed to be authentic. He certainly wasn't the charmer Jack had been, which was appealing. She was done with charmers. But that didn't mean she would fall for a newspaperman again. She absolutely wouldn't. She'd learned her lesson.

After Mr. Graham and Billy left, she locked the cottage door and then carried the lamp around the cottage. Everything seemed in order. It was as neat and tidy as she expected it would be.

She dragged her trunk into the second bedroom, which had the top sheet and covers turned down, waiting for her.

She went back to the kitchen and opened every cupboard. She found flour, cornmeal, and sugar, salt and spices, and cans of beans and vegetables and a tinned ham. But no bourbon or other alcohol. She returned to the hallway, this time turning into Uncle Edward's room. It was as immaculate as the rest of the house. The bed was made. His clothing was perfectly folded and placed in his bureau. His spare uniforms hung in his closet. On his nightstand was his Bible, the one he used to read to her from every morning when she was a child. Again, she didn't find any bottles of bourbon or other alcohol.

She ventured back to the kitchen and sat at the table. Uncle Edward had been framed. She was one hundred percent certain that he wasn't drunk and hadn't broken the lens. But how could she prove it?

What would Uncle Edward want her to do now? It didn't take long for the answer to come. He'd want her to put a light in the lens room.

She took the lamp into her room, opened her trunk, and pulled out a clean pair of stockings and bloomers, a work dress, and an old coat. Once she'd changed, she retrieved the lantern by the door and lit it. Then she grabbed the matches, blew out the lamp, and headed back to the lighthouse.

Julia gathered all the lamps and lanterns in the lighthouse and lit them too, placing them around the windowsills of the lens room. Then she sat against the wall where the shattered glass hadn't reached and hugged her knees to her chest.

Uncle Edward had worked for the US Lighthouse Service for twenty years, starting when she'd been a seven-year-old orphan. He insisted, relentlessly, that she concentrate on her studies. He would check her homework and quiz her on math problems and geography and spelling.

When she was in high school, one of her teachers told Uncle Edward not to press Julia so hard. "At best she might go to normal school and become a teacher. She won't need to know algebra for that."

Uncle Edward had bristled and told the man to mind his own business. On the way home, he told Julia she was going to college.

When she was accepted to Vassar, he took a week off work and accompanied her on the train. He seemed so out of place in his simple suit, sitting among the fathers who were bankers and doctors and lawyers. But not once did he act as if he was out of place. In fact, he shone brighter than the lighthouse beacon.

When she graduated from Vassar, she assumed she'd keep house for him again. *Don't you dare*, he'd written back to her. *I'm fine. Use your education. Do what suits you best—and I know that's not keeping house for me.*

She'd secured a position with the *Philadelphia Times* as a proofreader. Soon, she was promoted to reporter. Granted, she mostly wrote about society happenings, domestic products, and household tips. Every once in a while, she was able to interview a prominent woman who headed up a charity. But a few times she'd been allowed to assist Jack on a journalistic investigation.

He told her to befriend everyone. To take coffee to police officers—and secretaries. To sit with the bereaved. To flatter the society girls.

He didn't include to court the younger reporters, but that's what he'd done with her. He'd won her trust—and then her heart. And then he dumped her for a society girl he'd flattered who clearly could offer much more for him in Philadelphia than Julia ever could.

She couldn't stay after that. She missed Uncle Edward—he was all she had left.

Again, he'd told her not to come, but she insisted. *I'll find a job*, she'd written. *And hire someone to keep house for both of us.* Finally, she wrote and told him she needed to come. She wanted to be with family—the only family she had left.

If she'd come sooner, this never would have happened.

Or if it had, at least she'd have an idea of who might do such an atrocious thing.

The next morning, Julia awoke as light filled the lens room. The rain had stopped, and the clouds had shifted. She extinguished the lanterns and then, with hands on the windowsill, gazed out over the Pacific. She turned to the left, toward the Columbia River. There was the *Pacific Star*, with the hull smashed, bobbing in the water with lumber and other debris banging against it. She picked up the binoculars on the sill and focused on the ship. She didn't see any sign of life—except for a gull perched on the railing around the deck.

A racket on the first floor drew her away from the window. She walked around the glass and to the staircase and called out, "Who's there?"

"It's Lucien Graham, with Officer John Carlson from the US Custom House. Alexander Blake is with us too."

"I'm coming down." When she reached the first floor, Mr. Blake greeted her.

Mr. Graham crossed his arms. "What are you doing here?"

"I lit lamps and put them in the lens room," she said.

He shook his head. "You weren't authorized to do so."

"Someone might have needed a light, even though dim." She directed her attention to Officer Carlson. "I'm pleased to meet you." She offered him her hand. "I'm Edward Warren's niece, Julia Warren."

He shook her hand as he said, "Yes. I've been made aware of your presence here."

"I expected the agent," Julia said. "Why didn't he come?"

"Goodness, Miss Warren." Mr. Blake's voice was low. "Are you working for the US Marshal's office?"

She ignored him and addressed Officer Carlson again. "Who is your agent?"

"Agent Belville."

"Where is he? Obviously, your office received the telegram in good time for you to arrive at the crack of dawn."

"He's in Olympia for a week of meetings."

"Olympia?"

Mr. Blake whispered, "The capital."

Julia grimaced. "I knew that." After all, Uncle Edward had schooled her in geography.

"I'm sorry you're disappointed Agent Belville isn't here, but it can't be helped." Officer Carlson looked up the staircase and then back at Julia. "You need to vacate the premises. I'm opening an investigation into how the lens was broken and why Edward Warren abandoned his post."

"Certainly." Julia forced a smile. "Please also investigate who else was in the lighthouse with Mr. Warren last night and had the opportunity to push him down the stairs and break the lens."

"I'll look at every angle," Officer Carlson said.

"Thank you." Julia squeezed past the three men and headed to the door. "I'm going to the hospital now. I'm guessing you'll be following soon."

in Cape Disappointment, Washington

Officer Carlson nodded. "Do not speak with Mr. Warren about what took place last night. I need his memories to be fresh when he speaks with me, not tainted by your ideas."

Julia gave the man a curt nod and marched out the door.

One of the men closed the door behind her.

Chapter Four

After cleaning her boots, changing into a clean skirt and blouse, and eating breakfast, Julia left the cottage and headed toward the road to town. Walking out of a cabin was a woman carrying a basket.

"Excuse me!" Julia hurried to the woman and quickly introduced herself.

The woman shifted the basket in her arms. "My name is Maria. I do laundry for the soldiers at Fort Canby."

Julia asked if she had seen anyone the afternoon or evening before. "Going into or out of the lighthouse."

Maria shook her head. "I was scrubbing sheets in my cabin."

Julia thanked her and continued walking toward town. A few minutes later, she came across two soldiers on the road. They hadn't seen anything suspicious either.

She pressed on. Through the trees she could see the Columbia River below and Baker Bay. At least that's what she remembered Uncle Edward calling the bay in his letters. Soon she could see buildings and then the wharf. She guessed there was a shortcut to the town off the road, another muddy trail most likely. But the thought of sliding on her backside and grabbing at roots to try to stop herself as she'd done last night kept her from looking for it.

There was always something to be grateful for. Today it was the blue sky and sunshine. She didn't think she could survive more rain, not with her lack of sleep.

The brisk walk kept her warm, and soon the road veered down to the town. When she reached the outskirts, the sound of horses' hooves and wheels came from behind. She turned and saw Mr. Graham driving a buggy with Officer Carlson on the seat next to him. He stopped the horse. "Want a ride? I imagine we're going to the same place."

"Thank you, Mr. Graham," she said. "I would."

He jumped down from the buggy and hurried around to help her up as Officer Carlson scooted to the middle of the bench. As he let go of her hand, Mr. Graham said, "We don't stand much on ceremony in Ilwaco, Miss Warren. I'd be more comfortable if you'd call me Lucien."

"Lucien it is, then," said Julia pleasantly. She turned to the officer as she settled in her seat. "Lovely morning, isn't it?"

"Yes. It is. But rain is moving in again soon. Those clouds to the west appear ominous."

Julia heard another horse and buggy approach, and she looked behind them. "Is that Mr. Blake?"

Lucien chuckled. "It is, indeed, Alexander. He refused to ride to the lighthouse with me this morning. He said he needed to be 'unbiased.' I think you may have influenced him last night."

Julia smiled.

They reached the hospital, which was a converted house. As Lucien helped Julia down, she noticed in the back of the buggy a box that was mostly covered with a tarp. A tool handle stuck out of the uncovered corner.

"What's in the box?" Julia asked Lucien.

"A spade," he answered. "You can't imagine how often we get stuck in the mud around here."

Julia guessed that anyone driving a buggy would need a spade and perhaps other tools too, but the handle looked too short to be any type of shovel.

"Why is the handle so short?"

Lucien frowned at her. "It probably only looks short from that angle."

Officer Carlson chuckled. "We have the same problem with mud in Astoria. I've never seen so much rain."

After Lucien parked the buggy, he helped Julia down and then led the way to the hospital. The doctor's office occupied the front room. Doc Olsen greeted them and then turned to Officer Carlson. "Let me know if there's anything I can do to assist your investigation."

"I'll need a report on the patient's status last night when you examined him," Officer Carlson said. "How is he doing this morning?"

"He hasn't woken up."

"What do you attribute that to?"

"Well, if he was unconscious from the amount of alcohol he consumed, he would have either passed away or come to by now. I'm guessing it's his head injury."

Julia winced. "I'd like to see him now."

Alexander Blake slipped into the office.

"I'll take all three—" Doc Olsen nodded to Alexander. "All four of you back." He opened a door to a hallway.

Uncle Edward was in a bedroom at the end of the hall with a window looking out on the intersection of Main Street and First Avenue. A nurse, a middle-aged woman that Doc Olsen introduced as Miss Vera Atkins, sat in a chair next to the bed. She stood and said, "He stirred a few minutes ago but didn't open his eyes."

"Thank you," Doc Olsen said. "You may take a break while I examine the patient again."

Uncle Edward appeared to be wearing some type of nightshirt. Doc Olsen took his stethoscope from the table beside the bed and listened to Uncle Edward's chest. He lifted one eyelid, then the other, and then examined the back of his head.

Julia had never seen Uncle Edward so helpless.

The doctor addressed Officer Carlson. "His heart and lungs are sound, but his head injury hasn't improved. He's unconscious."

"So he's in a coma?"

"I'm not sure," Doc Olsen said. "There are many stages of consciousness. Mr. Warren's not responding, but fortunately, he can swallow, so we can keep him hydrated. I'm hoping he'll come out of it—either gradually or all at once. I've seen both."

"Could he be"—Officer Carlson glanced at Julia—"pretending to be injured to escape the consequences of his actions?"

Julia bristled at the man's accusation.

"Right now, his eyes aren't responsive. That fact indicates he's had an injury to his brain."

"I see," Officer Carlson said. "That's unfortunate." He turned to Lucien. "I'm ready to speak with the deputy now."

Julia stayed behind after everyone left. She took Uncle Edward's hand and said, "Please wake up. I know you didn't break the lens, but I need you to wake up and tell us what happened."

Uncle Edward didn't respond.

Finally, she said, "I'm going now, but I'll come again soon."

When she reached the front office, Alexander was leaving the building and the other two were already gone. Nurse Vera sat at the front desk, and the doctor stood at a cabinet across the room. "I'm going," Julia said, "but I'll be back later this afternoon. I'm staying in Uncle Edward's cottage up on Cape Disappointment. Please send for me if—" She paused. "When he wakes up."

"I will," he said.

She stepped out of the doctor's office and glanced to her right. She didn't see anyone. Then she looked to her left. Officer Carlson was following Lucien into a building a block away, with Alexander trailing behind. She hurried after them. A small sign on the front door read PACIFIC COUNTY DEPUTY SHERIFF.

When she entered, Lucien and Officer Carlson were standing while Deputy Martin and an older man with silver hair sat at a table. Alexander stood beside the door. He said quietly to Julia, "That's Captain Evert, from the *Pacific Star*."

Deputy Martin stood. "Miss Warren, what are you doing here?"

She squared her shoulders. "I'm here to observe the investigation."

"Just as a bystander?"

She nodded. "That's right."

"It doesn't work that way," Deputy Martin said.

"Why not?" she asked.

Alexander stepped forward. "I've hired Miss Warren to work for the *Cape Dispatch*. She is now a member of the press. She has a right to be here and observe what's taking place."

Julia did her best to hide her surprise. She couldn't imagine Alexander's motivation, but she'd go along with this, for the time being. Deputy Martin looked as if he didn't believe Alexander, but he said, "All right. But all of this is off the record. You can report about the wreck but not about the lighthouse or the lightkeeper until we've had a chance to interview everyone involved." He cleared his throat and said to Officer Carlson, "Do you want my report from last night now? Or would you rather interview Captain Evert first?"

"I'll speak with the captain first." Officer Carlson turned to the captain. "That way you can be on your way and get some rest."

Captain Evert sighed. "Thank you, son. I appreciate your thoughtfulness."

The deputy motioned for everyone to sit down around the table. Thankfully, Julia had a notebook and pencil in her bag, so she could look official.

"Tell me what happened last night," Officer Carlson said. "Why you decided to cross the bar when you did, what happened once you were on the bar, and what caused the wreck. Relay every detail that comes to mind."

Captain Evert laced his fingers together. "It was sunset and top of the tide. A storm, a bad one, was blowing in, and I knew I needed to get across the bar as soon as I could. I fixed my sights on the lighthouse and then the jetty, aiming for the best place to cross. A massive wave swept over the boat as darkness fell. The beacon flashed, as it should. But as I proceeded forward, the light went out. The waves must have pushed us south, but without the northern marker, I didn't realize it." He paused a moment and then said, "We hit the bar a few minutes later. At first I thought we could make it, but then the creaking began. I realized the ship was breaking apart. Thankfully, there was already a rescue crew on the beach. They sent a boat out and a rope, but it was too late for the ship. It was beyond rescuing. Miraculously, we didn't lose a single sailor."

"That's certainly a relief," Officer Carlson said. "Tell me about your experience as a captain."

"I've piloted ships up and down the West Coast for thirty-five years, and recently piloted the *Pacific Star* from San Francisco to the bar without incident. But most importantly, I've been a board-licensed Columbia Bar pilot for twenty-three years. I've never lost a ship."

"What made the difference last night?"

"The beacon being out. It is impossible to safely cross the bar in a storm without it."

After Captain Evert finished, he left, and then Deputy Martin read his report to Officer Carlson. "Mr. Warren was found unconscious on the stairway of the Cape Disappointment Lighthouse on the evening of February 3, 1899, at approximately 6:30 p.m. by Mr. Lucien Graham, Mr. Alexander Blake, and Miss Julia Warren. I was summoned by Lucien Graham and Alexander Blake at 7:45 p.m. and began my investigation at 8:30 p.m. I found Mr. Warren reeking of alcohol, both on his breath and uniform, in the first level of the lighthouse on the settee, where he'd been moved. A bourbon bottle, that I took as evidence, had been thrown at the lens, which damaged it. The beacon had been put out as the *Pacific Star* was crossing the bar."

He then listed all of the people on the premises of the lighthouse during his investigation. "Signed by Deputy Martin on this day of February 4, 1899."

"Thank you. I'll take over the investigation from here." Officer Carlson reached for the report.

The deputy handed it to him and said, "You'll need to speak with the sheriff about that."

"It's a federal matter," Officer Carlson said.

The deputy crossed his arms. "Still, the sheriff would like to be kept apprised of the situation."

Lucien held up his hand. "Think of it as a courtesy. That way if you need more information, Deputy Martin and even Sheriff Lowden will be at the ready to help."

Officer Carlson seemed to take a moment to absorb the information and then said, "I understand." He folded the paper and slipped it into the inside pocket of his uniform jacket. Then he said, "I'm going back to the hospital to arrest Mr. Warren."

"Has he regained consciousness?" Deputy Martin asked.

"Not when we saw him earlier," Officer Carlson said. "But clearly there's enough information to arrest him. When he comes to, lock him up until I can come and take him to Astoria."

As Julia spoke, her knees trembled under the table. "You haven't asked who else was in the lighthouse when the lens was broken."

Officer Carlson shook his head. "There's no evidence that there was anyone else in the lighthouse."

"But you haven't even asked. Several people live near the lighthouse. I saw the cabins when I walked into town." She didn't mention she'd questioned a few people herself. She turned to Lucien. "Who lives in those cottages?"

"I live in one," he said. "As the assistant lightkeeper. There's a barracks for Fort Canby and cottages for the lifesaving station crew. Also, there are some cabins that house people who work at the fort but who aren't in the military. That sort of thing."

"Did you notice anything suspicious last night?" Officer Carlson asked Lucien. "A stranger lurking around the area?"

"I was in town," Lucien said. "At the saloon, playing cards with a friend. I hurried to the beach when word came that the *Pacific Star* had stuck on the bar. That's when we all noticed the beacon was out."

Officer Carlson asked, "Can you think of anyone who might attack Mr. Warren and break the lens?"

Lucien thought for a moment and then shook his head. "No."

"Did he have a habit of drinking?"

Lucien glanced at Julia and pursed his lips.

Officer Carlson squared his shoulders. "Mr. Graham, please answer my question."

"He did drink. Not at the lighthouse, that I saw," Lucien said. "But a few times, perhaps several times, when I stopped by his cottage to visit, he had a bottle out, which isn't a crime. But a couple of times he seemed inebriated."

Julia turned to Officer Carlson. "Were Uncle Edward's supplies delivered by the custom house?"

"Yes."

"Was any kind of alcohol ever included in the order?"

Deputy Martin laughed. "No, but there are certainly other ways to acquire alcohol around here. We are a seaport, after all."

Julia placed the palms of both hands flat and looked at the men around the table. "There wasn't a single bottle of alcohol in his cottage. I checked last night."

"You shouldn't be in his cottage," Officer Carlson said. "I need to investigate it next. Now there's no way to know if you removed evidence or not."

"I most certainly did not."

"You'll need to vacate it immediately."

Julia felt as if she'd been slapped. "But where will I stay?"

"That's not my problem," Officer Carlson said. "It's yours." He glanced at Alexander. "Maybe your new boss can help."

Chapter Five

Two hours later, Julia headed straight to her room in Uncle Edward's cottage, fighting back tears. It had been the worst twenty-four hours of her life. At least the worst since her parents drowned when their sailboat capsized off Block Island, near the coast of Rhode Island.

But then she had Uncle Edward to comfort her and care for her. She felt inadequate to return that care, in this strange place.

She thought of Billy. She should have looked for him down at the wharf. She needed someone to recommend a boardinghouse and move her trunk into town.

Her dress from the night before had dried but was still muddy. She folded it and placed it in her trunk. Then she closed the trunk and dragged it down the hall to the sitting area.

She heard a knock at the door.

She hoped it would be Alexander with a lodging idea for her.

But it was Lucien. "How can I help you?" he asked.

Tears stung her eyes. "Do you know of a suitable boardinghouse in town? Or a woman renting a room?"

He thought a moment and shook his head. "However, there are a few cabins where women who work at Fort Canby live—a couple of cooks and laundresses."

Julia said, "I met one of the laundresses this morning."

"At the moment," Lucien said, "one is empty."

"Is it furnished?"

"Partially," he answered. "It has a bed and a table and chairs. Cooking pots. That sort of thing. You can take bedding from here. It'll need to be cleaned and swept, but it's adequate."

It would make more sense to be in town, close to Uncle Edward. But if Julia was on the cape, she'd be closer to Uncle Edward's cottage, where she could keep an eye on his things.

"Did you speak with Officer Carlson before he left?"

Lucien nodded. "I saw him down at the wharf. He's finished his investigation and headed back to Astoria."

"Did he find anything?" Julia asked. "Bourbon bottles?"

Lucien's eyes were filled with concern. "It's a pity Carlson didn't search the cabin before you did. He doesn't believe that you didn't clean the place up before he came."

Julia squeezed her eyes shut. "But I didn't."

"I believe you."

She opened her eyes. "Do you? You're the one who accused Uncle Edward of having a drinking problem."

"I only reported what I'd witnessed." He gestured toward the kitchen. "Gather up what you need, and then I'll help you with your trunk and show you the cabin."

Julia stowed the sheets and quilt from her bed in the trunk. Lucien sat on it to get it closed. Then she found an empty crate and filled it with a plate, a teacup, a kettle, a set of cutlery, a wooden spoon, a tin of tea, and some canned goods from Uncle Edward's shelves.

As she collected these things from the kitchen, Lucien left to retrieve a handcart from Fort Canby. When he returned, they loaded the trunk and box into it. Together, they pushed it along the path to the fort.

As they walked, Julia asked, "Who burdened this cape with the forlorn title of 'Disappointment'?"

"Lieutenant John Meares of the British Royal Navy in 1788," Lucien answered. "He missed the Columbia River, even though he was looking for the Northwest Passage, when he was heading south from Vancouver Island. He declared that—I have this memorized—'We can now with safety assert, that no such river as that of St. Roc exists, as laid down in the Spanish charts.' He therefore named this hunk of basalt Cape Disappointment."

"Fascinating. I do remember Uncle Edward writing that Captain Robert Gray was the first to discover the Columbia River."

"Yes. He was an American sea merchant. The year was 1792. However, Native tribes had been navigating the river and coastline for hundreds of years, if not more."

"Of course." Julia tried to imagine canoes powered by oars on the mighty river and crossing the crashing of the waves at the bar and continuing out to the ocean. The entire endeavor would have demanded a fortitude she couldn't even imagine.

"I need your opinion about something."

Lucien turned. "I'm always happy to share my opinion."

"Why do you think Alexander said I worked for the newspaper this morning? What could his motivation be?"

Lucien chuckled. "I'm sure he didn't do it out of the goodness of his heart. He must have some sort of ulterior motive."

"That's what I was afraid of," Julia said. "So, should I act as if I have a job? Show up for work on Monday and see what he does?"

"Do you need a job?"

"Yes." Julia paused a moment and then said, "I both need and want a job. And as I understand it, the *Cape Dispatch* is the only newspaper in town."

Lucien shrugged. "Alexander is an odd duck."

"I'll go into town tomorrow and ask him." Julia put her hand out to steady the trunk on the cart. "Except it will be Sunday. I guess I should wait until Monday."

"Alexander will likely be in his office tomorrow," Lucien said. "He doesn't go to church that I know of. Doesn't socialize much." He stopped and looked over his shoulder. "You're welcome to come to the community church tomorrow. The service starts at eleven."

"Thank you." Julia felt a wave of gratitude to Lucien for his opinions, advice, history lesson, and, even more, his continued help. Yet, she also felt frustration at his certainty that Uncle Edward had a drinking problem.

Uncle Edward had written about the joy and peace he felt on Cape Disappointment, feeling as if he were perched on the edge of a world so beautiful, he couldn't help but be aware of the Lord throughout every moment of the day. None of his letters indicated he was lonely or out of sorts.

Julia wished she could find the same joy. All she'd found on Cape Disappointment, so far, was, well, disappointment. She'd found absolutely no joy and certainly no peace.

After they hauled the trunk inside the cabin, Lucien offered to help clean. Julia insisted he'd done far more than enough for her and that she was perfectly capable of cleaning the one room. She walked him out the door as she thanked him.

"Lucien!" A young woman carrying a parasol in one hand and lifting her skirts with the other hurried to them. "I've been looking all over for you. Did you forget?"

"Minnie." Lucien smacked his hand to his forehead. "I'm so sorry. I've been working all day. And now I need to go clean the lighthouse and gather wicks and oil."

As the woman approached, Lucien motioned to Julia and then Minnie. "Julia, this is Minnie Winther. Minnie, Julia Warren."

"Pleased to meet you." Julia stepped forward.

Minnie put one hand on her hip. "Are you the lightkeeper's daughter?"

"Niece," Julia said. "Although more like a daughter. Uncle Edward raised me."

"Oh."

"Would you like to keep me company while I clean?" Lucien asked Minnie. "I have an order from the custom house officer in Astoria to do so."

Minnie wrinkled her nose.

Julia almost volunteered to help, but she stopped herself. It appeared that Minnie had been expecting to spend time with Lucien. Julia had taken enough of his day.

"I'll let you two go," Julia said. "Lucien, thank you so much for your help. Minnie, it was nice to meet you. I hope I'll see you again soon."

Minnie smiled sweetly, but once she and Lucien started to walk away, Julia heard her ask, "Why were you helping her?"

Julia stepped back into the cabin and started a fire in the cookstove, which was also the only source of heat in the cabin, and then swept—the ceiling, the walls, and the floor. Next, she hauled water from the pump and put it on to heat—both to clean with and for tea.

By the time the light began to wane, she had everything in order. The day had grown warmer, and the wind had died, making it surprisingly mild. The rain hadn't returned, much to her surprise. Perhaps clouds and a gray sky didn't always mean rain.

She stepped out of the cabin and walked along the path to the lighthouse, drawn by the setting sun. She stopped where Lucien's buggy was parked, next to the stable where he boarded his horse. She peered into the buggy. The box that had been in the back was gone. Why hadn't she ripped the tarp off when he'd parked the buggy at the hospital?

She stepped into the stable, expecting to see the stable hand, but no one was around. She didn't see Lucien's box, but there was a sledgehammer leaning against the wall next to the first stall. Was that what someone used to break the lens? Its handle seemed to be the same length as the handle she'd seen in Lucien's buggy. She picked it up and put it inside the stall in the far corner, on its side. Then she pulled a hay bale in front of it.

She slipped out of the stable and headed toward the ocean. She could see strips of yellow and orange and a fiery ball through the trees. She reached the last of the trees and hurried past the lighthouse, where oil lamps now burned in the lens room, to the edge of the bluff. It did feel like the end of the world. Ahead of her was the

Columbia Bar, the jetty at the north end, and then—straight ahead and to the right—the vast Pacific.

The wind and rain of the night before were only a memory. No wonder Uncle Edward loved this area so much. The coastline was rocky and rugged, with only a few sandy beaches. The terrain was nearly as treacherous, with cliffs rising straight from the ocean and gullies and ravines cutting through the bluffs.

Cape Disappointment *was* a disappointment to her—but it was also the most spectacular place she'd ever seen.

Julia spent a restless night in her cabin. The sunny day had turned into a freezing night, and she rose several times to feed the fire. In the morning, which dawned gray and drizzly, she stoked the fire again and made herself a pot of tea. She cradled the hot mug in both hands as she sat at the table.

She'd go into town and find Alexander. She had enough money for a few weeks, unless whoever owned the cabin started charging her rent. A job was a must. And she'd rather work at the *Cape Dispatch* than anywhere else.

Soon, wearing her boots and coat, she stepped into the dreary morning. She followed the road into town again and found the shortcut down the hill. Large stones were wedged into the slope to form a staircase. Once she reached the street closest to the Cape, she headed toward downtown. On the way, she heard music. Halfway up the block was a church. A man, perhaps in his late forties and wearing an expensive coat and shoes, strolled up the church stairs.

He had a thick head of dark hair and carried a big Bible. The sign outside the building read COMMUNITY CHURCH. The church Lucien attended. Most likely, Minnie attended it too.

Julia hesitated a moment, debating whether she should go in or not. Uncle Edward would want her to—but she wasn't ready. It had been months since she'd been inside a church, since Jack had announced his engagement to Suzanne Harris, the Philadelphia socialite. It wasn't that she was angry with God. She just wasn't sure she could trust Him.

When she reached the hospital, Nurse Vera was in the front room at the desk and Doc Olsen was out on a house call. "There's been no change," Nurse Vera said.

"Has he been taking water?"

"Some. And a little broth," she answered. "But, as I said, there's been no change. There's no need for you to see him."

"I'd like to anyway."

"Suit yourself."

Nurse Vera continued sitting at her desk, and Julia stepped through the door, down the hallway, and into Uncle Edward's room. He was on his side, facing the door. He appeared peaceful. Julia sat in the chair next to his bed and took his hand.

"I hope you're feeling better." She paused. "We really need you to wake up. The lens is broken, so I set up lamps in the lens room night before last, and Lucien Graham did the same last night."

Uncle Edward stirred. Could he hear her?

She held his hand a little longer and then said, "I'll come back tomorrow and see you again." She bent and kissed his forehead. "Please wake up."

She thanked Nurse Vera on her way out and headed to the newspaper office.

When she reached it, the curtains were drawn across the one window. She knocked on the door. When no one responded, she turned the knob. It was unlocked, so she opened the door and walked in.

Alexander sat at the desk, reading a book. He looked up with a startled expression on his face. Then he closed the book and slipped it into a side drawer.

"Good morning, Miss Warren," he said.

Julia smiled. "Good morning." She closed the door. "I do wish you'd call me Julia. Lucien told me people don't stand on ceremony in Ilwaco."

He stood. "Julia. How is your uncle?"

She shook her head. "He seems the same."

"Come on in." He seemed much more subdued than he had the last two days. "I need to speak with you."

"Oh?"

"I wanted to apologize for how I acted the other day when you stopped by, asking about a job. And then I've realized I was harsh that evening surrounding the circumstances of your uncle and the lighthouse." Alexander steepled his hands. "You're right—I did jump to conclusions. I got caught up in the circumstances. Thank you for pointing out that I needed to be unbiased. Honestly, if I was a betting man, I'd say it looks as if your uncle had been drinking, but I can't show that in my reporting. I appreciate your honesty."

"Thank you," Julia managed to say. "That was most unexpected. Will it affect your article about the lighthouse?"

"*Did* it affect the article. The newspaper came out yesterday afternoon."

"I see."

He stood and walked to the table by the wall. He picked up a newspaper and handed it to her. "I only wrote the facts. Who, what, when, where, and why."

The five Ws, which could be traced all the way back to Aristotle. Julia knew them well.

She unfolded the newspaper. The two front-page articles were about the *Pacific Star* wrecking and the lighthouse lens being damaged. She skimmed the second article. The writing wasn't bad. Alexander had included the approximate time the beacon went out. And exactly what had been found in the lighthouse—the broken lens and the lightkeeper, unconscious and with a head wound. Alexander finished the article with *The investigation is ongoing*. That was fair.

"Thank you." She held the newspaper out to him.

He smiled. "Keep it."

She returned the smile.

"What did you need to speak to me about?"

"The fact that I am, as of yesterday, employed in this office."

He rubbed the side of his head.

"Am I now employed as a reporter?"

He shook his head. "I can't afford a reporter."

"What do you need? Or, rather, what can you afford?"

"I need a typesetter, like I said."

"Of which I have no experience, like I said."

"I understand that," he answered. "I also need someone to sell and write advertisements, so I can bring in more money to hire a reporter."

Her heart fell. "I also have no experience selling and writing ads."

"But you could do it," he said. "I'm certain."

Julia inhaled sharply. She probably wouldn't find anything better. "All right," she said. "I'd like to give it a try."

He gave her a curt nod. "Good. I'll see you tomorrow morning at nine. I'll give you a rundown of the job, and then you can get started."

"I'll be here." As she left the newspaper office, she wasn't sure if she'd just sold her soul or simply acquired a means to survive.

Chapter Six

Monday morning dawned gray again. Julia dressed in her work suit—corset, white blouse, black tailored jacket, petticoat, forest-green skirt, boots, and a wide-brimmed black hat with a green ribbon. She placed her notebook and her pencil in her bag and arrived at the *Cape Dispatch* office to find Alexander hiring another typesetter. He was an older man who'd recently arrived in the area.

After a few minutes, Alexander turned his attention to Julia and presented a list of regular advertisement buyers and prospective buyers. Then he gave her a quick tutorial on selling ads. When he finished, she asked, "What about writing the ads?"

"It's easy. You'll do fine."

"May I go through a few copies of the newspaper and look at examples before I go out?"

"Of course." He nodded to the shelves against the wall. "There are past copies over there."

Julia picked up several and sat down at the worktable. The general store ran several ads—one for men's boots, one for women's hats, and one for children's toys. Doc Olsen had a small ad, most likely out of support for the newspaper. She doubted he needed to advertise. Another ad was for a saloon in town. She'd never been inside a saloon before.

A cannery had an ad, advertising fresh fish for local buyers. That would be much easier.

Julia gathered her notebook, pencil, list, and copies of newspapers.

"Are you all set then?" Alexander asked.

"Yes."

He cleared his throat and met her eyes. Then cleared his throat again. Was he nervous?

Finally, he said, "Miss Warren—Julia, I want you to know how pleased I am to have you working for the *Cape Dispatch*. I'll do all I can to give you a chance to work as a reporter. I've had a few challenges lately, as far as the newspaper, that I need to overcome first."

"Thank you," she replied. "I appreciate the job—and the future opportunity to write."

"The good news is that newspaper sales were way up on Saturday." He smiled. "Make sure you let people know about the increased sales when you're selling ads."

"I will."

He brushed his hair from his forehead. "I'm hoping everything works out, including your uncle's health. He's in my prayers."

"Thank you." Tears stung Julia's eyes. "I'll come back if I have any questions." She decided to go to the restaurant on the same block as the newspaper office first, but the owner wasn't in, so she continued to the millinery, one block to the east.

Julia stepped through the door into a bustling shop. Several customers examined hats on the shelves, and two clerks worked with two women at the counter on designs. A third woman approached Julia. "May I help you?"

"My name is Julia Warren, and I'm working for the *Cape Dispatch*, selling ads. I need to speak with the owner about updating her current ad."

"Are you the niece of the lightkeeper, Mr. Warren?"

Julia's face grew warm. "Yes."

"Well," the woman said, "I never would have taken him to be a drunk. It's a good thing the investors in the *Pacific Star* all have insurance."

Julia gathered her courage. "Is the owner in the shop today?"

"The owner's busy," the woman said. "I'll let her know you stopped by. Come back later."

"All right." Julia smiled as broadly as she could manage, hoping to hide her sense of defeat—and doom. What if everyone in town shunned her because they believed Uncle Edward was responsible for the *Pacific Star* breaking up on the bar?

She decided a brisk walk might calm her, so she headed down to the canneries. When she reached the wharf, she veered right to the Cape Cannery and then to the door with a sign that read OFFICE over the top.

As she entered, a woman sitting at a desk asked, "May I help you?" Julia assumed she was the secretary.

Julia explained who she was. "I'd like to speak with the owner."

"He's in a meeting," she said. "But he won't be long. Would you like to wait?" She motioned to a chair.

Julia sat down. The woman opened a door and stepped into a hallway to the left. Julia couldn't help but overhear a conversation going on in a room beyond the door.

"You're my attorney." A man spoke forcefully. "Why didn't you notify me?"

Another man spoke calmly. "You never presented the contract to me to review."

"This is unacceptable."

"I'm sorry," the calmer man said. "But the insurance policy isn't legitimate, and I had a telegram this morning from a colleague in Astoria that the owner has fled town, taking the business account with him."

"That lightkeeper should be tarred and feathered and run out of town," the first man said.

The secretary had returned. She quickly closed the door. Then she turned to Julia, her face pale and her hands clasped. "I think it's best if you return at another time."

A wave of doubt swept over Julia as she headed to Hawk's Saloon across the street from the wharf. Uncle Edward was persona non grata in the area.

She stopped outside the saloon and inhaled sharply. She was a supporter of the temperance movement. She'd never entered a drinking establishment in her life.

But the place did serve food too. Everyone needed to eat, especially sailors and fishermen and lumberjacks, who all worked hard providing for others.

Besides, if she could establish that Uncle Edward didn't frequent the saloons in town, she might be able to prove the bourbon bottle didn't belong to him.

She squared her shoulders and marched into the saloon, which wasn't yet open for the day's business. A man and a woman sat at the bar talking. She asked to see the owner.

"Take a seat," the woman said. "I'll tell him you're out here."

Julia sat at the end of the bar.

When the woman returned, she said, "He'll be with you in a few minutes." Then she sat down again next to the man and said, "Several of the sailors came in yesterday. One said Alexander Blake sabotaged the *Pacific Star* when he was down in San Francisco for the christening. Remember the big article he wrote for the newspaper, praising the investors? He toured the ship."

Julia didn't dare breathe, not wanting to give away her shock at what the woman was saying.

"But how?" the man asked.

"He could have planted a bomb. It could be coincidental that they were on the bar when the ship wrecked. It could have happened anywhere along the way—Blake wouldn't have cared."

The man frowned. "But why would he do that?"

"To get a big story," the woman replied. "The article he wrote about the christening was picked up all the way back east. So was Saturday's article about the wreck. Each new story will be reprinted too. This is big news. He's been struggling to keep the newspaper going."

If a bomb had been planted, it would be big news. Was Alexander Blake that desperate to sell newspaper stories?

A man came out from the kitchen, and the two stopped talking. He appeared to be Uncle Edward's age and even had a white head of hair and a white beard. He wore a muslin shirt and an apron over his trousers.

Julia introduced herself.

"Pleased to meet you." He took her hand and gave it a firm shake. "I'm William Hawkins. Everyone calls me Hawk—thus the name of this place." He sat down next to her. "You aren't from around here, are you?"

"I'm new to the area. I'm selling ads for the *Cape Dispatch*."

"I see," he said.

"This is a good time to buy. Newspapers are selling like hotcakes thanks to the recent happenings."

"I can imagine." He sighed. "We do have extra sailors in town until they can find positions on other ships. Some of them are bound to be reading the paper, interested in what the investigations show. I haven't bought an ad before. What do you recommend?"

Julia squared her shoulders and talked through the sizes with him. He opted for the smallest. "What are you known for here?" she asked.

"The usual," he said. "But our fish stew and sourdough bread are what bring people back."

"Perfect," she said. "Let's put that in the advertisement." She met Hawk's gaze. "And who are you trying to get to come into your saloon? To give it a try?"

"Sailors," he said. "But the saloon at the end of the wharf gets more of them."

"You could give sailors a 10 percent discount."

He thought for a moment and then said, "That might be worth a try."

"Do you want me to add it to the advertisement?"

"Sure," he said. "Let's see what happens."

As she jotted down notes, Hawk said in a low voice, "Julia Warren. Any chance you're related to the lightkeeper?"

Again, her face grew warm. "Yes. He's my uncle. In fact, I was wondering if I could ask you a question about him."

"Of course."

"Did he ever frequent your saloon? In particular, would he have purchased a bottle of bourbon here?"

"No." His voice grew a little louder. "Don't listen to the rumors in town. Your uncle isn't a drunk. He didn't drink. Not at all."

Surprised, considering the reactions of everyone else, Julia asked, "How can you be so sure?"

"Not once has he stepped foot in here or any other saloon in town. I keep track of my customers and everyone else's too. And there's no way he's making his own drink under the watchful eyes of the US Custom House, even if the closest one is in Astoria. And they wouldn't be including bottles of anything in his delivered supplies—except maybe cod liver oil."

"Thank you," Julia said. "You've been very helpful."

She liked William Hawkins as much as anyone she'd met in Ilwaco so far. And not because he resembled Uncle Edward—even though he did. She liked him because he'd defended Uncle Edward.

That afternoon on her way to her cabin, Julia stopped by the hospital. Nurse Vera greeted her and then with a sigh said, "There's been no change."

Julia felt defeated. "Surely this can't be good."

"No," the nurse said, "it's not. Usually if a person is going to wake up, he has by now."

"Is he continuing to take water and broth?"

"Yes."

"I'll go sit with him for a few minutes." Julia headed down the hall and into Uncle Edward's room. He was on his back now, propped up on a stack of pillows.

"Hello, Uncle Edward." She told him about her day selling ads. Then she said, "Alexander Blake wrote an article about what happened at the lighthouse Friday night."

Uncle Edward remained still.

Julia continued. "Alexander, thankfully, only reported the facts, since we don't know what happened and won't until you wake up."

Uncle Edward's head tilted forward, slightly. Did he hear her? Did his reaction mean anything?

She waited another half hour, but nothing more happened.

After she told Uncle Edward goodbye and then told Vera that he'd moved his head a little, Julia started the trek back to Cape Disappointment. When she neared her cabin, she saw a figure in the distance. As the person came toward her, she saw it was Lucien.

"Hello, Julia," he said. "Where have you been all day?"

"Working," she answered. "Selling ads for the *Dispatch*."

"Ah, working for Alexander? So he was serious about a job?"

She nodded.

"How did it go?"

"All right."

He frowned. "I hope you didn't hear too much gossip."

"A few things," Julia said. "I ignored them." Which wasn't true. She wished she could ignore them.

He returned her smile, and then his face grew serious. "How's your uncle?"

"The same." The slight movement of his head wasn't enough to report.

"I'm sorry." Lucien's expression turned even more serious.

She shrugged. "At least it's not worse."

He agreed. "I'm on my way to light the lamps. See you later."

That night, once she was under the quilt in her bed with the hot brick she'd warmed in the fire and then wrapped in a towel at her feet, she stared at the open-beamed ceiling. It had been months since she'd prayed, since Jack had betrayed her. All she could think of after that fateful day was fleeing to the safety of Uncle Edward. But he couldn't help her now. He needed help. She folded her hands under her quilt and managed to whisper, "Dear God…"

Dear God, what?

"Dear God…" All she could manage to add was, "Help. Please, help me find the truth."

In the morning she walked to town through a drizzle and arrived at the office early. Alexander sat at the desk, reading again. As he had on Sunday, he slipped the book into the desk drawer when she entered the office.

"Do you have some ads for me?" he asked.

"I sold three. I need to write the copy though. That's why I came in early."

"You can work at the table," he said.

"Thank you." As she walked across the room, she said, "I'm afraid once some people know I'm Edward Warren's niece, they won't buy an ad from me."

"Don't tell them you're related," Alexander said.

Julia shook her head. "That won't help. People are figuring out who I am."

"Ignore them."

"That's hard to do."

"Do your best."

She put her things on the table and then turned to Alexander again.

"Is there something else?" His voice was kind.

She hesitated, weighing whether she should bring up the rumor that he'd sabotaged the ship for a big story. She decided not to.

"It's just that—" She paused. "That I'm praying for the truth to come out regarding my uncle."

Alexander's eyes brightened. "That's what I'm praying as well. That at some point, the truth will come out."

She wasn't sure whether to believe him or not. She found Alexander endearing in a more honest way than Jack had been, but she couldn't take a chance on being fooled again. Just like Jack, Alexander could likely have ulterior motives. Jack wanted more status in Philly. It seemed Alexander wanted more status as a reporter, nationally.

Julia continued to the table, pulled out a chair, and got to work on the ads.

Fifteen minutes later, Alexander approached her with a cup. "How about some tea?"

"Thank you." She took the cup, letting it warm her hands, touched by the gesture.

Until it occurred to her that he could be trying to earn her trust to protect himself.

She felt a chill come over her despite the warmth of the steam rising from her cup. It seemed there was no safe haven for her here in Cape Disappointment.

Chapter Seven

As Julia continued to sell ads throughout the week, she heard about several other *Pacific Star* investors who had purchased fraudulent insurance policies. The more she talked with people, the more it seemed as if a figurative, along with a literal, dark cloud hung over the town. Several cannery owners had invested in the *Pacific Star,* as had one of the Ilwaco Railway owners. So had the owner of a shipping company. And the owner of the general store next to the newspaper office, who also owned a cannery, had invested, or so she'd heard. There were rumors that not all the policies were fraudulent, but Julia couldn't determine who had bought valid ones.

Friday morning, she arrived at the office early to write up the ads she'd sold the day before. Alexander was, once again, reading at his desk. After he slipped the book into the drawer, he said, "Good morning." Without pausing, he asked, "How many ads did you sell yesterday?"

"Two," she said.

He smiled. "That's better than one. Or none."

He was either trying to encourage or—or perhaps flatter her. She couldn't tell which. "Any new developments on the insurance fraud story, the wreck, or the attack on my uncle and the vandalism at the lighthouse?"

"Nothing," he answered. "How is your uncle?"

"The same." She'd stopped by the hospital for a report on the way to the newspaper but didn't take the time to see Uncle Edward. She'd do that after work.

Alexander brought her a cup of tea, which she accepted. "Thank you."

"I appreciate your work," he said. "I know you feel as if the townspeople are judging you, but you're doing a fine job. Each week will get better."

She thanked him again. She couldn't believe Alexander would sabotage the ship. He didn't seem the type of person to do such a thing. But maybe her gratefulness that he'd hired her made her biased.

An hour later, her ads written and her day planned, she headed to the millinery once more, after having been put off again on Monday afternoon. She'd been told to return at the end of the week. Suddenly, someone called out her name. She turned.

"Julia!" Lucien called again as he hurried to her. "How are you doing?"

"All right."

"How is your uncle?"

"The same."

"I'm sorry."

"How are you?"

"Good. I worked last night." He appeared bright-eyed nonetheless. "I have a few errands to run before I sleep for a few hours."

"Do you have time for a quick question?" Julia asked. "I promise it won't take long."

"Sure," he answered.

She lowered her voice. "What are your impressions of Alexander Blake?"

"What do you mean in particular?"

"His integrity."

Lucien laughed. "So, you finally want the scuttlebutt on Mr. Blake. Let me guess—you've heard the rumor about him sabotaging the *Pacific Star*?"

She nodded.

"Alexander and I worked at the lifesaving station together a decade ago."

"Is that connected to the rescue brigade?"

He shook his head. "The brigade is volunteer and is activated when there's a big wreck or the crew from the lifesaving station is out on a call."

"I see," Julia said.

"Anyway," Lucien said, "Alexander was a little unreliable at the time. You know, he grew up rich and didn't really know how to work."

"He grew up rich?"

"Filthy rich. In Chicago."

Julia wouldn't have guessed that.

Lucien continued. "By the time Alexander ended up here, he had one wild scheme after another. One in particular backfired on him—before he tried to execute it, thankfully. Otherwise, he might be serving time in the state penitentiary over in Walla Walla."

Julia winced.

"But he was young, and people change, right?" Lucien continued.

She wasn't sure how common it was for a man to change, at least not when it came to his character.

Lucien shrugged. "Could Alexander have sabotaged the *Pacific Star*? Probably not alone, but with help, sure. Would he?" Lucien smiled. "I have no idea, but I also think it's hard to know what anyone is capable of. That said, like most communities, people around here have a long memory. There are some who don't trust Alexander, which has never been good for his business. They may feel they don't have reason to trust him now."

Julia thanked Lucien and continued on her way. Perhaps she needed to be more suspicious of Alexander, not less. She also still needed to find an opportunity to investigate what tool with a short handle Lucien had in the box in his buggy.

Julia continued on to the millinery shop. As she waited for the owner, she overheard a customer say, "My daughter told me the lightkeeper colluded with an insurance agent in Astoria. They planned the wreck, and they're going to split the premium payments the agent stole from the investors."

Julia sighed. That theory didn't make sense. The agent couldn't have made that much money off the insurance premiums. Sure, he might have colluded with someone, but it seems it would have been with someone who actually had a viable insurance policy, one that would pay out on the wrecked ship.

Julia stared at a hat with a cloth peony on the top. Perhaps the insurance agent had sold one of the investors a viable policy.

Finally, a woman came out of the back room and, without introducing herself, said to Julia, "Could you come again this afternoon? I'm busy right now."

Julia smiled and said, "Of course. Two o'clock?"

"Make it three."

As Julia left the shop, she wondered if Captain Evert had an insurance policy. After all, the captain was responsible for both the vessel and the cargo. From growing up around ships, she knew many captains carried marine policies on the vessels they piloted. She decided to go down to the wharf and look for Captain Evert.

Once she reached the wharf, Julia stopped in and saw the secretary at the cannery and asked her if she had any idea where she could find Captain Evert.

"I have no idea," she answered.

Someone yelled, "Do you have those papers for me?"

"You need to leave," the secretary said to Julia.

Julia slipped out the door. Billy and his buggy came to a stop on the roadway. Julia waved and hurried toward him. He smiled and waved back. As she neared his buggy, she called out, "Billy, how are you?"

He tipped his hat. "Just fine, Miss Julia. How's your uncle?"

She stopped at the buggy. "He's the same."

His face fell. "I'm sorry."

"Thank you," she replied. "I have a question for you. What kind of tools do you carry in your buggy?"

"A shovel in case I get stuck."

"Anything else?"

He shook his head. "If I break a wheel, I have to take it in to the blacksmith to fix."

"Do you ever carry a sledgehammer?"

"I don't," he said. "But some people do. Or a mallet, plus an axe for cutting trees. A sledgehammer could be used to repair a wagon wheel or perhaps an axle. People carry all sorts of tools around here."

"So a lot of people would have a sledgehammer?"

He nodded and smiled at her. "Any other questions?"

"Yes, I have one more. Do you know where I can find Captain Evert?"

A confused expression passed over his face, and he shook his head. "I have no idea. I haven't seen him for a few days."

She smiled. "Thank you anyway."

She had a copy of yesterday's newspaper with the ad for Hawk's Saloon. She'd ask Mr. Hawkins if he knew Captain Evert.

Julia waved goodbye to Billy and continued down the road.

When she entered the saloon, the owner stood behind the bar. "Hello, Mr. Hawkins," Julia called out.

"Ah, Miss Warren," he said. "How are you today?"

"Just fine." She sat down on the last stool at the bar. "I have a copy of your advertisement here."

"I saw it yesterday. A couple of sailors came in with it." He stepped closer. "The discount worked."

"Oh, good." She handed him the newspaper. "Take it anyway."

He took it from her and tucked it under his arm.

"Do you mind if I ask you a couple of questions?" she asked.

"Go ahead."

"Does Lucien Graham play cards here on Friday nights?"

"No. He frequents the saloon at the end of the wharf."

"How about Captain James Evert? Does he come in here?"

He laughed. "Are you set on selling him an advertisement?"

Julia couldn't help but smile. "Not today."

"Well," Mr. Hawkins said, "this isn't his saloon of choice either."

"Does he go to the one at the end of the wharf too?"

He nodded, winked, and handed her back the newspaper. "Maybe you should give him the newspaper and see if my advertisement will lure him away."

Julia took the newspaper and smiled. "I'll give it a try."

Again, Julia hesitated before going into the second saloon. But if it meant finding Captain Evert, she needed to do it. Once she stepped inside, she stopped, giving her eyes a chance to adjust. There was a man at the bar and another at a table. She squinted. The man at the table was the captain.

She approached, and once Captain Evert raised his head, she asked, "Would it be all right if I asked you a few questions?"

Captain Evert cocked his head. "And who are you?"

"I work for the *Cape Dispatch*. I met you Saturday."

He stroked his beard. "You're the lightkeeper's daughter."

"Niece."

He shrugged.

She stepped closer and joined him at the table. "I've heard some rumors that the insurance policies some of the investors purchased for the *Pacific Star* were fraudulent."

He finished his drink. "That's not my concern. Nor yours. Hasn't anyone ever told you to mind your own business?"

Julia didn't flinch. "Anything to do with the wreck of the *Pacific Star* is certainly my business. My uncle is fighting for his life, and we need to know why."

"Probably because he was drunk while on duty."

"That hasn't been proven." She sat up as straight as she could. "Did you take out a policy on the ship?"

He harrumphed. "Of course I did."

Julia leaned toward him. "I don't know how this works. Why would you, as the pilot, take out a policy?"

"In case they sued me. In case the wreck was my fault." He locked eyes with her. "Which it clearly wasn't."

"But the investors who bought fraudulent policies will lose everything."

He leaned away from her. "It's not my fault those investors didn't check out the legitimacy of the agent they bought policies from."

"What company did you go through?"

"Lombards of San Francisco." He glared at her. "I keep hearing all this speculation about fraudulent insurance policies. But what does it have to do with me? I won't benefit in any way because they won't be paid. It's not as if I'll get more money."

Julia understood that. But would someone else benefit in some way from the fraudulent claims, besides the agent who supposedly ran off with the insurance company's money?

"What will you do with your settlement?" she asked.

"Stay right here," Captain Evert said, placing both hands on the table and pushing himself to his feet. "I'll be right back."

He weaved a little as he walked through the door, probably on his way to the outhouse. Perhaps he wouldn't return. She stepped to the bar. "Excuse me," she said to the bartender. "Are you the owner?"

"Yes, ma'am," he said.

"I work for the *Dispatch*, and I'm looking into the wrecking of the *Pacific Star*. Do you recall if Mr. Edward Warren, the Cape Disappointment lightkeeper, visited your saloon or purchased a bottle of bourbon from here?"

"No, ma'am," he answered. "I've never seen Mr. Edwards in this saloon or entering the other one in town either."

"How about Lucien Graham? Does he frequent this saloon?"

"Yes, ma'am. He sure does."

Julia asked, "Was he here the night the *Pacific Star* wrecked?"

"That was a Friday, right?"

She nodded.

"Yes, ma'am. He's here every Friday night, unless he's working."

"Thank you." Julia walked back to Captain Evert's table and waited. And waited. Finally, just when she was ready to leave, surmising the captain had snuck out on her, he returned. He grinned when he saw her. "You're still here?"

She smiled back. "I'm still waiting for you to answer my question."

He plopped down in the chair. "And what was your question?"

"What will you do with your insurance money?"

"Well," he said, "if I didn't have any scruples, I'd buy a business in town." He chuckled. "I'm sure a few of the investors will be selling their businesses soon enough. The recovery from the Panic of '93 arrived here late, so the prices are already low. Combine that with desperation from their losses, and I should be able to afford at least one."

"What business would you buy, if you chose to do so?"

"The wharf."

"That would certainly be a good investment."

"The owner, John Hoffman, invested heavily in the *Pacific Star*."

"Oh?"

"Yes." Captain Evert waved his empty glass at the bartender. "He'll be looking for a buyer in a few weeks, no doubt."

Julia cocked her head.

"But I would never do that to Hoffman nor to anyone else in town." Captain Evert tipped his head back. "Maybe I'll find someone who's floundering in Astoria. Or Seattle. It's probably time I retire."

Buying up businesses could certainly be motivation for someone else to be involved in fraud, even if it wasn't for Captain Evert. "Do you think someone could have sabotaged the ship and caused the wreck?"

He dragged his hand across his mouth. "I examined the ship from top to bottom and found nothing on board and nothing wrong with its construction. I missed my mark on the bar because the light was out."

"Should you have waited?"

He slammed his palm down on the table. "I couldn't wait. It was the top of the tide, and I'd already started across when the storm blew in like a hurricane. I know the ropes. If the light had been on, I would have known where I was on the bar. It was the keeper's fault."

Julia stopped by to see Deputy Martin next. He was in the office, at the front desk. As she entered, he stood. "Is your uncle conscious?"

"I'm afraid not," she said. "I stopped by to let you know I found a sledgehammer in the stable up on Cape Disappointment, and I'm pretty sure Lucien Graham had a sledgehammer in his buggy the day after the lens at the lighthouse was broken."

Deputy Martin narrowed his eyes. "And this proves what?"

"That you should examine the sledgehammer. I'll tell you where it is."

"Do you know how many sledgehammers there are in the area? Everyone has a sledgehammer. Blacksmiths. Lumberjacks. Shipbuilders. Stonemasons. Farmers. Demolition crews. Finding a sledgehammer in a stable is proof of nothing."

"If it was used on the lens, perhaps there's something that was left on the head."

He laughed. "I heard you were a writer, but not one of those novelists."

Her face grew warm. "Won't you at least take a look at the sledgehammer?"

He shook his head. "But I'll send Officer Carlson a telegram and let him know you found one."

"Tell him also that both of the saloon owners in town said Uncle Edward never frequented their establishments. He didn't drink at either place or purchase alcohol from them."

"That doesn't prove anything. All he had to do was ask someone else to purchase it for him." Deputy Martin smirked. "But I'll make sure and let Officer Carlson know that too."

He was laughing again as she left the office.

Next, she headed to the general store, which took up three-quarters of the building where Alexander rented his office and printing shop.

She opened the door to the general store. Inside she saw a ready-made clothes section, bolts of fabric, shelves filled with thread and notions, and rows of housewares. Near the back, there was a section of canned goods, staples, and barrels of pickles and soda crackers.

Behind the counter was the young woman who'd been looking for Lucien on Saturday—Minnie Winther. She wore a white frilly apron over a lavender print dress and waited on an older woman at the counter.

The woman asked, "Your father didn't buy one of those policies from the company in Astoria, did he?"

"No, ma'am," Minnie answered. "He's not that foolish. His policy is legitimate."

"That's a relief," the woman said. "I'm afraid my brother-in-law is going to lose his entire business."

"Oh dear," Minnie said. "I'm sorry."

The woman shook her head, causing her hat to bounce around. "That lightkeeper. He should be behind bars."

Minnie nodded in agreement.

As the woman left the store, Julia said, "Hello, Minnie."

"Oh, hi. I didn't see you there."

No doubt. "How are you doing today?" Julia asked.

"Good." Minnie smiled sweetly. "How are you?"

"Just fine." She held up her notebook. "I'm selling advertisements for the *Dispatch*. I wondered if someone is here I can talk to about your ad for next week."

"My father is busy today," Minnie said, crossing her arms. "But I need to speak to Alexander anyway. Tell him to come talk to me and sell me the ad himself. I don't feel right buying from you."

Chapter Eight

When Julia returned to the newspaper office that afternoon after being rebuffed at the millinery, Alexander was too busy printing the paper to speak with her.

"Can you come back in the morning?" he asked.

"Sure." She'd planned to work a few hours on Saturday anyway. "When you have time, Minnie Winther wants you to sell her the advertisement for the general store. She won't buy from me."

He cringed. "Sorry about that. I'll speak with her."

Julia stopped by the hospital again and sat with Uncle Edward. Several times she started to speak, but her words trailed off. What if he didn't recover? What if he wasted away in this bed for the little time he had left on earth? It wasn't what a good man like Edward Warren deserved.

When she arrived at her cabin, she peeled off her jacket, blouse, and skirt. She put on a nightgown and her robe, stoked the fire, and made herself a cup of tea and then a corncake and a couple of pieces of bacon. That would do for dinner.

After she ate, she took out her notebook. It had been exactly a week since someone damaged the Cape Disappointment Lighthouse Fresnel lens and injured Uncle Edward—and since the wreck of the *Pacific Star.*

It was up to her to figure out who was responsible for all three. Perhaps it was one person—or many. She didn't know, not yet. What she did know was that Uncle Edward wasn't responsible for any of them.

Who, what, where, when, and why. Those were the questions that needed to be answered when writing a newspaper article, according to Jack, as well as when solving a crime. She knew who was attacked—she needed to know who the attackers were and what exactly happened. She needed to know where all the suspects were that night and any alibis they had. She needed to know when the planning for the attack began. She needed to know why the crime was committed and what the motivation was, and if it was connected to the fraudulent policies.

Alexander was first on her list. A big national story could have been his motivation, and theoretically, he could have sabotaged the ship while touring it in San Francisco. She guessed he would have needed to have an accomplice on the ship. Then again, Captain Evert said he examined the ship and found nothing wrong with it. Perhaps Alexander and Captain Evert were in cahoots.

Alexander's alibi was being on the beach at the time Uncle Edward was injured.

Was being on the beach an alibi? Couldn't Alexander have sneaked up the hill, attacked Uncle Edward and the lens, splashed bourbon all over the place, and then returned to the beach? She needed to ask around to see who actually saw Alexander on the beach, and when. She finished her notes about Alexander.

Next on her list was Captain Evert. He could have wrecked on the bar on purpose, but he would have had to have been working with someone else—like Alexander. Someone who could sneak into the lighthouse, attack Uncle Edward, knock him down the stairs, pour bourbon on him, and damage the lens. If someone else—meaning Uncle Edward—was blamed for the accident, Captain Evert could retain his good reputation. But would he profit enough off his insurance money to make it worth wrecking the *Pacific Star*? Only if he bought a business at a low price, as he'd suggested he could do—but said he wouldn't.

The next name on her list was Robert Winther. She felt bad about her suspicion of the man since she hadn't actually met him. But he had invested in the *Pacific Star*, and his insurance policy would pay out, unlike the fraudulent ones. As far as an alibi, she had no idea where he was when Uncle Edward was attacked and the lens was damaged. She needed to investigate that.

She wrote down Lucien's name. He had the motivation—the head lightkeeper job, although she didn't know if he would get it or not. When it came to an alibi, he said he was playing cards at the saloon. Once she knew which saloon, that should be easy enough to verify. He could easily be the perpetrator when it came to Uncle Edward's attack—he did have a tool in the back of his buggy that he could have hidden there that night—but she didn't see any connection between Lucien and the wrecking of the *Pacific Star*. She needed to put more thought into that.

Who else? She couldn't think of anyone, but she needed to be open to more possibilities.

What connections could she make? As a newcomer to Cape Disappointment, she was probably missing all kinds of connections. She needed to be looking for those. In the meantime, Lucien and Minnie/Robert Winther was an obvious connection.

Were there business connections she didn't know about? What connections did Captain Evert have in town? Likely, many. Were there any connections between those on the list and the insurance agent who sold the fraudulent polices and fled Astoria?

Julia put her pen down. There were lots of possibilities. And yet, Officer Olsen and Deputy Martin didn't seem to be investigating any of them.

The next morning, the rain poured again. But at least she remembered her umbrella.

It hardly mattered. The rain flew sideways and pelted her face and sent the cold straight through to her bones.

Instead of going to the *Dispatch* office, she headed to Hawk's place, hoping Mr. Hawkins would be available to speak with her. She squinted in the dim light as she entered. No one was at the bar. "Mr. Hawkins?" she called out.

He appeared at the door of the kitchen.

"Goodness," he said. "You're soaked and shivering. Let me get you a cup of tea. Come in here and dry yourself by the stove."

"Thank you." She followed him into the kitchen.

He pulled up two chairs to the stove at the far end of the room. "Put your coat on one and sit in the other." He poured a cup from the kettle on the stove and added a splash of milk.

As he handed it to her, he asked, "What brings you in here on a stormy Saturday morning?"

"I have a question for you. Do you know if Lucien Graham and Captain Evert know each other?"

"I'm sure they're acquainted. They both spend a good amount of time at the other saloon. Beyond that, I wouldn't know."

Julia took a sip of tea and then another, feeling warmer already. "It seems Lucien was playing cards at the saloon the night the *Pacific Star* wrecked."

Mr. Hawkins's eyes sparkled. "Are you establishing alibis?"

"I'm trying to." She took another sip of tea.

"Well, my guess is that would be accurate, although it might be more difficult to establish whether or not he was there the entire evening."

"He was on the beach soon after the *Pacific Star* wrecked. I saw him there."

Mr. Hawkins thought for a moment and then asked, "Who did he say he was playing cards with?"

"A group of friends. His usual Friday night game, he said. He headed to the beach when he heard the news of the wreck. That's when I saw him. But that was after the beacon went out."

Mr. Hawkins crossed his arms. "Best of luck establishing alibis around here. People are more loyal to each other than the truth."

"How about Alexander Blake? What do you know of him?"

"He seems to be a nice enough fellow. But I don't know him very well—he's never come in here, and I doubt he goes to the other saloon either." Mr. Hawkins gave her a questioning look. "Is he on your list of possible suspects?"

"Have you heard people saying he sabotaged the *Pacific Star* to create a big story?"

He nodded. "I've heard that—but you hear a lot of things around here." He took the kettle from the stove. "How about more tea?"

"I'd like that very much," she said gratefully. "Thank you."

When she arrived at the newspaper office fifteen minutes later, the door was locked. She knocked and knocked, but no one came to the door. After she'd waited a few minutes, the typesetter arrived and pulled out a key.

Julia sat at Alexander's desk. The side drawer was ajar. She peered inside at the book he read every morning. Then she opened the drawer a little farther. The book was a Bible. Was it a prop? Or was Alexander genuine in his faith? She closed the drawer and began writing up ads.

When Alexander came through the door carrying a briefcase, she stood and gathered up her things.

He startled when he saw her. "Sorry, I forgot you'd be here. How did you get in?"

"The typesetter." She headed to the table.

"Ah, of course." He put his briefcase on the desk and walked to her. "How are you doing on the advertisements?"

She held up three pieces of paper with ads sketched out on them. "Almost done."

He took them, read them, and handed two back. Waving the paper he still held, he said, "This one is good." It was the new one for Hawk's Saloon, with a 15 percent discount this time. "But you need to work on the other ones. Oh, and the one for the general store too." He returned to his desk, placed the Hawk's ad on it, and then pulled a piece of paper from the top drawer.

"Doesn't Minnie want you to write up that advertisement?"

"Sorry about that." He handed her the paper. "The Winthers get special treatment if they want it. After all, they're my landlords."

"And they own half the town," she added.

Alexander winced. "Something like that."

"And he was one of the few people who bought a legitimate insurance policy on the *Pacific Star*."

Alexander lowered his voice. "I heard that too."

"Speaking of insurance policies, what do you think of Captain Evert?" Julia asked. "Is he respected around here?"

"Yes."

"How much does he drink?"

"I've never heard of him drinking when he's working."

"But he drinks when he's not?"

Alexander shrugged. "At times. But he's well respected. He's a good pilot."

Julia waited for Alexander to say more, but he didn't elaborate. "Is the respect deserved?" she asked.

Alexander didn't answer at first but then said, "Mostly."

"What does that mean?"

"I'm not at liberty to say anything more about that."

Julia crossed her arms, annoyed with Alexander for withholding information from her. Perhaps he had collaborated with Captain Evert. Was that what he was trying to hide? She'd waited long enough. She had to ask Alexander about the gossip she'd been hearing concerning him.

She took a deep breath. "Have you heard the rumor about yourself? That some people suspect you sabotaged the ship?"

He shook his head. "You can't believe everything you hear around here."

Julia bristled. "But you believe my uncle is responsible for the wreck of the *Pacific Star*?"

"The two accusations are not the same," Alexander said. "There's no evidence I sabotaged the ship. In fact, I think it would be impossible for someone to do so. How would I have detonated a bomb? It's simply an outlandish rumor. However, there is evidence your uncle broke the lens. He reeked of alcohol. The lens was broken, and there's no evidence of anyone else in the lighthouse. He fell down the stairs."

Julia crossed her arms. "As outlandish as someone sabotaging the ship sounds to you, I find the idea that Uncle Edward was drunk and vandalized the Fresnel lens just as outrageous."

"Touché," he said. "Hopefully the truth will come out." His voice grew softer. "I realize it's hard to accept that a relative, someone you've always respected, could do something so horrible. I hope the evidence is wrong."

"I can assure you that my uncle was not drinking Friday night, nor did he damage the lens."

Alexander took a step backward. "I think we both want the same thing, like I said before. We both want the truth. Time will tell."

Julia didn't respond. Did he really want the truth? Or was he intent on hiding something?

She'd wait to ask him about who could corroborate he was on the beach during the time in question. She didn't want to make him more defensive and therefore more suspicious of her than he already was.

However, it was obvious she needed to guard her feelings when it came to Alexander Blake. Yes, regardless of him being misguided about Uncle Edward, she was attracted to his kindness and faith in her abilities. Unless he was a fake, just as Jack had been.

Time would tell.

After work, the sun came out just before dusk, so Julia headed to the bluff to see the sunset. As she neared the lighthouse, Lucien walked out, holding a piece of paper in his hand.

He held it up. "I received a telegram from Officer Carlson."

"What did he say?"

"To continue lighting the lamps."

"Did he say anything about Uncle Edward's cottage?"

"No. They'll probably appoint a new keeper soon."

Julia smiled, just a little. "Are you working tonight?"

He shook his head. "The relief lightkeeper from the North Head Lighthouse is."

"So, you have Saturday night off?"

He did a little jig. "I'm going to the dance in town. Want to come? Minnie and I are going with a few friends."

"Oh, I don't want to intrude."

"You wouldn't be intruding. In fact, we always have more men than women. You'd be welcomed."

Julia doubted that, at least on Minnie's part, but she said, "I'll go watch the sunset and think about it."

Lucien took a step toward his cottage. "I'll stop by your cabin on my way, in about an hour, and see what you've decided."

The sunset wasn't as spectacular as the Saturday before, but it still moved Julia's soul. As the sun sank, an eagle soared beyond the bluff, silhouetted against the streaks of pink and orange. She gasped at the beauty before her, and for a glorious moment forgot her troubles. Enough so that she decided to go to the dance.

Chapter Nine

An hour and a half later, Julia rode with Lucien into town. She glanced to the rear of his buggy and said, "Where's your box of tools?"

He turned his head. "It's not back there?"

"No."

He returned his eyes to the road. "That's odd. I didn't take it out."

"What was in it?"

"My spade. Sometimes I carry an axe and mallet in case I need to chop a tree that's fallen across the road, although that doesn't seem to happen as much as it used to." He shook his head. "I don't know who would have taken my box of tools."

Was he covering for himself by mentioning a mallet? Sledgehammers and mallets were around the same size.

Fifteen minutes later, they arrived on the north edge of town at Minnie's three-story house, which was made of brick and wood with a wraparound porch and was on at least an acre of land.

Lucien left Julia in the buggy and ran up to the front door. A man opened it—the same man she'd seen walking into the church with his big Bible the Sunday before.

Lucien spoke with the man for a few minutes. They laughed a few times, and then Lucien pointed to the buggy. Minnie appeared, and all three spoke for a few more minutes, and then the man, who was most likely Minnie's father—making him Robert Winther—pointed to the buggy. Lucien said something to her, and she frowned. Lucien said something else, and she smiled. Then she kissed her father on the cheek. She took Lucien's elbow, and they started down the steps.

Julia stopped staring and climbed down from the bench to allow Minnie to sit in the middle.

"Hello, Julia." Minnie wore a pink gown with ruffles on the skirt and blouse and a very wide hat, with heart-shaped displays of flowers.

"Hello, Minnie," Julia said, stepping away from the buggy. "Thank you for letting me tag along with the two of you."

"Oh, we're happy to have you," Minnie gushed. "Aren't we, Lucien?"

"Indeed." He helped Minnie up into the buggy and then Julia.

Minnie's gown took up as much room as her hat, and Julia scooted to the end of the bench to make room.

When they arrived at the dance hall, Lucien stopped the buggy and helped Julia down and then Minnie. "I'll take care of the horse and buggy and be right back."

"Julia, what are you doing here?"

She turned toward the dance hall. Alexander stood to the side of the front door with a young woman, who was also wearing an elaborate gown and hat.

"I came with Minnie and Lucien." Julia stepped to him.

"This is Eliza Petersen." Alexander made the introductions. "Julia Warren. She's selling advertisements for the *Dispatch*."

"It's a pleasure to meet you," Julia said.

Eliza answered, "Likewise." Then she turned to Minnie and took both of her hands. "I'm so glad to see you. I need to speak with you."

The two walked to the corner of the building, leaving Alexander and Julia alone. Alexander cleared his throat and said, "I need to go talk with one of the fiddlers before they get started."

"All right." Julia watched him take the steps two at a time. Was he that eager to get away from her?

She moved to the edge of the pathway and then turned to the two women.

Eliza dabbed at her eyes with a hanky. "We're losing everything. The timber contracts. The log ponds. The sawmill. The house. Everything. All because of that horrible ship."

"Because of the insurance policy," Minnie corrected.

"What do you mean?"

"Your father's policy was fraudulent."

"But I don't understand. You're not losing everything."

"No, because my father's insurance policy was legitimate."

"It's not fair," Eliza said.

"Well," Minnie said, "you should talk to Alexander about the ship. Some people are saying he's responsible for the wreck."

"But he wasn't even on the ship."

Minnie lowered her voice and stepped closer to Eliza. Julia walked up the steps to the front door of the dance hall and stepped inside. Lamps illuminated the hall. Alexander stood on the stage, speaking with a man holding a fiddle. Another man sat at a piano, while a third man tuned a guitar.

Some people sat on chairs around the perimeter of the hall, and others stood. Julia continued to stand, not sure what to do. She didn't belong at the dance and wished she hadn't come. Finally, Alexander stepped away from the fiddler. As he started down the

in Cape Disappointment, Washington

stairs, the fiddler stepped to the front of the stage and said, "Welcome, welcome! Who's here to dance?"

People began to clap.

Lucien, Minnie, and Eliza came through the door and stood beside Julia.

"Can your father help us?" Eliza asked Minnie.

"I know he'd like to." Minnie put an arm around the girl. "Have your father talk to him. I know he'll do what he can."

Julia couldn't imagine what Minnie's father could do to help Eliza's. No doubt, Eliza was taking Minnie's words literally when she simply meant them as a momentary salve. Still, Julia couldn't help but wonder about it as she danced with a man who worked on the railway and then one, who by the looks of his boots, was a lumberjack. She didn't think of it while she danced with Lucien. He was graceful and kept a dialogue going, prattling on about nothing, really, but it was comforting.

Next, she danced with a man a few years younger than she, who was, by the smell of his hands, a fisherman. Then she asked a sailor to dance, who blushed and stumbled over his words as he said, "Jah, ma'am, I would like to dance with you."

Once they were on the floor she asked, "Any chance you were on the *Pacific Star* when it wrecked?"

"Jah," he answered. "I was."

"What are your thoughts about Captain Evert?"

"He is a good captain. We had plenty of food and even time to rest."

"Did anything unusual happen crossing the bar?"

"Besides the wrecking of the ship?"

Julia nodded.

He concentrated on his steps for a moment and then said, "It was my first time across the bar. I cannot answer your question with any knowledge. I do know, once the beacon went out, that we were in trouble."

"Where are you from?"

"Sweden," he answered. "Can you not tell by my accent?"

She shook her head. "Your English is just fine."

"I left home at fourteen. Been gone twelve years."

Julia asked him his thoughts about Cape Disappointment.

"It is beautiful, although I am not impressed with this 'Graveyard of the Pacific,' as it is called. Did you know hundreds of lives have been lost on the Columbia Bar alone? Along with over a thousand vessels? Maybe more?" The sailor shook his head. "I just received a contract for a ship that is leaving next week to go around Cape Horn. I am happy I will soon be working in the Atlantic again."

Alexander asked her to dance next. She guessed it was obligatory because Lucien was dancing with Eliza.

Alexander wasn't as talkative as Lucien. In fact, he wasn't talkative at all. Finally, she asked, "Are you and Eliza courting?"

"Courting?"

"Yes."

"Um, no."

When he didn't say anything more, Julia said, "But you asked her to the dance."

"Not exactly."

"What do you mean?"

"She asked me."

As Julia walked back to the women's side, the fiddler called out, "Time for a little break. See you all in a half hour."

Eliza was talking to the girl next to her and, at the moment, Minnie wasn't speaking to anyone.

"I'm curious," Julia said to her. "How will your father make things right for Eliza's father?"

"Maybe he'll buy their sawmill at a fair price, if he can."

"But that would only be a short-term solution for the Petersens."

Minnie shrugged. "My father doesn't have to do anything, but he wants to because he cares about our community. How can you fault that?"

Julia couldn't. But it sounded as if a lot of people were going to lose everything. Just like Uncle Edward. She swallowed the lump in her throat.

Just like herself.

A half hour later Lucien approached Julia and said Minnie was feeling upset about Eliza's family and that he was taking her home. "Come with us," he said. "After I drop her off, I'll take you up the cape."

"That's all right," Julia said. "I'll find a ride."

"How?" Lucien asked. "The only other person you know here is Alexander."

"I know Eliza now." She smiled at Lucien. "I'll be all right. Stay with Minnie."

She waited until Lucien and Minnie would have had time to reach his buggy and be on their way, and then she retrieved her coat and slipped out of the dance hall, hoping no one noticed. She'd had enough socializing.

Thankfully there was a moon out, but she wouldn't trudge up the shortcut. She needed to take the road.

As she walked along, under the dark canopies of the gigantic evergreen trees growing on each side of the plank road, Julia thought about Uncle Edward's situation. She guessed, if he survived, he wouldn't be eligible for his lightkeeper's pension. Not if he was found guilty of being inebriated while on duty and of destroying the lens. She hoped he had money saved, but she didn't know for sure.

She needed to prove him innocent. Not only for his good name but also for his livelihood and his future.

She wondered about Alexander and Eliza Petersen. Was there a connection between Alexander and Eliza's father? She needed to explore that further. She'd make a note when she reached her cabin. And she hadn't entirely explored if there was a connection between Alexander and Captain Evert.

She stepped out of the shadows of the tree and into the middle of the road. It didn't appear anyone used it on a Saturday night.

But then the sound of hooves and buggy wheels startled her, and she scurried to the edge of the road again.

"Julia!" For a moment, she thought it was Lucien, but as she turned she saw it was Alexander. "Why are you walking home?"

She stepped out into the road. "How else will I get there?"

"Get in. I'm giving you a ride."

She hesitated.

"Julia," he said. "There are all sorts of reasons you shouldn't walk home in the dark. There are wild animals. And wild people. It's not safe."

As she climbed into the buggy, she asked, "Where's Eliza?"

"I took her home."

They rode silently for a few minutes as Julia tried to phrase a question about Alexander's whereabouts on the day the *Pacific Star* wrecked, both in the afternoon and evening. Finally, she blurted out, "Who are the other men in the volunteer rescue brigade you belong to?"

"Well, Billy."

She remembered that, but he wasn't on the beach Friday. He was with her.

"And Robert Winther," Alexander added.

"Was he on the beach when the *Pacific Star* wrecked?"

"No. He had something at the church. An Easter service rehearsal, I think."

"Who else?"

"Eliza's father, George Petersen, was on the beach for both incidents, although I don't know if he stayed the entire time. You might have seen him."

Mr. Petersen wouldn't be a reliable witness then to whether Alexander was on the beach the entire afternoon and evening. Perhaps Mr. Petersen and Alexander were in cahoots, and Eliza was spreading misinformation about her father losing everything, as a ruse. Perhaps establishing alibis among the suspects would be harder than she thought.

Julia asked, "Where does Mr. Petersen work?"

"He owns the lumbermill." Alexander shook his head. "Although he might not for long."

"Who else is part of the brigade?"

"Usually, Robert Winther's son, but he's been in California on business for the last year."

"Minnie has a brother?"

"Yes, he's a few years older than she is. He's in business with Mr. Winther, although he's been working in San Francisco."

"Interesting. What's his name?"

"Bobby Winther."

Julia paused a moment and then said. "Robert Winther Jr.?"

Alexander nodded. Julia imagined her list in her notebook. She would add both George Petersen and Bobby Winther to the list of connections. It could be coincidental Bobby was in San Francisco, where the *Pacific Star* had been built and launched, but it was worth noting.

When they reached the cabin, Alexander asked, "Would you like to go to church with me tomorrow morning?"

"I heard you don't go to church."

"Who did you hear that from?"

"Lucien. Plus, you were working last Sunday."

Alexander set the brake. "Maybe Lucien doesn't see me at church. I usually come in late and leave early. And yes, sometimes I do work on Sunday mornings. When I'm short a typesetter."

There was an awkward pause.

Alexander said, "I'll pick you up."

"Thank you for the invitation, but I'm going to sit with Uncle Edward all day tomorrow. It doesn't feel right not to." More importantly, it didn't feel right to go to church with Alexander. But she wasn't going to tell him that.

Chapter Ten

On Sunday morning, when she awoke, Julia thought of Minnie's father. Then she thought of his Bible and his swift trip up the steps of the church the week before. She felt a pang of loss. Her own father had been tall with a full head of dark hair, like Mr. Winther. He'd been a man of God too. She thought of Uncle Edward and his own relationship with the Lord and the scriptures he'd read to her through the years.

Then she remembered his Bible on his bedside table. She needed to retrieve it.

Once she was dressed, she hurried over to Uncle Edward's cottage in the drizzling rain. She opened the door to a scent of dampness. A mouse ran across the floor. She shuddered.

She walked down the hall, glanced into the room that was to have been hers with the stripped bed, and then stepped into Uncle Edward's room. Being in the cottage brought her no comfort. She retrieved the Bible and placed it in her bag. Then she searched for a bankbook. She'd need to pay his hospital bill at some point and, sadly, she didn't have enough money on her own to cover it. However, she couldn't find a bankbook anywhere.

She headed into town, but when she reached the hospital, she kept walking. Uncle Edward would want her to go to church. It was time for her to move on from feeling betrayed by Jack—and not trusting God because of it.

The music had already started when she came in. She scanned the congregation for Alexander.

She found him three rows from the back, with Eliza. Next to Eliza was the man she'd seen on the beach when the *Pacific Star* wrecked. *Eliza's father.* Julia slipped into the last row.

When the scripture was read, she opened Uncle Edward's Bible to Mark, chapter four. The pastor read, "'And he was in the hinder part of the ship, asleep on a pillow: and they awake him, and say unto him, Master, carest thou not that we perish? And he arose, and rebuked the wind, and said unto the sea, Peace, be still. And the wind ceased, and there was a great calm. And he said unto them, Why are ye so fearful? how is it that ye have no faith?'"

"Lord," the pastor prayed, "we ask for your faith today."

Julia whispered, "Amen" as the pastor started his sermon about practicing faith and trusting the Lord. The fate of Uncle Edward weighed heavy on her, but she was reminded to trust God in all things. He'd give her the strength to handle what the future might bring. But she also knew He was a God of justice. *Lord,* she silently prayed, *show me—or someone—what really happened in the lighthouse that night.*

At the end of the service, Julia said hello to Alexander and Eliza and then introduced herself to Mr. Petersen. "I saw you on the beach the night the *Pacific Star* wrecked."

"I remember seeing you," Mr. Petersen said. "I was on the beach after the sailboat wrecked and then returned when I heard about the *Pacific Star.*"

Alexander leaned around Eliza. "Miss Warren is checking up on me. To make sure I was on the beach that afternoon and evening."

Julia's face grew warm, and she gave Alexander an annoyed glance.

Mr. Petersen chuckled. "I'm guessing he was there the entire time, until you showed up with Billy and you all ran up to the lighthouse, but I was at the church for a while during that time. Mr. Winther and I are directing the Easter pageant."

"How lovely," Julia said. Then she smiled at Eliza and gave Alexander a nod before slipping out of the church. Mr. Petersen couldn't verify Alexander's alibi—but he had Mr. Winther's.

"Julia!"

She turned, expecting that Alexander had followed her, but it was Lucien.

As he approached, she asked, "Where is Minnie?"

"Still not feeling well," Lucien answered. "She's sensitive that way."

Julia pondered that. Eliza's father was losing everything. Julia's uncle lay injured. Both young women faced an uncertain future. Yet it was Minnie who felt ill.

"Where are you going?" Lucien asked.

"The hospital."

"I'll walk with you."

As they headed down Main Street, Julia asked, "How long have you and Minnie been courting?"

"Two years. Since she returned from back east. I'd marry her—and I think she'd have me—but, although I've won her brother over, her father doesn't think I'm good enough for her." He grinned. "Not yet."

"Why?"

"Oh, you don't want to hear about a young man's foolishness."

"Of course I do," she answered.

"Well, unfortunately it has to do with Alexander."

Her breath caught. "Yes…go on."

"We worked at the lifesaving station together. He came up with this wild idea to smuggle wine into Canada."

"Is this the same scheme you alluded to before?"

Lucien nodded. "Crazy, huh?"

"How far is Canada from here?"

"Nearly three hundred miles. He was on a break from college, and I took a job on a fishing boat. He knew about a shipment of wine that he wanted to commandeer—or something. I nearly went along with him, until I heard that there were rumors around town and Mr. Winther found out about it. I bowed out before anything happened."

Julia was dumbfounded. "But Alexander tried to go through with it?"

"Oh no. It all fell apart."

"This is the episode that you mentioned before that you said could have landed Alexander in the state penitentiary?"

"Yes."

"So, nothing actually happened?"

"Nothing, except that we all knew what Alexander hoped for." He laughed. "And then he bought the *Cape Dispatch News* the next year and became a newspaperman. I have no idea where he finally got the money—perhaps from his family." He laughed again. "His past makes me question everything he writes. Every action has a consequence, right?"

She nodded. That was certainly true.

When Julia reached the hospital, the nurse was in the front office, speaking with a patient, and Doc Olsen was leaving on a call.

Julia headed back to Uncle Edward's room and spent much of her time reading to him from his Bible, going through his favorite passages. Jonah and the whale. Jesus calming the storm. Jesus walking on the water. Yes, there was definitely a theme to his favorites.

Several times, Uncle Edward stirred, and a few times he turned his head to her. It seemed his mouth slanted to the left side. Julia propped him up and spooned water into his mouth, which he swallowed. When the nurse brought broth, Julia asked how he could drink when he was unconscious.

"He's partly conscious," she said. "He's definitely improving. I'm certain he can hear what we say. He's what they call 'locked in.'"

"What will it take for him to wake up completely?"

"Time," she answered. "Unless there's permanent damage."

"When will we know if he's going to wake up or not?"

"If he's going to, I imagine it will be soon."

"How soon?"

"Within the next few days."

Julia felt as if a clock was ticking—or a bomb. She tied a bib around her uncle's neck and fed him the broth.

When she was done and was getting up to leave, the doctor returned. He asked to speak with her in the hall. "If your uncle regains consciousness in the next few days, you'll need to plan to take him home and care for him."

"Take him home?"

"I can't keep him here indefinitely."

"But I don't have a home. We can't stay in the lightkeeper's cottage, and I'm staying in a one-room cabin."

"You don't have to do anything for a couple of days, and that's only if he wakes up," he said. "Don't fret."

Don't fret. That was easier said than done.

Monday morning, Julia headed straight for the general store, intent on setting up a meeting with Robert Winther. When she arrived, an older woman was behind the counter and Minnie was nowhere in sight.

She introduced herself to the woman and then said, "I'm working at the *Cape Dispatch* and need to speak to Mr. Winther about his ad."

"He's down at his office," the woman said.

"Where exactly is his office?"

"At the cannery."

"I'm new in town," Julia said. "Which cannery?"

"Win-Win Cannery," the woman said. "At the south end of the wharf."

"Thank you," Julia replied.

She had to wait a few minutes for the train to pass by in order to cross to the south side of the wharf. She passed the last saloon and kept going. Finally, she reached Win-Win Cannery, a large building painted bright blue. There was an open barnlike door leading into the cannery. She looked inside and could see all the way to the dock, where men unloaded a boat. In between were rows of tables loaded with fish and lined by men wearing aprons. There was a single door on the far side of the front of the building.

Julia walked to it. When she entered, Minnie asked, "Julia, what are you doing here?"

Julia smiled as sweetly as she could. "I'm looking for your father. To figure out the advertisement for the store for this week. Or should I ask Alexander to come down here?"

Minnie waved. "I think we're past that." She glanced at a door. "I do think Daddy has some ideas."

"Great." Julia hiked her bag higher on her shoulder. "Do you work here or at the general store? Or both?"

"Wherever Daddy needs me for the day. I'll tell him you're here." She returned a minute later and said, "You can go in now."

As Julia walked through the door, Robert Winther stood and walked to her, his hands outstretched. "Miss Warren, welcome!" He grasped both of her hands.

"Mr. Winther, I'm so pleased to finally meet you."

"The pleasure is all mine." He let go of her hands and motioned to the chair in front of the desk. "Please, sit down."

She did.

"Lucien told me about your predicament. I'm so sorry about your uncle. Regardless of the circumstances, I've been praying for his recovery."

"Thank you."

"The wreck of the *Pacific Star* was a tragedy for the entire community." He sat down, and Julia noticed his Bible on his desk.

He must have tracked her eyes, because he said, "I have a Bible study I lead on Mondays at noon for businessmen in town." He met her gaze. "Are you a woman of faith, Miss Warren?"

She hesitated. She certainly had been in her youth, and she was trying to reclaim it now. "Of uncertain faith, at times, I'm afraid."

"Ah, aren't we all." His eyes were full of kindness. "I'll pray for your faith during this trying time. And make sure and let Minnie or me know how we can help. It sounds as if you're without friend or family, besides your uncle."

Had Lucien told Minnie that? "Thank you." She took her notebook from her bag. "Before we talk about your advertisement, do you mind if I ask you a question?"

He leaned toward her. "Is this for an article for the newspaper?"

"Oh no," she said. "I'm strictly selling advertisements."

His eyes twinkled. "I was teasing you. I can answer your question, I'm sure."

"It is about the night the *Pacific Star* wrecked. Because of my uncle, I'm trying to piece together what happened that night, around town." Mr. Petersen had corroborated where Mr. Winther was, but she wanted to hear it from him too. "Where were you that evening?"

He cocked his head and smiled. "Surely, Miss Warren, you don't suspect me of having anything to do with the wrecking of the *Pacific Star*?"

She smiled back, keeping her head high. "Of course not, Mr. Winther. Not a single thing would make me question your involvement. I'm trying to establish the whereabouts of Lucien Graham that afternoon and evening."

"Aw, yes. Lucien. I'm often trying to establish his whereabouts myself, now that Minnie has taken a liking to him. What do you want to know?"

"Did you happen to see him in town that day?"

He folded his hands on the table. "Come to think of it, I did. Lucien plays cards at the saloon every Friday starting around five when he's not working." He nodded to the end of the wharf. "I saw him as I left my office to go to the church." He chuckled. "He ducked into the saloon, no doubt hoping I didn't see him. But I see him nearly every Friday late afternoon, doing the same thing." Mr. Winther lowered his voice. "Don't tell anyone this, but I think more highly of Lucien than I let on. Yes, he plays cards, but I'm guessing he'll give that up soon. He's won Minnie's trust and her brother's, and he's winning mine too."

Julia smiled. But inside she felt befuddled. Either Lucien or Alexander was lying about the other and probably about a lot more too. She forced another smile and then said, "Now let's talk about your advertisement."

It turned out Mr. Winther wanted to buy three ads: his usual one for the general store, one looking to hire workers at his cannery, and one for a meeting on Wednesday evening at the Community Church for those affected by the wreck of the *Pacific Star. Let's come together as a community and figure out how to help each other* was the wording he wanted across the top of the full-page ad.

As Julia finished writing his instructions, she said, "What are your thoughts about the investors who ended up with fraudulent claims?"

He shook his head. "I don't know why they didn't take a better look at their policies. I feel ill about what happened. Not only will good men lose their businesses, but it's bound to hurt our local economy. That's why I'm trying to figure out how to help."

Ten minutes later, in the bright sunshine, she turned her head up to the blue sky as she walked back to the newspaper office.

She heard her name and glanced up the street. Lucien's buggy came racing toward her.

He waved frantically. "Julia! Get in the buggy. Your uncle's awake!"

Chapter Eleven

Julia rushed down the hall of the hospital and into Uncle Edward's room. The doctor stood at the end of the bed, speaking slowly in a loud voice. "Mr. Warren, you've indicated you can hear me. But can you respond?"

Uncle Edward opened his mouth, and it seemed he was trying to speak, but nothing came out.

Julia stepped to the side of his bed and took his hand.

He looked at her, and she felt a gentle pressure on her hand.

She turned to the doctor. "When did this happen?"

"While Lucien Graham was visiting him. I heard a cry and hurried down the hall. It was Mr. Warren regaining consciousness. I sent Lucien to retrieve you immediately."

Julia sat on the edge of the bed and brushed the white hair from Uncle Edward's forehead. "We were so worried about you."

Uncle Edward nodded.

Doc Olsen shuffled some papers. "Officer Carlson told me to contact Deputy Martin when your uncle awoke. Lucien left to go get him."

"So soon?" Julia asked. "Uncle Edward obviously hasn't regained his health. He still needs care."

"That's up to the deputy to decide," Doc Olsen replied.

Uncle Edward made a moaning sound.

She turned to him. He had a puzzled expression on his face.

"There was an incident at the lighthouse over a week ago, on the day I arrived," Julia said. "You were found on the stairs, unconscious, with a head wound. The Fresnel lens was damaged."

He gave her another questioning expression.

"I know you didn't do it," Julia said. "I'm trying to figure out who did, and who injured you. When you've regained your speech, you can help."

He opened his mouth, but no sound emerged.

"Do you have any memory from that night?"

His brow wrinkled.

"Let's give it some time," she said.

He leaned back against the pillow and closed his eyes. Julia continued to hold his hand.

Doc Olsen slipped out the door.

Uncle Edward sighed.

"Don't worry," Julia said. "We must have faith that everything will be all right. We're in the boat in the storm right now, waiting for Jesus to calm the waves."

Uncle Edward nodded.

He fell asleep soon after, and Julia slipped out of his room. She told the nurse she needed to go to the newspaper office for a minute. She stepped out of the hospital to find the sun behind a cloud and the sky turning gray. When she arrived at the office, Alexander was in the back room with the typesetter.

"May I speak to you for a minute?" she asked.

He followed her into the office. She pulled her notebook and the drafts of Mr. Winther's ads from her bag.

"He bought three?"

"Yes."

"He's never done that before."

She put her hand on the chair to steady herself.

"Are you all right?" Alexander asked.

"No." She inhaled sharply. "Uncle Edward has regained consciousness."

Alexander's eyes widened. "What did he say happened?"

"He's not speaking."

"Can he write?"

"I don't know. I need to go back there now. Lucien went to get the deputy, who apparently might arrest Uncle Edward and take him to the jail."

"Go," Alexander said. "I'll be there in just a minute."

Julia wasn't sure whether she wanted Alexander at the hospital or not. Did he really want the truth? Or was his motive to protect himself?

When she returned to the hospital, Uncle Edward was still asleep, and Lucien and Deputy Martin hadn't arrived. But a few minutes later, both came into the room, followed by Doc Olsen and Alexander.

Deputy Martin stepped to the side of the bed, forcing Julia to move to the corner. "Mr. Warren?"

"He's asleep," Julia said.

"I thought he'd regained consciousness?"

"He has," Doc Olsen said. "But he's sleeping."

"I see." Deputy Martin shook Uncle Edward's shoulder.

Uncle Edward stirred. Finally, he opened his eyes and then scooted up on the pillow a little.

"Mr. Warren," Deputy Martin said, "you're under arrest for vandalizing the lens of the Cape Disappointment Lighthouse, being drunk while on duty, and dereliction of duty on the night of February 3, 1899."

Uncle Edward blinked a few times.

"I'm moving you to the Ilwaco jail."

"No." Julia stepped forward, wedging her way between Deputy Martin and Lucien. "He's unwell, as we can all see."

"My instructions from Officer Carlson were to move Mr. Warren to the jail once he regained consciousness."

Doc Olsen said, "I'll get the stretcher and then pull the wagon around."

"No!" Julia said again.

"It's the law," Doc Olsen said. Was he anxious to get Uncle Edward out of the hospital before the townspeople realized he'd awakened?

Julia turned to Lucien. "Talk some sense into everyone. Who's going to care for him in the jail?" Julia caught hold of Deputy Martin's arm. "Are you going to feed him? Dress him? Tend to his needs?"

Deputy Martin shook his arm, forcing Julia to let go. "Oh, I bet he can do that for himself. I'm guessing he could talk too, if he wanted. I think a night in jail will be the best thing all around."

A few minutes later the men had transferred Uncle Edward to the stretcher. Julia hurried alongside as the group moved him, holding Uncle Edward's hand. "I'll figure out what to do," she said. "You won't have to spend the night in the jail, I promise."

A crowd had gathered outside of the hospital. A man yelled, "Lock up the lightkeeper!"

in Cape Disappointment, Washington

Someone else yelled, "Make him pay!"

The men slid Uncle Edward into the bed of the wagon, and then Alexander climbed in after him. As Doc Olsen began driving the wagon away, the crowd followed.

Alexander yelled, "Stay back!"

Julia followed along behind the crowd. Could she trust Alexander with Uncle Edward? It appeared Alexander was trying to protect him, but what if he had ulterior motives?

Tears stung Julia's eyes.

Rain began to fall as she walked to the jail. At first just a few drops, but then the sky opened up and a downpour began. It scattered the crowd, but soaked Julia.

She couldn't stop the tears. Uncle Edward, the kindest soul she knew, had been arrested and was on his way to jail, as ill as he was. Alexander might well be responsible, and yet he was protecting Uncle Edward, or pretending to. Perhaps he was really gathering information for his next national news story. *Lightkeeper Jailed for Dereliction of Duty and Breaking Fresnel Lens of Cape Disappointment Lighthouse.*

Tears streamed down her face. She'd never felt so helpless, so hopeless, and so alone.

When Julia reached the jail, Deputy Martin refused her entrance.

Julia waited until Alexander exited the jail.

"How is he?" she asked.

"All right. We put him on a cot."

"Does he have a blanket?"

"He does," Alexander said. "He'll be all right."

"You're wrong." Sparks of anger shot through her. "He's ill. And immobile. He's not going to be all right."

Alexander's eyes grew wider. "Look, I know this is hard. But I don't know what more we can do at the moment. You need to find an attorney. The sooner the better."

"I don't have money for an attorney. I need to access Uncle Edward's bank account, but I couldn't find a bankbook in his cottage. Since he can't speak, I need to see if he can write." Julia wrung her hands.

He frowned. "I tried to get him to write something before I left him. He can't."

"Can you help me find an attorney? One that I can pay later?"

"Attorneys don't like to work for free."

Obviously, Julia needed someone who could help her more than Alexander could. Or would.

She started marching away from him.

"Where are you going?" he called out.

"To find someone who can help me." She started to run toward the wharf.

Alexander hurried after her. "I'd hire a lawyer for you myself if I had the money."

She waved him away and kept on going, heading straight for Mr. Winther's cannery. When she reached the office, Minnie wasn't at the desk. She hesitated a moment but then strode across the room and knocked on Mr. Winther's office door.

"Who's there?" he called out.

"Julia Warren. May I speak with you?"

The door swung open. "Miss Warren," he said. "Are you all right?"

"I need help," she said.

"Come in." He pointed to the chair. "Whatever is the matter?"

"My uncle woke up—"

He smiled.

"Yes, that's positive. But when Deputy Martin was alerted, he came and arrested Uncle Edward and hauled him off to the jail."

Mr. Winther leaned against his desk. "Well, that was expected, wasn't it?"

"Except that he can't talk or walk. He can't see to any of his needs. We don't know how bad his head injury is."

"I see." Mr. Winther stood up straight. "What does his attorney say?"

"He doesn't have an attorney. I don't have the money to hire one."

"What about your uncle's money?"

"I couldn't find a bankbook. I need to go to the bank here and see about his account."

"Oh dear." Mr. Winther tapped his chin. "They wouldn't let you access it immediately, in any case. What do you need help with the most?"

"Convincing Deputy Martin to move Uncle Edward back to the hospital."

"Sounds like a tall order, but I'll see what I can do to help." He stepped to the coat tree by the door and retrieved his coat and an umbrella. "I'll have Billy get the buggy. Wait here for a minute."

She stood, followed him to the door, and watched as he left the building. Did Billy work for Mr. Winther? If so, why had he been available to drive Julia the day she arrived?

Five minutes later, Billy came into the office.

He seemed surprised to see her. "Mr. Winther told me to come let the young lady know the buggy had arrived, but I didn't realize it was you."

Julia followed him out the door.

"Where are we headed?" he asked.

"The jail."

"Ah. Your uncle?"

She nodded.

"I'm sorry."

When they reached the buggy, Billy helped Julia up to the rear seat where Mr. Winther sat. After they arrived at the jail, Billy set the brake and then helped Julia from the buggy. She followed Mr. Winther into the building.

"Hello, Mike," he said to the jailer. "How are you today?"

"I can't complain. What can I help you with, Mr. Winther?"

"I need to speak with Deputy Martin."

"He's in the back."

"Would you let him know I'm here? I have some questions about Mr. Warren's condition."

"Of course," the jailer said.

When the man disappeared through the door at the far end of the room, Mr. Winther told Julia to stand by the woodstove. "You're shivering," he said.

She stepped to the stove, took off her gloves, and tried to warm her hands.

Finally, Deputy Martin appeared. "Mr. Winther, what a nice surprise. What can I do to help you?"

"I'm here with Miss Warren," he said, nodding to Julia. "I need to know what Mr. Warren's condition is."

"He's resting."

"I'd like to see him."

"On what grounds?"

"As a concerned citizen."

Deputy Martin took a step backward. "What is your intention?"

"To determine whether the jail is the best place for an injured man."

"The doctor didn't have a problem with it."

Julia couldn't keep quiet. "The doctor was following your instructions."

Deputy Martin was silent for a long moment but then said, "I'm guessing the sheriff would want you to assess the situation. Come along."

Mr. Winther gave Julia a smile and followed Deputy Martin, leaving her befuddled. Obviously, Mr. Winther had some sort of connection to the sheriff.

A few minutes later, Mr. Winther led the way, followed by Deputy Martin and three other men carrying Uncle Edward on the stretcher that Doc Olsen must have left behind.

"We're taking him back to the hospital." Mr. Winther turned to Deputy Martin. "Put him in my buggy. Miss Warren and I will walk and meet you there."

Julia followed Mr. Winther out the door. The rain had stopped, and the sun was shining over Cape Disappointment. Above the trees, an eagle soared.

For the first time since she arrived at the Cape Disappointment Lighthouse, she felt a glimmer of hope as she offered up a prayer of thanks.

Chapter Twelve

"Let's stop by the bank on our way to the hospital and speak to the manager," Mr. Winther said. "Surely your uncle has an account there."

When they arrived, Mr. Winther stepped up to the teller. "Would you please tell Mr. Barrett that Mr. Winther needs to speak with him immediately?"

The teller said, "Of course," and hurried to the back of the bank.

Immediately, a plump man with gray hair appeared, making a beeline to Mr. Winther. He extended his hand and said, "Robert, so good to see you. How may I help you today?"

"I'd like you to meet Miss Warren, Mr. Edward Warren's niece." Mr. Winther let go of the man's hand and turned to Julia. "Miss Warren, this is Mr. Barrett, the manager of the bank."

Julia extended her hand. "I'm pleased to meet you."

A sour expression formed on Mr. Barrett's face. "Likewise."

Mr. Winther said, "Miss Warren needs to access her uncle's bank account."

"I'll need permission from Mr. Warren."

Mr. Winther stated, "He's incapacitated."

"A note will do."

"He isn't able to write—yet."

"Do you have his bankbook?" Mr. Barrett asked Julia.

"No, but I'm his next of kin," she answered. "I'll be his guardian if necessary."

"You'll need your attorney to present your case to the president of the bank in Astoria. To Mr. Paul Fredrick."

"I don't have an attorney. May I consult with the president of the bank in person?"

Mr. Barrett managed to smile, just a little. "You could try. The bank is on Jefferson and Main."

"Thank you," Julia said.

As they left the bank, Mr. Winther said to Julia, "If I were you, I'd visit Charles Moore, an attorney in Astoria, before going by the bank. Tell him I sent you."

Julia smiled. "I can't thank you enough."

"Nonsense," he said. "Let me know what else I can do."

After seeing Uncle Edward settled back in his hospital room, Julia returned to the newspaper office, still damp and cold but relieved. She had the names of both an attorney in Astoria and the president of the bank. Uncle Edward was safe. Obviously, Mr. Winther had connections.

As she entered the newspaper office, Alexander stood, pushing his chair away. "Where have you been?"

She explained what happened. "Perhaps I can convince the president of the bank in Astoria. Mr. Winther also gave me the name of an attorney to speak to, plus I'd like to investigate the insurance agent in Astoria to see if he really fled the area."

"That's a good idea." Alexander paused and then said, "We could go to Astoria together."

Julia nodded. "How about tomorrow?"

The next morning, Julia met Alexander on the wharf, and they boarded the steamship for Astoria. Julia stood on the port side, near the stern, and kept her eye on Cape Disappointment. In the distance, an eagle soared and then dipped down to the water in the bay. When it came back up, the eagle had a fish in its talons.

It was an answer to a prayer to have Alexander suggest they go to Astoria together. She'd get far more accomplished going with someone who knew the town. God was working, she was sure. She needed to keep waiting on Him and His direction.

As the steamship made its way to the river, Julia joined Alexander on the starboard side. There were several fishing boats on the river and a cargo ship that had just crossed the bar. Julia wondered where it was from. California? Canada? Across the Pacific?

As the steamship picked up speed, the wind began to tug at Julia's hat and then her hair. "I'm going to go sit down," she said to Alexander.

"I'll come with you."

They sat on a bench near the bow as the boat turned into the rising sun. Once they'd settled, Julia asked Alexander if Mr. Winther was as upstanding as he seemed.

He gave her a questioning look.

"Is he sincere?" Julia clarified. "Does he really care about people?" He'd certainly seemed to care about Uncle Edward.

"Yes," Alexander said. "I believe he does."

"Do you find it alarming that he has an insurance policy that is viable while so many don't?"

"No. His son, Bobby, is in California, working for an attorney. I imagine he facilitated the marine policy with Lombards of San Francisco."

"How about Captain Evert? Does he have a connection with the Winthers?"

"Not that I know of, and I like to think I'm aware of most of the connections in town."

"What about Lucien?" Julia asked. "He said that Mr. Winther isn't thrilled about him dating Minnie."

"Right. That's well-known in town. I think Mr. Winther was hoping Minnie would find a husband from one of Bobby's classmates at Santa Clara. Lucien isn't exactly what he had in mind."

"Any reason that Mr. Winther wouldn't trust Lucien?" Julia desperately wanted Alexander's side of the story as far as the near-smuggling incident years ago.

"Yes. There was a situation, one I was involved in too."

Julia tilted her head, hoping to encourage him to keep speaking.

He sighed. "I haven't thought about this for a while. Let's see..." He crossed his arms. "Lucien and I were both working at the lifesaving station at the time. I'd been writing some articles for the newspaper, on the side, including ones about shipwrecks. The owner wanted to sell the newspaper, and I was interested in buying it. Lucien told me about a job he had coming up on a ship to Canada. I had a couple of weeks off before I needed to return to college, and he asked me if I wanted to go. I'd never been to Canada, so I said yes. Then the next day I overheard Lucien talking with someone else, and it sounded as if the idea was to smuggle goods into Canada without paying the taxes. I confronted him about it, and he told me to relax, that it happened all the time. I backed out of the trip and reported what I'd heard to the custom office."

"Interesting," I said. "Because Lucien told me the smuggling plan was your idea."

"Really?" Alexander shook his head. "I wonder who else he told that." He was silent for a long moment and then said, "There's a record of my report at the custom house in Astoria. Maybe I should speak with Officer Carlson about it."

"Why?"

"To see if anyone followed up on the report, found any additional information."

"Good idea," Julia said. After a moment of silence, she wondered what he would tell her about his upbringing and if it would match what Lucien told her. She took a deep breath. "Where did you grow up?"

"Chicago." That matched.

"How did you end up out west?"

"I came out to Santa Clara for college."

"Did you meet Bobby Winther there?"

"It's as if you already know my story." He chuckled.

"I really don't. I just heard he went to Santa Clara." Julia smiled. "From you."

He laughed. "I started coming up here with him in the summer. He worked for his father, and I worked at the lifesaving station. When I graduated, I came up here for good."

Julia shifted her face to Alexander and the warmth of the rising sun. "Why didn't you return to Chicago?"

"The short story is my grandfather was a newspaperman in Chicago. He always hoped my father would take over the business, followed by me. But Father was a drunk, and my mother left him. When my grandfather died, Father sold the business—even though he knew I hoped to run it someday."

"That must have been quite a shock."

"Yes, it was a bit of a shock. My senior year of college, my grandmother died—so I really didn't have anything to go back to. She'd set aside a little money for me, enough to buy the *Cape Dispatch*." He gave Julia a wry smile. "But not enough to run it."

"But you have been," Julia said.

"Barely," he answered.

Alexander was alone in the world too, even more alone than she was.

"How about you?" he asked. "What's your story?"

Julia hesitated as a cool breeze danced across the deck. She wasn't sure she wanted to tell Alexander about her life. But he'd told her about his, including that his father was a drunk. Was that why he was so quick to assume Uncle Edward was too?

She took a deep breath and then said, "My parents died in a sailing accident when I was seven."

"I'm sorry."

Julia murmured, "Thank you." After a pause, she said, "Uncle Edward piloted ships up and down the East Coast at the time, but he quit and took a job as a lightkeeper in Rhode Island so he could raise me."

"No wonder you're so loyal to him."

"He's been both father and mother to me," she said. "When I left to go to Vassar, he took a job as a lightkeeper in Maryland. Two years ago he transferred here, saying he wanted one last big adventure before he retired. He read the book *Astoria* by Washington Irving when he was a child growing up in Connecticut. Then, in his twenties, he worked on a passenger ship from San Francisco to Astoria for a year. It was 1860, when the Cape Disappointment Lighthouse was only a few years old. He thought it was one of the most beautiful locations he'd ever seen. He spoke of it often while I was growing up."

"Fascinating that your uncle had a connection going back that far." Alexander looked toward the bow. "I wish I'd gotten to know him. I should have interviewed him for the newspaper when he first arrived." He turned to Julia again. "What made you decide to follow him here?"

"That's a bit complicated." She sighed. "To be honest, I wanted to get away from Philadelphia."

"You didn't like your job?"

She shook her head. "I loved my job."

"Your living arrangement?"

"That was fine. I lived in a boardinghouse with other women."

"So…" Alexander said, "do I have to keep guessing why you wanted to get away from Philadelphia?"

"No." Julia pulled her bag closer. "It was a courtship gone bad."

"I'm sorry."

Julia turned to him. "I'm not. Not at all. In fact, I'm relieved. But he worked at the newspaper, and I didn't want to see him every day."

Alexander nodded. "That makes sense."

"Uncle Edward always told me to follow my intuition when it came to men. This one, Jack, was a superb journalist but not so great a beau. I didn't realize it until he announced his engagement to a socialite."

"That's tough," Alexander said.

"It was," Julia said. "Jack only cared about using people to advance his career. After that, I vowed to never become involved with another newspaperman."

A pained expression dashed across Alexander's face, but he quickly composed himself.

Finally, he said, "Clearly you did the right thing to come west."

"I agree." Julia searched Alexander's face for more of a reaction to her declaration against newspapermen, but he simply smiled at her as kindness filled his eyes.

Julia had her notebook with her and made a list of what they needed to accomplish while they were in Astoria as they neared the dock. *Attorney. Bank. Insurance agent. Custom house.* As the ship slowed, Julia and Alexander stood and waited to disembark.

"Where should we go first?" she asked.

Alexander considered for a moment. "Let's go to the attorney first."

Julia grew more and more restless as they waited in the attorney's outer office. "This is taking too long," she said. "We're wasting precious time."

"No need to be anxious." Alexander's tone soothed her. "We don't have any control over how long an attorney takes."

in Cape Disappointment, Washington

After an hour, the attorney—Charles Moore—called Julia into his office. "Want me to go with you?" Alexander asked.

"Please," she said.

After introductions, Julia told the attorney she needed to access her uncle's bank account to be able to care for him.

"I had a telegram about this," Mr. Moore said. "From George Barrett."

Julia stifled a groan. Mr. Barrett must have assumed Mr. Moore was the attorney Mr. Winther would recommend and sent him a telegram alerting him that Julia would be wanting to see him.

"You shouldn't waste your money—that you can't access anyway—on me," Mr. Moore said. "George told me about the federal investigation."

"Everyone deserves representation," Alexander said.

"That's true," Mr. Moore said. "But any money Miss Warren can access is better used on her own support instead of on representing a man who will surely be found guilty. Your uncle doesn't have a chance."

"Can you recommend another attorney?"

He shook his head. "No."

"Any advice for getting access to my uncle's money?"

He stood. "No. I'll waive the fee for this meeting, considering the circumstances."

Julia stood too. "We'll see ourselves out." Alexander followed her.

When they reached the street, Julia seethed. "That was unconscionable."

Alexander put his hand on her shoulder. "I'm sorry."

She met his eyes. "It feels as if everything is stacked against Uncle Edward."

Alexander nodded. "I can see why you feel that way."

"I doubt the bank here will let me withdraw any money either," Julia said, "but I still need to try."

Alexander removed his hand from her shoulder. But he stayed close by her side, like an anchor keeping her steady in a storm.

Julia was right about the bank.

The teller gestured to Alexander, who stood behind her. "Is this your husband?"

"If he is, could he withdraw the money?"

The teller leaned forward. "Is he?"

Julia refrained from rolling her eyes and shook her head. "May I speak to Mr. Fredrick?"

"He's not in today, but you can come back tomorrow."

Julia turned to Alexander. "Let's go to the custom house. Hopefully, we won't have three failures today."

When they reached the custom house, Alexander led the way. Officer Carlson was behind the counter.

"Mr. Blake. Miss Warren." He smiled. "Welcome."

"Were you expecting us?"

He nodded. "A telephone call alerted me that you were in town."

Julia put her hands on the counter and leaned forward. "Mr. Fredrick, no doubt?"

Officer Carlson smiled again. "Actually, I had two phone calls. I also heard your uncle regained consciousness and that he's back at the hospital after a trip to jail."

Julia stared at Officer Carlson.

His face reddened. "I had a telegram from Deputy Martin."

She still didn't say anything.

"As soon as Agent Belville returns, we'll transport your uncle here to stand trial on federal charges...." His voice trailed off under Julia's glare.

Finally, she asked, "When will Agent Belville return?"

"Tomorrow."

Julia straightened her shoulders. "I'm looking forward to speaking with him."

Officer Carlson shifted from one foot to the other. "I doubt you stopped in to say hello. What can I do for you?"

"We're looking for records from eight years ago—a report on a possible smuggling operation," Alexander said. "July of 1891."

"Why do you need the information?"

"For a story I'm working on."

"We don't keep records that far back."

Alexander squared his shoulders. "Please check."

Officer Carlson retreated into a room at the rear of the building. About ten minutes later he returned. "I was correct. We only have records going back five years."

"That can't be." Alexander took a step closer to the counter. "Perhaps they're stored in another room."

Officer Carlson shook his head. "I've never seen any other records in the building." He smiled. "I'm afraid I can't help you."

Julia spoke up. "I have another question. Why didn't I hear from you about the sledgehammer I found in the stable near the lighthouse?"

Officer Carlson grinned. "Deputy Martin sent me a telegram about that too. He said there wasn't any proof as to the owner of the sledgehammer nor any indication that it was used to break the lens."

"Did you investigate its owner? Question the stable owner? Or the stable hand?"

"Of course not," he said. "We have the bottle. No further investigation is needed."

"So much for that," Alexander muttered under his breath. He took Julia by the elbow and escorted her to the door.

"Tell your uncle I'll see him soon," Officer Carlson called out.

Alexander muttered something else under his breath, but Julia couldn't make out what he said.

Once they left the custom house, Julia explained that she'd found the sledgehammer in the stable and reported it to Deputy Martin.

"It would be hard to prove who owns it," Alexander said. "But you're right, it should be investigated. That said, I don't trust Officer Carlson. How about you?"

Julia spoke quietly. "I haven't from the first, but I was afraid it might have been because I felt protective of Uncle Edward."

"Well, I don't have that bias, and I think he's about as insincere as can be." He pointed to the right. "The office of the Columbia Marine Insurance Agency is this way. There's a café a block before it. How about some lunch?"

After vegetable soup and ham sandwiches, the two continued on their way. Three blocks later, Alexander pointed at a small run-down wooden building with peeling white paint. "This is the address for the insurance agency."

Alexander knocked on the door. When no one answered, he stepped to the building next door—a shoe repair shop.

A man wearing a leather apron with a boot in his hands looked up.

Alexander said, "I'm looking for the man who owns the insurance agency next door."

The man put the boot on the table. "You and everyone else."

"Is there any information you can share about him?"

"I haven't seen him since February sixth."

Alexander asked, "What's his name?"

"Clarence Jones."

"What kind of man was he?"

"Nice enough," the man said. "Didn't talk much."

"Who else worked in the office?"

"No one as far as I could tell. I never saw anyone else."

"Thank you for the information," Alexander said. "We appreciate it."

As they continued down the sidewalk, Alexander said, "The courthouse is on the way. Let's stop there and see how the insurance business was registered."

At the Clatsop County Courthouse, after Alexander made his request, the clerk pulled up the business ledger. After a few minutes, he said, "Here it is. The Columbia Marine Insurance Agency was registered March 8, 1898."

Julia leaned closer. "So, less than a year ago?"

The clerk nodded.

"Two owners registered the business. Clarence Jones was one."

Julia craned her neck, reading *Clarence Jones* upside down. She said the second name out loud. "Lucien J. Graham."

Chapter Thirteen

Once they were on the steamship for the trip back to Ilwaco, a storm blew in from the Pacific and the river grew rough. The sun's descent added to the icy afternoon. Julia shifted on the bench, struggling to keep her eyes on the horizon past the bow of the ship as her throat grew tight.

"I'm going to confront Lucien," Alexander said.

Julia nodded. It needed to be done. But she was feeling too ill to think about the next step.

"I thought he'd given up nefarious pursuits," Alexander said. "But obviously that isn't true."

Julia swallowed, trying to overcome the nausea. But she couldn't deny it any longer. For the first time in her life, she was seasick. As the bow waves grew larger, so did the rise and fall of the sickness roiling inside her.

"Are you all right?" Alexander asked.

Without answering, she fled to the side of the ship, clutched the railing, and was sick over the side. After a few more bouts of heaving, Alexander left.

Julia was so mortified she didn't even think about where he'd gone, but when he returned with a cup of water, she felt only gratitude.

"It happens to the best of us," he said.

After she rinsed and spat, he took the cup and gave her his coat.

"Are you being nice to me so I won't be suspicious of you?" She meant to sound as if she was teasing, but her tone was as serious as a shipwreck.

"No," he answered earnestly. "I'm being nice because I care about you."

Julia believed him. He seemed genuinely kind. It had been so long since anyone had cared for her. Then she remembered him "hiring" her so she could listen to Captain Evert talk about the wreck of the *Pacific Star*. She thought of the cups of tea he had made her in the newspaper office. The time he sought her out on the road to give her a ride home from the dance. He'd been caring for her since she first arrived. Another bow wave forced the ship up and then dropped it violently, sending Julia crashing into Alexander.

He caught her and held her until the ship righted. Then he let go. Except for her elbow, which he held tightly even as she heaved over the railing again. Although this time she had nothing more to expel. Finally, he helped her back to the bench and sat beside her for the rest of the trip, as if guarding her from harm.

When they reached Ilwaco, Alexander helped Julia off the boat. Ahead, Billy waited on the street in his buggy. Or was it Mr. Winther's buggy?

"Can you give us a ride?" Alexander called out to him. He and Julia walked slowly up the dock, with her holding on to his arm as the wind and rain whipped at their coats.

"Sure." Billy jumped down from the buggy. "Have you been to Astoria for the day?"

Alexander nodded. "We had a rough crossing on the return trip."

Billy looked kindly at Julia. "I thought you looked a little green."

She felt too ill to respond.

As the buggy bumped over the cobblestones, she concentrated on not getting sick again. When they reached the newspaper office, Lucien came out of the general store. He called out, "Hello, Alexander! Where have you been?"

Alexander hopped down from the buggy while Billy helped Julia.

"Astoria." Alexander approached him. "I have a question for you."

Julia thanked Billy and stepped around the back of the buggy to the boardwalk.

"We stopped by the Columbia Marine Insurance Agency," Alexander said, "while we were in Astoria. What do you know about the owner?"

Julia stepped to where she could see the expression on Lucien's face. It was as calm as ever. "Nothing more than what Mr. Petersen told me. A Clarence Jones owns the agency. He came west from New York, where his father has a marine insurance agency."

"Interesting," Alexander said. "I hadn't heard about the connection to New York."

"Glad I could clear that up."

"There was another name on the registry," Alexander said.

"Oh?"

"Your name."

Lucien cocked his head. "My name? What are you talking about?" His expression appeared genuinely confused.

"Both Julia and I saw your name and a signature. Lucien J. Graham."

Lucien clutched the back of his neck. "That's unbelievable. Surely, Clarence Jones forged my name. But why? I've never even met the man."

"Is *J* your middle initial?"

Lucien nodded.

"How would he have that information if he doesn't know you?"

"Good question." Lucien crossed his arms. "And it's interesting he just used the initial."

"What does it stand for?" Julia asked.

"James." A puzzled expression settled on Lucien's face. "You two don't think I had anything to do with the fraudulent claims, do you?"

Alexander shrugged. "We're simply investigating all the leads we come across."

"Of course." Lucien shook his head. "I'd better go to Astoria tomorrow and sort this out."

Julia continued to watch Lucien. He didn't seem as if he was upset about them finding his name associated with the insurance agency. Maybe this was just another dead end in a series of dead ends today.

Before walking home, Julia stopped by the hospital. Nurse Vera sat at the desk in the office. After greeting Julia, she said, "He has a visitor."

"Oh?"

"Mr. Winther is sitting with him." Nurse Vera gestured toward the hall. "Isn't that nice?"

"Yes. That's wonderful." Julia couldn't help but be surprised. Mr. Winther was a busy man. "Is Uncle Edward speaking?"

"I'm afraid not."

"Responding to questions?"

The nurse shook her head. "But he's eating better. He had noodle soup for lunch."

"That's good to hear."

When Mr. Winther saw Julia at the door of Uncle Edward's room, he stood. "Miss Warren, come in. I was just getting ready to leave."

"Oh, don't go yet." She stepped up to the bed and took Uncle Edward's hand. "How are you today?"

Uncle Edward turned his head to her but didn't respond.

Mr. Winther picked up a leather briefcase from the floor. "I'm headed to the church for a meeting."

"Do you have just a couple of minutes? I'm trying to figure something out." She thought of what Jack used to tell her about getting information from someone, whether it was an officer or a suspect. *Put them at ease. Treat them like an expert. Make them think you need them.*

She sat down on the edge of the bed. "Uncle Edward, Mr. Winther has been so kind. He's the reason you're here and not in jail. And he's helping investors in town who are in financial problems because they were sold fraudulent insurance policies for the *Pacific Star*."

Uncle Edward turned his head away from her.

"Thankfully, Mr. Winther had a valid insurance policy, which is why he can help others." Julia smiled at Mr. Winther.

He met her eyes, smiled back, and asked, "Does that seem suspicious to you that I'll recover my investment and others won't?"

Julia shook her head. "Captain Evert has a valid policy too, or so I've heard. From the same agency as you."

Mr. Winther shrugged. "It's purely coincidental, I can assure you. I don't know the man. Other investors hired him to pilot the *Pacific Star*, not me." He stood. "I used Lombards of San Francisco because my son works with an attorney who recommended them."

Uncle Edward stared straight ahead.

"Well, I need to be on my way." Mr. Winther then addressed Uncle Edward. "It's been a delight to see you, Mr. Warren." He smiled at Julia. "And you too." Then he placed his briefcase on the chair and faced her. "I want to assure you that I've had no involvement in the fraudulent insurance or the sinking of the ship. I'd like to make it clear. I sense that you doubt me."

Julia's face grew warm. "Oh no," she said. "I believe you." He was an upstanding citizen, and he'd been so helpful to her.

His eyes met hers.

"I'm only asking questions," she said. "I'm neither judge nor jury. Everyone I've spoken to has told me you're trustworthy."

He smiled kindly. "I can assure you that I am, and I'm thankful for your trust in me too."

During the night, Julia tossed and turned, waking to the question of Lucien. Was he lying about not being one of the owners of the Columbia Marine Insurance Agency? Finally, she knew what she needed to do. If Lucien was, in fact, going to Astoria, she needed to return too, regardless of how seasick she'd become on the return trip.

In the morning, she left a note on the newspaper office door for Alexander and then waited to board the steamship to Astoria until Lucien boarded first. She wished Alexander could go with her to Astoria, but she couldn't ask him to go again. He had a newspaper to run. Five minutes before departure, Lucien appeared and bought a ticket. Four minutes later, Julia bought a ticket and boarded as the final whistle blew. Instead of going to the bow of the ship, she stayed near the stern, sitting on a bench that was out of the way. Thankfully, the river was smooth.

When the ship reached the dock in Astoria, she waited to be the last to disembark. As she walked up the hill from the river to the town, she saw Lucien ahead, walking with another passenger. She decided to follow him, thinking he was headed to the courthouse. But when he turned the opposite direction, she decided to go ahead to the custom house again to see if Agent Belville had arrived, and then circle back to the courthouse.

When she entered the building, an older man stood over Officer Carlson's desk, speaking with him.

"Hello, Officer Carlson," Julia said.

He stood. "Miss Warren."

"Warren?" The older man studied her curiously.

She extended her hand. "Julia Warren. I'm Edward Warren's niece."

"Good to meet you," the man said. "I'm Agent Belville."

"You're just the man I wanted to see."

"I can imagine," he answered. "Officer Carlson and I are talking about the destruction of the lens at the lighthouse. I've sent a telegram to the Fresnel Company, asking them to send a technician to assess the situation."

"I'd also like the lens evaluated," Julia said. "The two officials who've investigated so far seem convinced a bourbon bottle could have done the damage, but I'm wondering if something more substantial was used."

"Such as?"

"A sledgehammer."

Officer Carlson laughed. "Sir, I can assure you that wasn't the case."

Agent Belville scowled. "That's a question worth exploring. I'll be coming to Cape Disappointment tomorrow to investigate the situation myself."

"Excellent. Because there's a sledgehammer in the stable near the lighthouse. I found it there the day after the lens was smashed. It's in the first stall, behind the hay bale." Julia smiled, hoping to communicate her appreciation. "I have another matter I came to ask you about concerning a report of a smuggling plan eight years ago. Alexander Blake filed a claim about the incident."

Officer Carlson looked at her impatiently. "We went over this yesterday. The records don't go back that far."

Agent Belville cocked his head. "Some of the records do, but if we had the report what good would it do?"

"We'd like to know exactly what the report included."

Agent Belville shook his head. "Let's not go down a rabbit hole," he said. "I'll investigate the breaking of the lens, but I'm not wasting my time on a report from eight years ago."

"All right." Julia forced a smile. "Thank you for your time today and committing yourself to fully investigate the incident at the lighthouse."

"You're welcome," Agent Belville said. "How is your uncle doing?"

"He's conscious but not speaking. He's still in the hospital."

"I'll stop by tomorrow and see him."

As Julia left the custom house, she saw Lucien a block away heading toward the courthouse. She followed.

Chapter Fourteen

When Lucien entered the courthouse, Julia waited a couple of minutes and then entered, hurried down the hall to the clerk's office, and slipped behind the open door. From that spot she listened.

Lucien was saying, "—I need to have it corrected."

"Wait right here," the clerk said. "I need to attend to something and then I'll be back."

A few minutes later, Julia heard the clerk say, "This is the Clatsop County Sheriff, Alvin Lansing. He has a few questions for you."

"Does this have to do with the Columbia Marine Insurance Agency?" Lucien asked.

"Yes." The voice belonged to the sheriff. "Do you have any knowledge of Clarence Jones's whereabouts?"

"None whatsoever," Lucien said. "I've never met him."

"Oh?"

"Minnie Winther, the woman I'm currently with, courted Clarence Jones for a short time. I believe revenge is the reason he forged my name and connected me to the business registry." Lucien spoke rapidly. "Let me show you my signature to compare to the one you have on record."

"Here's a piece of paper," the clerk said.

There was a long moment of silence, and then the sheriff said, "The one in the business registry is definitely different."

"Yes," the clerk agreed.

"Where can I find you if I need you?" the sheriff asked.

"I'm a relief lightkeeper at the Cape Disappointment Lighthouse," Lucien answered. "I live on the property."

"All right," the sheriff said. "I'll be in touch if I have any further questions."

"I'll take this piece of paper with me," Lucien said. "I don't want my real signature floating around where someone can get it."

Why not? Julia wondered as she scurried down the hall and into a broom closet. Did he expect someone else to try to forge his signature? Or was he afraid someone might use it to prove his signature hadn't been forged?

She heard footsteps going in the opposite direction and then waited for a few more minutes before she exited the courthouse from a side door. As she turned onto the sidewalk, she saw Lucien. He stood looking at a piece of paper. After a moment, he folded it and placed it in the breast pocket of his suit jacket. Then he headed in the direction of the docks.

She stayed two blocks behind and boarded the steamship after Lucien.

When she sat down in the middle of the ship, she saw him near the bow. Soon, the steamship was headed west. Today, the water was as smooth as a cup of tea. A half hour later, Lucien walked toward her. She raised her head and smiled. "Lucien. How are you?"

He stopped. "What are you doing here?"

"I had some business to attend to in Astoria, again. Unsuccessful, I'm afraid."

"I'm sorry."

"What about you?" she asked. "Did you sort things out?"

He frowned. "It took me all of two minutes. It's ridiculous I had to spend so much time correcting the misuse of my name."

Julia agreed. "I'm sorry."

"Well, at least I was successful."

Lucien sat down next to her. "I hope things will turn around for you soon. Do you think you'll stay here, regardless of what happens with your uncle?"

"At least for a while." She dabbed at her eyes with her index fingers.

"Are you all right?"

"I will be." She searched in her bag. "This has all been so much. Do you have a handkerchief? I seem to have misplaced mine."

"Yes." He pulled his handkerchief from his pocket with a bit of a flourish. "Here it is."

Julia took it, hoping the piece of paper was folded inside. As she opened the handkerchief, her eyes fell to the deck. A piece of white paper had landed in front of her right foot.

She slid her boot over it.

That evening, Julia knocked on the lighthouse door, not knowing if Lucien would be working or if it would be the relief lightkeeper from the North Head Lighthouse. She hoped whoever was working was on the lower level making dinner or a cup of tea.

After no one answered, she decided whoever was on duty was in the tower, and she started to leave.

The door opened. "Hello?"

It wasn't Lucien.

She turned. "Oh, hello. I'm Julia Warren. My uncle is Edward Warren."

"I'm the relief keeper from the North Head Lighthouse. Eugene Maxwell. How can I help you?"

"May I look at the logbook? Uncle Edward still isn't talking, and I want to know how many shifts he worked in the last few weeks before he fell. If he'd been ill. Or overworked. That sort of thing."

He hesitated a moment but then said, "All right." He opened the door wider. "Come on in. The logbook is on the desk upstairs."

When they reached the lens room, which still had the fourteen lamps placed around the sill, she stepped to the lens. "Do you think a bourbon bottle could have done this much damage?"

He shrugged. "A bourbon bottle could do a lot." He pointed to the desk. "There's the log."

She scanned it until she found Lucien's signature. It was exactly as she remembered the signature in the book in the Clatsop County Courthouse. It was nothing like the signature she had in her bag, from the steamship.

She continued to look through the log. Uncle Edward worked five times each week. There didn't seem to be anything amiss. No gaps. No drunken days.

"Thank you," she said to the relief keeper. "I'll see myself out." As she hurried to her cabin, she said another prayer of gratitude to the Lord. Step by step, she was waiting on Him to reveal the truth and exonerate Uncle Edward.

The next morning dawned bright and glorious. It was the warmest day since Julia arrived on Cape Disappointment. On her way to work, she stopped by the hospital.

"He's still asleep," Nurse Vera said as Julia stepped into the office. "Go on back if you want to."

Julia knocked on Uncle Edward's door and then opened it. He stirred. She stepped to the window, lifted the shade, and said, "Good morning."

"Mornin'."

Julia spun to Uncle Edward. "What did you say?"

"Mornin'," he repeated.

She hurried to his side. "You're speaking."

He pushed himself up in the bed.

She sat down beside him. "How are you feeling?"

"Foggy."

"What do you remember?"

"You being here. And a man," Uncle Edward said. "I can't remember his name."

"Robert Winther."

"Ah, that's right."

"What do you remember about falling down the stairs in the lighthouse?"

"I fell?"

"Yes."

"Did I trip?"

"I don't think so," Julia answered. "It happened on Friday, two weeks ago. You were working."

He exhaled slowly.

"Do you remember if anyone else came to the lighthouse that night?"

He didn't answer.

"It was the day I arrived. I'd sent you a telegram that I'd arrive on Saturday, but then I made the connection in Portland and arrived a day earlier. A storm blew in that night. You may have seen it come in from the lighthouse."

"I remember being excited that you were arriving soon…"

Julia stayed silent. It had to be difficult for Uncle Edward to remember after being unconscious and then unable to speak.

He rubbed the side of his face. "Someone came that evening to the lighthouse…"

"Can you remember who?"

He shook his head.

"Was it Alexander Blake?"

Uncle Edward asked, "The newspaperman?"

She nodded.

"No."

"Was it Mr. Winther?"

He made a funny face and shook his head.

"One of the other lightkeepers?"

He wrinkled his nose and then whispered, "Yes." He rubbed his eyes. "That nice young man. Light hair. Smiles a lot. Big laugh."

Julia whispered back, "Lucien Graham?"

"Yes."

"Do you remember what happened?"

He shook his head.

"Do you remember that the lens was broken?"

in Cape Disappointment, Washington

He gasped. "Broken?"

"Yes."

Uncle Edward shook his head as tears filled his eyes. "No. What happened?"

Julia explained that the lens was broken, supposedly by a bourbon bottle, and then he'd been found reeking of alcohol.

"But I don't drink."

"I know."

She went on to explain that the *Pacific Star* wrecked on the bar.

He shuddered. "Were any lives lost?"

"No."

"Still, a ship was lost." He reached for her hand. "No wonder the deputy keeps coming around. He's going to arrest me again, isn't he?"

As Julia thought about how to answer Uncle Edward, she heard a racket outside the window.

"Just a minute." She stood. "I need to see what's going on."

She stepped to the window. Lucien was standing in the middle of the intersection, yelling something. A crowd had gathered around him.

Julia pushed open the window to hear.

"—responsible for the wreck of the *Pacific Star*, for the devastation of our economy. He sabotaged the ship, causing it to wreck. Now he's selling more papers, and his articles are spreading across the entire country along with his byline." Lucien pointed down the street toward the newspaper office. "Alexander Blake will move on from here, back to Chicago where's he's from, back to his family's newspaper business.

All of us, no matter our professions, will suffer from the wreck. But Alexander Blake, the newspaperman, will benefit."

Lucien pointed around the circle. "Who will march with me to the newspaper office to see Alexander Blake arrested? Sheriff Lowden will meet us there."

Julia turned away from the window. "I'll be back," she said to Uncle Edward as she dashed into the hallway, down the hall, and through the office.

By the time she reached the street, Lucien led a group of sailors, lumberjacks, and fishermen down the street. He must have started at the wharf and worked his way to the middle of town.

Julia picked up her skirts and pushed through the crowd. Just as they reached the newspaper office, she neared Lucien. "What are you doing?"

Lucien lowered his voice. "Your uncle isn't the only one to blame. It seems there really was a bomb on the ship. That's what an independent investigator hired by the investors determined. Alexander had ample opportunity to plant a bomb while he was in San Francisco."

"What kind of bomb?"

"That hasn't been determined yet."

Julia asked, "Does Alexander know anything about bombs?"

"He's a newspaperman," Lucien replied. "He knows a little bit about everything."

"You're being ridiculous," Julia said. "Alexander didn't sabotage the ship."

Without answering, Lucien brushed past her. The mob reached the general store and turned down the alley.

Alexander stepped out of the newspaper office. "What's going on?" he asked.

Coming down the opposite end of the alley was Deputy Martin and another man. Julia assumed he was Sheriff Lowden. "Alexander Blake," the sheriff said, "you're under arrest for planting a bomb on the *Pacific Star*."

Alexander began to chuckle. "Sheriff Lowden, it appears someone's fed you a story."

"That's right!" Julia called out, although her voice was muffled by the men around her, yelling, "Arrest the newspaperman!"

"It appears you've fed the entire nation a story." The sheriff held out a pair of handcuffs. "You can come willingly or by force."

Alexander shrugged and held out his hands. "I'll come willingly. But I know nothing of explosives and don't plan to be in jail long."

Chapter Fifteen

Julia watched as the sheriff and the deputy led Alexander through the crowd.

"I heard his family in Chicago has a lot of money," a fisherman said. "A few of the investors plan to sue."

Julia felt ill. Where was Lucien? She glanced around and saw Lucien running down the street, away from the crowd. She followed. Was he going into the hospital? He was a block ahead, but it appeared he was—or had turned down the street.

When she reached the intersection, she looked down the cross street. She didn't see Lucien. She continued to the hospital.

Agent Belville sat in the chair near the window.

Julia ignored him and gasped to Nurse Vera, "Did Lucien Graham come in here?"

She nodded. "He went down the hall to see your uncle."

Julia turned to Agent Belville. "Come on."

"I'm waiting to speak to the doctor."

"Have you spoken to Uncle Edward yet?"

He shook his head.

She reached down and grabbed his arm. "Come on."

Thankfully, he cooperated. She pushed through the door into the hall. When they reached Uncle Edward's room, she flung open the door.

Lucien stood at the head of the bed, a pillow in his hands. "Julia!" he said. "There you are."

He dropped the pillow on the floor.

"What's going on?"

Uncle Edward cleared his throat. "I'm not sure."

Lucien took a step backward. "When did he start talking?"

Uncle Edward pushed himself up to a sitting position. "I have more to say."

Julia took her uncle's hand. "Have you remembered anything more about that night?"

Uncle Edward shook his head. "Not anything other than Lucien stopping by the lighthouse."

"I did," Lucien said. "On my way into town. But it wasn't evening—it was still afternoon. Around four or so."

"I remember it being later," Uncle Edward said.

"No doubt." Lucien's voice grew louder. "But you've had a head injury, so we wouldn't expect your memories to be accurate."

Something had changed in Lucien. He'd been so unflappable since she'd met him. So suave. Was he beginning to panic?

She faced Agent Belville. "I implore you to thoroughly investigate the wrecking of the *Pacific Star* and question Lucien. There's evidence that he and a partner, Clarence Jones, sold fraudulent insurance policies on the *Pacific Star* to all but one of the investors and Captain Evert. Lucien claims that his signature was forged when the insurance agency was registered, but I have evidence that it wasn't."

Lucien guffawed.

She continued. "The evidence suggests that more than one person colluded to sell fraudulent policies on the *Pacific Star*, wreck the ship, collect the insurance money from their own legitimate policies, and buy up businesses in town from the investors who lost money on the fake ones. Plus, the claim that a bottle broke the lens hasn't been proven. As I've already reported, there's a sledgehammer on the property that should be evaluated as the possible weapon. If that sledgehammer was used, Uncle Edward couldn't be the culprit. He was injured and couldn't have hidden it in the stable after the lens was destroyed."

Lucien took another step back. "Miss Warren's claims are ludicrous. She's been unstable since she arrived here." He motioned to Uncle Edward. "I don't blame her, because of her distress over her uncle's crimes, but don't believe her lies. Edward Warren was drunk that night and vandalized the lens. That was the reason Captain Evert hit the bar, which caused a bomb on the *Pacific Star*—that was planted by Alexander Blake—to explode."

Agent Belville thought for a moment and then asked, "Wouldn't someone on board have needed to detonate the bomb?"

Lucien shrugged. "If that's the case, then most likely Blake was working with one of the sailors on the ship."

"Has the wreckage been examined to confirm there was a bomb?"

"Yes," Lucien said. "An investigator from Seattle determined there was an explosion in the hull. Mr. Blake is now in the city jail."

"I see." Agent Belville paused a moment and said, "I need to examine both the remains of the ship and the lens at the lighthouse."

"Please determine if a bottle could have done the damage to the lens," Julia said. "It seems something more substantial would have had to have been used."

Lucien's eyes narrowed.

"I'll investigate the damage to the lens and examine the sledgehammer." The agent motioned to Lucien. "Come with me. I'll need to speak with the captain too. Where can I find him?"

"I have no idea where he is."

"But isn't Captain James Evert, in fact, your maternal great-uncle? Aren't you, Lucien James Graham, named after him?"

Lucien shook his head. "I have no idea what you're talking about."

"I found a report yesterday crammed in Officer Carlson's desk drawer," Agent Belville said. "It linked you and Captain Evert in a failed smuggling plan in 1891."

"I can assure you the report was fabricated."

"Sir," Julia said. "I don't mean to interrupt, but I know Captain Evert frequents the saloon at the end of the wharf. He might be there."

"Thank you." He turned to Lucien. "Come along. We can talk more about your bomb theory and Mr. Blake and Captain Evert as we walk."

"I need to get some sleep before I work tonight."

"We'll have the relief lightkeeper from North Head take duty tonight. I'll send a message to him."

The shipwreck bell began to ring.

"What's that for?" Agent Belville asked.

"A ship is wrecking," Lucien said. "I need to go."

Agent Belville put his hand on Lucien's shoulder. "No. You need to come with me."

Even though Lucien was with Agent Belville and Julia doubted he'd be returning to the hospital, she asked Nurse Vera not to let him back into

Uncle Edward's room. Then she left the hospital and hurried toward the beach, where a ship had broken up on the bar, the pieces washing up on the beach. Alexander couldn't report on it. He needed her to.

"Want a ride?"

She turned.

Billy was coming up behind her.

"Are you headed to the beach?"

"Yes, ma'am." Billy stopped the buggy, and Julia climbed up onto the front bench.

As they passed the jail, someone yelled, "Julia!"

"Stop," she said to Billy. "For just a minute."

Alexander was at the window of the jail, clutching the bars. "I didn't do it!"

Her heart raced at the sight of him. "I know." She pulled the notebook from her bag and held it up. "I'm going to the beach to report on the wreck. Agent Belville is here. He found your report from eight years ago. He's keeping Lucien with him as he investigates Captain Evert, the *Pacific Star*, and the broken lens."

"Thank you!" Alexander yelled.

"You'll be out soon," she replied. Then to Billy, she said, "Let's go."

As the buggy began rolling again, Julia asked, "Did you just happen to be at the wharf the day I arrived, or did someone ask you to look for me?"

Billy's face grew red, but he didn't answer.

"Did someone tell you to take me to the North Head Lighthouse instead of the Cape Disappointment Lighthouse?"

"I'm sorry," he said. "I was told you might be coming from Astoria that Friday. Or maybe the next day. If you arrived on Friday,

I was to take you to the North Head Lighthouse no matter where you asked me to take you."

Julia inhaled sharply. "Did Mr. Winther give you those instructions?"

"No."

Julia exhaled, remembering Lucien saying something to Billy right before they left for the lighthouse. "Lucien Graham?"

He nodded. "But please don't tell him I told you. He might convince Minnie to get me fired."

"I won't speak of it to Lucien." But she would need to tell Agent Belville.

When they reached the end of the road, as close to the beach as they could get, Billy jumped down from the buggy and helped push the rescue cart while Julia ran ahead, trying to get a good view of the ship. It bobbed on the bar as men jumped into a lifeboat. An inexperienced captain must have tried to cross. There wasn't a rogue wave in view.

A large boat heading west, ready to cross the bar, caught Julia's attention. Was that Captain Evert at the helm? She shaded her eyes from the midmorning sun. The man stared straight ahead until a gust of wind tossed his hat off his head. He bent down, grabbed the hat, and stood. As he pulled it down over his silvery hair, he turned. When he saw Julia, he grinned.

She headed toward the dry dock at the north end of the wharf. Agent Belville faced the remains of the *Pacific Star*. Lucien was looking out over the river, his arms crossed. Julia couldn't make out his expression, but she could guess. No doubt, he felt betrayed as his uncle escaped.

Lucien would likely get what he deserved. Whether Captain James did or not would be up to the Lord.

At the end of the day, Julia walked back to the hospital, passing the jail on the way. Alexander wasn't at the window.

Uncle Edward was asleep when she arrived. She stood at the window of his room for a few minutes and then sat down and picked up his Bible. She thought of Mr. Winther and how kind he'd been to her and Uncle Edward and others. She saw no signs that he was in cahoots with Lucien, and yet she couldn't help but wonder.

A knock on the door startled her and woke Uncle Edward. Julia stood and said, "Come in."

Agent Belville opened the door.

Alexander stood behind him. She wanted to rush forward and give him a hug.

Instead, she said, "I'm so relieved."

Alexander smiled. "I told you I wouldn't be in for long."

Agent Belville stepped to Uncle Edward. "Your niece saved the day. Her investigation pointed to Lucien Graham and Captain James Evert masterminding an insurance scam that included Clarence Jones of Astoria to keep others from recouping their investment in the *Pacific Star*, and then wrecking the ship for their own profit, with the intention of buying up businesses at low prices in town."

Uncle Edward looked at Julia, admiration in his eyes. "You figured that out?"

"Yes," she said. "With Alexander's help."

Agent Belville gave Julia an appreciative look and then addressed Uncle Edward again. "I examined the lens and doubt it can be repaired, but we'll see what the technician says when he arrives." He turned to Alexander. "Lucien Graham did his best to direct the blame away from himself, mainly toward you. But that's all sorted out now."

Alexander nodded and asked, "Any word on Captain Evert?"

"Only that he headed north. I've sent telegrams all the way to Canada. Hopefully, he'll be caught."

"What about the possibility of Lucien attacking Uncle Edward and framing him for damaging the lens?" Julia asked.

Agent Belville shook his head. "Without Mr. Warren's memory returning or a confession from Lucien, there's not enough evidence to accuse Mr. Graham at this time. We can't prove the sledgehammer in the stable was used to break the lens. It's a common tool in these parts." He turned to Uncle Edward. "However, there is enough evidence to acquit you, sir. The charges have been dropped."

Julia's heart rose at the news of Uncle Edward no longer being a suspect—and then fell at Lucien not being charged with attacking Uncle Edward and the lens. "What will happen to Lucien, as far as the insurance fraud charges?" she asked.

"There will be a trial on that matter, I'm sure. If he's convicted, I'm guessing he'll be sentenced to five years or so."

"That's not very long…"

"Remember," Uncle Edward said, "justice belongs to the Lord."

Julia hesitated. Hadn't God already taken care of Uncle Edward through all of this? And directed Julia? Hadn't the truth of Uncle

Edward's innocence prevailed? "You're right," she said. "I'll continue to trust Him."

Agent Belville stepped closer to Uncle Edward. "We'll talk soon about your future. You may return to your cottage, and I hope you'll be able to return to work. If not, I'll do what needs to be done to start your pension."

"Thank you." Uncle Edward's eyes shone. "I'm hoping I have a few more years of work left in me."

After Agent Belville left, Julia told Uncle Edward that she'd see him the next day. "We'll talk with Doc Olsen about taking you home."

He smiled up at her. "I'd like nothing more."

Alexander said, "Julia, in the meantime, I'd be happy to give you a ride to your cabin now."

"I'll gratefully accept," she said.

Soon they were on their way up the plank road through the trees to the clopping of the horse's hooves, winding their way up Cape Disappointment. The sun shone through the canopy of budding leaves and towering evergreens. Alexander had his jacket off and his sleeves rolled up to his elbows. Julia glanced at him sideways. His dark hair was mussed a little, his cheeks were rosy, and his eyes bright.

Julia asked, "Is the typesetter printing the paper this afternoon?"

"It's not going out today."

"Alexander! Are you sure?"

"Positive," he said. "We'll put out an extra-large issue tomorrow. I'll get started on it tonight."

"I'll help you in the morning." She slid nearer to him on the bench as the buggy rounded a corner. "I'll write up the article about today's wreck and get it to you first thing in the morning."

Alexander gave her a quick grin. "I appreciate that."

"What do you think will happen with Lucien, if he's sentenced?"

"I'm guessing he'll be paroled after a couple of years, due to his charming smile and good behavior." Alexander rolled his eyes. "Or Bobby Winther will defend him on appeal, and he'll get out even sooner. Then he'll return here and marry Minnie. He'll end up managing one of Robert Winther's businesses. In another twenty years, a few people in town will remember what he did and still resent him. Others will believe he was wrongfully convicted, thanks to Minnie's endless defense of him, which has already started. And the rest, the majority, won't remember the wreck of the *Pacific Star* in 1899 at all."

Julia's shoulders sagged.

"Chin up," Alexander said. They passed through a patch of shade and back into the sunshine. "What you've done is amazing. Not only would I still be in jail and headed for prison, but no one else could have revealed Lucien to be a collaborator in the insurance fraud. If you hadn't returned to the custom house, Agent Belville wouldn't have found the report from eight years ago in Officer Carlson's desk and investigated further."

"Lucien was good at deceiving all of us," Julia said. "He acted so concerned for me and Uncle Edward. He reached out to me. Consoled me. All, I'm assuming, so I wouldn't suspect him." She should have seen it. In retrospect, Lucien's charm reminded her of Jack's. Both pretended to care while working to further their own interests alone. Had she been so set on not trusting another newspaperman that she trusted another scoundrel instead?

"Some people can lie without flinching," Alexander said. "And flatter those they intend to harm. It's uncanny."

Julia agreed.

"You know who else was kinder to me than I would have expected him to be?"

"Who?" Alexander asked.

"Robert Winther."

Alexander met her gaze. "I think he's genuinely kind."

Julia wasn't so sure. "He feared I suspected him of somehow being involved in the insurance fraud, and that seemed to trouble him."

Alexander shrugged. "He was probably just trying to protect his good name. I can't even remember all the things I heard at the jail today." He sighed. "I need to hang out there more often. Besides hearing that Nancy was saying Lucien had been framed, I heard that Robert Winther presented an offer to John Hoffman to buy the wharf."

"That was fast." Julia shook her head. "And you don't believe Mr. Winther is involved in all of this somehow?"

"Not unless there's solid evidence," Alexander said. "If you have any information that involves Robert Winther, go to the authorities but don't spread any rumors, whatsoever. No one in town is thinking that Robert Winther was involved. People will accept that your uncle is innocent, but if they hear you talking badly about Robert Winther, they'll be appalled."

Julia mulled over what Alexander said. He was right. She had no evidence when it came to Robert Winther. Just a feeling—which didn't count when it came to the law or justice or, of course, journalism.

Alexander continued. "For example, I heard from several people today that John Hoffman said Robert Winther was doing him a favor in buying the wharf—and that's how most of the townspeople feel. Of course, time will tell."

Alexander reached for Julia's gloved hand as the buggy rolled onto the plateau leading to the lighthouse. "Speaking of the future... I know you said you'd never get involved with another newspaperman..."

Julia's heart fluttered as her hand clasped his. "I may have been a little impetuous when I said that."

He grinned. "That's good to hear."

Ahead was the silhouette of the lighthouse against the setting sun as orange and pink streaked across the sky. Two eagles soared over the ocean.

She turned to him. "What were you saying about the future?"

He leaned nearer and in a deep voice asked, "Do you plan to stay on Cape Disappointment?"

"Yes," Julia answered. "Yes, I do. There's nowhere else I'd rather be."

He put his arm around her. "That's all I needed to know."

She scooted closer to him and raised her face to his. The horse continued clopping along the wooden planks as Alexander leaned down and kissed her. Courting a newspaperman—the right one—was in Julia's future after all.

Love's Light Returns

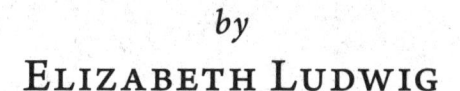

by
Elizabeth Ludwig

"Every moment is made glorious by the light of love."

—Rumi

Chapter One

Cape Disappointment, Washington
Present Day

Fat, fluffy snowflakes—the kind Marnie Stewart liked to catch on her tongue—piled on the windowsill of the Greater Pacific Tourism Agency. At least three inches had accumulated since she arrived early that Thursday morning, partially obscuring her view of the Port of Ilwaco and the naked ship masts jutting into the gray sky. They were expecting at least another six or seven inches by nightfall.

"Have you heard?"

Marnie startled and turned to the door where Kate Winther was brushing some of those fluffy snowflakes off her shoulders and onto the floor. Which gave Marnie an idea. She held up one finger, typed the last words on her post for the City of Ilwaco blog, and hit publish.

"Sorry. Seeing all that snow reminded me I wanted to say something about keeping the sidewalks clear outside of businesses to make it easier for customers and tourists to navigate downtown." She sank against the back of her chair and motioned to Kate. "You were saying?"

Kate looked across the office at Brandon and rolled her eyes. "How does she do it?"

"Wait until the last minute and then write killer articles just in time to meet her deadline?" Brandon shrugged. "No idea."

He grinned at Marnie over the lid of his laptop, keys clacking as he put the finishing touches on his own post.

"Anyway." Marnie quirked an eyebrow at Kate. "What haven't I heard?"

Kate shrugged out of her coat and hung it on the rack along with her scarf and gloves. "Lucien Graham is back. It's the talk all over town."

At Brandon's desk, the typing instantly stopped. Marnie slid a glance at him. His face remained unreadable...stoic...the words on his computer screen reflected in his glasses.

"Lucien?" Despising how her voice cracked, Marnie trained her gaze on Kate and tried again. "Lucien is back?" She picked up a pencil and twiddled it between her fingers. "How...um...where did you hear that?"

"Buddy Thompson told me."

Marnie's mouth went dry. Buddy was a reservist at the Coast Guard station at Cape Disappointment, so that could only mean one thing. She replaced the pencil carefully in its cup and laced her fingers on the desktop. "So, he's stationed here?"

Sympathy flashed in Kate's gaze. She nodded then flicked her long hair over her shoulder and circled around to her desk. "That's what Buddy said."

"Great. Just what we need." Growling, Brandon ripped his glasses off and slapped his laptop shut. "Ilwaco was better off without him."

Marnie lifted her hand. "Hold on now, he's military. It's not like he has a choice about where he's stationed."

"Actually, I heard Ilwaco *was* one of his choices." At Marnie's glare, Kate shrugged. "What? Buddy said Lucien submitted three station requests, and Cape Disappointment was one of them."

Not helping, Marnie mouthed, then looked back at Brandon. "Regardless, Lucien isn't his father. Or his great-grandfather, for that matter. People can't keep assuming he'll turn out like his relatives."

Brandon stowed his laptop under his arm and stood. "I think I'll finish up at home." He shot a glance in Kate's direction. "Will you let the mayor know my article's gonna be a little late?"

Not waiting for her reply, he shoved his chair into the desk with a bang. A second later, he yanked open the office door and walked out, and a blast of frigid February air swirled the papers on Marnie's desk.

"Wow." Kate turned wide eyes to Marnie. "The cold front in here is almost as bad as the one outside."

Marnie dropped her shoulders and sighed. "It was probably to be expected, given our history."

Kate's gaze changed from sympathetic to severe. "Which history is that? The one between you and Lucien…or the one between you and Brandon?"

When she didn't answer, Kate crossed to Marnie's desk, her tall heels clicking on the slate floor, and laid her hand on Marnie's shoulder. "I'm sorry. You know I didn't mean anything by that."

At Marnie's nod, Kate pushed aside a stack of papers and sat on the desk, one leg swinging. "Brandon's a good guy, and he cares for you. He just doesn't want to see you hurt again. Besides, it's not like he's the only one unhappy about this news. Most of the people in Ilwaco will be less than thrilled to know he's back. Best if you stay as far away from that guy as possible."

Marnie dropped her gaze and tucked her hair behind her ear. "I know."

The space heater on the floor beneath her desk hissed softly.

Kate sighed and crossed her arms. "But you aren't going to listen to me, are you?"

"Kate."

Her tone warned against more questions. Kate raised her hands. "Okay, okay. Your business is your business. I won't say any more about it." She slid off the desk and poured herself a drink from the watercooler.

Watching her, Marnie felt the tiniest tinge of envy. Kate was always perfectly put together. Perfectly poised and in control of her emotions. Perfectly...perfect.

"How's your mom?" Marnie asked.

The cup in Kate's hand rattled against the cooler, revealing the smallest crack in the veneer. She licked a drop of water from her thumb and shrugged. "She's doing okay. This first Valentine's Day without Pops will be hard, but I figured I'd take her out to eat to keep her mind off things."

Marnie instantly felt bad for resenting her friend's self-confidence. She pushed up from her chair and rested her hand on Kate's back. "What can I do?"

"Nothing." She sniffed and shot a watery smile in Marnie's direction. "The meal train you set up was enough. Really. The rest is just gonna take some time."

"Okay." Marnie drew in a deep breath and gestured to her computer. "I worked on a few more tourism ideas for the mayor. If you have a minute, I'd like to go over them with you before we present them so we can cull any you don't think will work."

"Yeah. That's fine. Let me grab something to write with." Kate's desk drawer groaned as she riffled through it.

Marnie shot her a cross look as she pulled up a chair. "You know, if you got a new keyboard, you wouldn't have to mess with writing things down longhand."

"Oh, but then I couldn't dot my i's with all these tiny purple hearts." She drew one and flipped her notepad around for Marnie to see. "What do you think?" She waggled the notebook from side to side.

"Cute."

"I thought so."

"I meant you, not the hearts."

"I know."

A laugh burst from Marnie at Kate's antics. The two had been friends since high school, and still Kate could win a smile from Marnie no matter her mood.

"Okay, here's what I have so far."

Marnie swung the screen around and started through her list—from ideas for an ice festival and clam digs in the winter to craft shows and fish fries in the summer—but even with Kate tossing suggestions her way, a part of Marnie's brain remained locked on the idea that Lucien was somewhere nearby. Was he thinking about her? Had her presence played even the smallest part in his return to Cape Disappointment?

She closed the lid on her computer when they finished and tugged her coat off the back of her chair. "It's getting late. I think I'll I head home."

"Uh-huh." Kate lifted her feet to the desk and crossed her ankles. "You gonna swing over to Brandon's place to see how he's doing, or are you heading in the opposite direction?"

The opposite direction being the Coast Guard station.

And none of Kate's business.

Marnie avoided her gaze as she stowed her laptop and swung her backpack over her shoulder. "Have a good weekend."

Kate's heels thumped to the floor, but Marnie ducked through the door before she could protest. All three of them had keys to the office. Kate could lock up.

Outside, very few tracks rutted the freshly fallen snow along Howerton Way. Brandon's place was in one direction. She could go there, as Kate had suggested or…

For several seconds, falling snow melted on Marnie's cheeks as she stared past the boats bobbing in the boatyard, across the water, toward Fort Canby.

No.

The memory of Lucien's leaving—and the sweetness of his kiss—was still too fresh. Kate was right. It *was* best if she stayed away. Except Ilwaco wasn't that big. They'd run into each other eventually. Still, she didn't need to go looking for trouble. She could just…avoid any places she thought he'd show up. Or find out when he was on duty and—

"Marnie, is that you?"

A shiver that had nothing to do with the weather traveled her spine. She knew that voice. She'd spent the better part of six years driving it from her head.

Chapter Two

Not yet.

It was a weak prayer but sincere, nonetheless. Marnie wasn't ready to face Lucien. After all, she'd only just learned he was in town. She hadn't prepared herself—hadn't steeled her heart against his slow grin that melted over her in stages or trained her brain from dwelling on his penetrating gaze that seemed to drill straight through to her core.

"Marnie?"

She blinked hard then turned, her muscles tightening defensively, as though she were bracing for a punch to the gut.

"Lucien." His name breathed out of her. "You're back."

She sounded happy about the fact. It infuriated her. Filled her with heartache. And rage. Mostly rage.

Whirling, she stalked to her car. Lucien called to her, but she wouldn't listen. Because the last time they'd seen each other, her heart had been broken into a million pieces. And she just wasn't sure she could put it back together if it happened again.

"Marnie, hold up. Please."

It was the "please" that froze her in her tracks. If there was one thing she remembered clearly about Lucien Graham, it was that he never, ever, said please.

She straightened her shoulders. Focused on slowing the white, wispy puffs of air escaping from her lips. On clamping a stranglehold on the fury simmering in her belly so she could think. Speak.

Composing her face into something like a rational human, she turned. A few feet away, Lucien slid his hands into the pockets of his red and white Coast Guard coat. It was unzipped, and the collar was tucked half in and half out, like he'd thrown it on in a hurry. He wasn't wearing a hat, so the flakes that settled on his black hair and lashes looked startlingly white.

"Thanks for stopping." He jerked his thumb across the street toward the café. "I saw you come out—"

"I heard you were back."

They stared at each other a long second, and then Lucien nodded. "Yup. Got here about a week ago."

He shifted on the sidewalk but didn't draw closer. She was glad for the distance. It let her breathe.

"I came to take care of Dad. He's not doing so well."

George was sick? She hadn't known that either.

As though reading the question on her face, he shrugged and looked past her toward the boatyard. "I guess all that drinking he did when I was growing up finally caught up to him."

So, it was still there...the loneliness and pain tangled up inside him that had drawn her in. Somehow, she managed to mumble, "I'm sorry."

He looked at her, his gaze as dark and penetrating as she remembered. "Me too."

"Hey, Luc!"

He looked over his shoulder in the direction of the voice. Another coastie waved from the door of the café. "You coming, or what?"

"Yeah. Be right there."

When he looked back, Marnie raised her eyebrows. "'Luc'?"

The slow grin she remembered washed over her. "Yeah. I go by Luc now."

She wanted to ask why but didn't. She wanted to ask about George but couldn't. There were so many questions piled up inside her, she knew if she released one, they'd all come flooding out. She rubbed her hands over her arms and stamped her feet against the cold. "Well, I should get going."

"Me too." He angled his head toward the café. "The guys are waiting for me."

"Okay." She bit her lip then started to turn.

"Marnie, before you go"—he waited for her to look at him before continuing—"it's really good to see you. I wanted to tell you—I need to explain—"

She held up her hand. "You don't need to explain."

Except…he did. And she wanted him to. Didn't she?

His jaw hardened, and he nodded. "Okay. Take care of yourself, Marnie."

"You too."

He turned, looked both ways, then jogged across the street. That was it? She'd waited six years to confront him, and all they had to say to each other was "take care"?

Behind her, the door to the agency rattled open and Kate stepped out. "Was that Lucien? What did he say to you? Did he tell you why he was back in town?"

Marnie swung her gaze to Kate shivering next to her on the sidewalk. "He goes by Luc now."

"What?" Kate clutched her arms around herself.

Oddly, Marnie now felt impervious to the cold. She gestured to the door. "You should get your coat if you're going to be outside."

Kate frowned. "Marnie, what were you and *Luc* talking about?" She stressed the name as though she found it distasteful.

"Nothing." It wasn't much of an answer, but it was true. Six years, and the first time they spoke, they talked about nothing. She sighed and hiked her backpack higher on her shoulder. "I'm gonna go. Don't forget to lock up."

Kate studied her face. "Hey." Stepping closer, she touched Marnie's elbow. "Hey, are you okay?"

If anyone would know what seeing Luc again meant to Marnie, it was Kate. Images of late nights spent crying on her shoulder came winging back. But that was in the past. Marnie had sworn a long time ago she'd never shed another tear over Lucien Graham, and she'd meant it.

She lifted her chin. "I'll be fine. We'll talk tomorrow, all right? I'll call you in the morning."

Worry creased Kate's forehead, but she dropped her hand. "Okay. Tell your mom I said hi."

"Will do." Marnie hurried to her car, then waved to Kate through the windshield as she backed onto the street.

Somehow, Marnie made it all the way home without driving into a ditch. It would have been easy enough to do, distracted as she was. And with the wind picking up and the falling snow making it hard to see, well, she was glad to make it home in one piece.

She pushed open the mudroom door and hung her keys and backpack on a quirky shelf she'd picked up at a craft fair. "Mom?"

"In the kitchen."

Sliding out of her coat, Marnie added it to the items hanging from the shelf then wound her way to the kitchen where the savory scents of meat loaf and gravy wafted. As she entered, her mother looked up from the stove, steam fogging her glasses.

"Hi, honey."

Marnie smiled and handed her mom a towel. At fifty-four, Corinne Stewart was still a striking woman, with bits of silver starting to streak her raven hair—when she couldn't make it to the salon for a color. After Marnie's stepfather passed away, Mom had moved in with her. The arrangement had been awkward at first, but over time, both she and Marnie had come to appreciate the closeness produced between them because of it.

"Are you hungry? Supper's almost ready."

"Starving." Marnie rounded the counter, pulled the lid off the pot, and took a whiff. "Mmm. Mashed sweet potatoes?"

"Uh-huh."

"Yum." Marnie replaced the lid and then gave her mom a hug. "How long have you been home?"

"About an hour. Doug let us off early since the bad weather was keeping people from venturing out."

Her mother worked part-time giving lessons at a local art studio in Ilwaco. Doug was her boss, but every now and then, Marnie got the distinct impression he hoped for more.

"Well, I'm glad." Marnie rubbed her hands together. "Anything you need me to do?"

"Nope, I think I've got it." Mom gave her a measuring look as she took the cinnamon from the cupboard. "You okay, honey? You look a little flushed."

Ugh. Her mother had an uncanny ability to spy trouble brewing, but that didn't mean Marnie was eager to talk about it. "I'm fine, Mom. If you don't need me, I'll go ahead and get washed up."

"Go." Mom shooed her with a dishcloth.

The escape gave Marnie a chance to collect her thoughts, and by the time she returned to the kitchen for supper, she felt better. More in control. Both she and her mother dished up their plates, then sat down at the small table next to a large bay window overlooking the backyard. In the winter, it was the perfect spot to sit and watch the rabbits scurrying from their burrows. Marnie often found her mom there, a cup of coffee in one hand and her worn Bible in the other.

"So? How was your day?" Mom dragged a bite of meat loaf through a pool of gravy on her plate. "Anything exciting happen?"

Exciting? That was one way to put it. A grunt escaped Marnie's lips before she could stop it.

Her mom shot her a curious look. "Marnie?"

She set her fork down and reached for her water glass. No sense putting off the inevitable. Mom would hear about it eventually, and better if it came from her. "I saw Lucien Graham today."

To her surprise, Mom refused to meet her gaze. Marnie lowered her glass and eyed her suspiciously.

"Mom? Did you know he was back in town?"

Her mother licked her lips and lifted one shoulder in a shrug. "I may have heard something." She peered at Marnie over the frames of her glasses. "How did it go?"

"About as good as could be expected, I suppose." She fiddled with her napkin, peering at her mother. "Did you know his father isn't doing well?"

"Uh…"

Marnie's mouth fell open. "Seriously?"

"I run into him sometimes at the community center where I walk when the weather is bad. Every now and then, we grab coffee and chat."

"You *chat*. With George Graham?" Disbelief made her voice sharper than she'd intended.

Mom reached across the table to clasp her hand. "He's different than you remember. Not so angry."

Marnie snorted.

Mom pulled her hand away and picked up her fork. "Anyway, he told me a while ago that he'd talked to Luc—he goes by Luc now—about moving back. I guess he finally agreed."

"I guess so."

"Hopefully, he and his father will be able to put some of their past issues behind them."

She didn't answer.

Mom pushed a bite of meat loaf around her plate but kept her gaze trained on Marnie. "Maybe now, the two of you will also."

"Mom."

"What?" Her mom's fork rattled against her plate. "I always thought the two of you made such a nice couple."

"Me too. Until he left."

"He didn't *leave*, sweetheart. He enlisted."

"Yeah, without telling me." Anger tightened her throat. She swallowed hard and uncurled her fingers from her glass. "Anyway, it's all water under the bridge. *Luc* has moved on, and so have I—"

The ringing of the telephone cut off the rest.

"I'll get it."

Laying her napkin on the table, Mom rose and crossed to the antique rotary dial phone mounted to the wall in the hallway. Though they rarely used it, her mother insisted they keep a landline in case the power went out. A few of her older friends still called on it. Marnie heard her answer, and then she went silent for a long time. When she did speak, she instantly snared Marnie's attention.

"Was anyone hurt?" Concern pinched her voice.

Marnie left her plate of cooling meat loaf and joined her mother in the hall. *Who is it?* she mouthed.

Doris, Mom mouthed back.

Marnie pressed her hand to her chest. Doris Abernathy's husband ran a charter fishing business. She tapped her mother on the arm and waited until she looked at her. *Did something happen to his boat?*

Mom shook her head, then returned her attention to the call. "Okay, thank you so much for calling, Doris. Yes, I'll see you Sunday. Bye-bye." She replaced the receiver and looked at Marnie, her eyes wide. "That was Doris Abernathy."

"Yes, you said that. What did she want?"

"She was calling to let me know...my goodness...I can hardly believe it."

"Mom."

Mom shook her head again and then looked at Marnie. "She was calling to let me know the fire trucks have been called out to the Grahams' place. Doris thinks Luc and George's house is on fire."

Chapter Three

Marnie felt a moment of shocked disbelief, quickly replaced by rising urgency. "Luc was with another coastie. They were in uniform, so I think they were headed to the station. Do you think he knows what's going on?"

"I don't know, but if Luc's on the water, George will be alone." Mom whirled and headed down the hall.

"Where are you going?" Marnie called.

"To check on him." She yanked her coat off one of the hooks and held out Marnie's. "You coming?"

Of course she was, but not because of Luc, or even George. Her mother didn't need to be out driving alone in bad weather. She hurried forward and snatched her keys from the shelf. "We'll take my car. It has better tires."

Her mom didn't argue. Within minutes, they were pulling to a stop on the road in front of the Grahams' gray clapboard house. As Doris had said, fire trucks had been called, the red and white lights flashing a pattern against the snow. But why couldn't they smell smoke on the air or see flames?

"Did they put it out already?"

Her mom asked what Marnie was thinking. "I don't know." She put the car in park and peered at the house. There were several firefighters clustered in groups near the front door and around the garage, but none of them seemed to be in a hurry.

"There's George." Mom pointed out the window to a hunched figure standing alone on the snow-covered lawn. Her door latch clicked. "I'm going to ask him what happened."

She scrambled out of the car without waiting for a reply, letting in a blast of cold air even the heater couldn't fight.

Marnie shut off the car. On either side of the Grahams' house and across the street, bystanders in fur-lined boots and coats had gathered to watch the spectacle. Marnie felt their stares as she followed her mom through the snow.

"I appreciate you coming, Corinne," George grunted as Marnie drew close. "You didn't have to, but I'm grateful, nonetheless."

"Of course, George. I'm glad you're okay," Mom said kindly. "Are the fire crews heading out?"

"Yeah, they're done here. If you ask me, them coming was a waste of time."

Even in the dim light, Marnie could see his scowl. He was upset they'd come? How did he think they felt, getting pulled out of their warm homes? And why was he being short with Mom when all she'd done was exhibit concern?

She hid a frown and shoved her hands into her pockets. "So, what happened, if you don't mind me asking?" George's gaze swung to her. Marnie pointed at the house. "It doesn't look like there was any damage."

"The fire wasn't in the house. It was on the porch. No damage except for a few scorch marks." He shuffled over to a blackened lump in the snow, grabbed a stick, and used it to lift the lump into the air. "Someone left this in a can and set it on fire."

Both Marnie and her mother leaned closer, then drew back quickly at the stench of melted plastic and fiber.

Mom lowered her glasses. "What is that?"

"Is it…" Marnie bit her lip. Though the item was tattered and scorched, there was no mistaking the spots of distinctive red color. "A Coast Guard coat."

George snorted and let the garment slide off the stick onto the ground. "Yeah. Some prank, eh?"

"Is that what you think it was, George?" Mom asked.

"Mom." Marnie gestured at the curious onlookers. "Maybe we should—?"

"Come inside?" George waved his hand toward the house.

Marnie had been about to say leave the discussion for another time, but her mom was already moving to the porch, leaving Marnie little choice but to follow. And she would have liked another choice. Because what she could remember of the Graham house was darkness from shuttered windows, a living room littered with takeout trays, and gloom mixed with anger and—

Marnie's mouth fell open. Was this even the same place? It was startlingly clean. Cleaner than her own place. And airy, with light-colored paint on the walls that opened up the hallway into the living room. New carpet and doors. There was even a plant on a table near the front door. A plant! And it was real, not one of those fake ones she saw in the housewares aisles.

"Marnie?"

She snapped her gaze to her mother, who was looking pointedly at her.

"Your coat?"

"Oh." She shrugged out of it and handed it to George. "Sorry."

"No problem." He cleared his throat. "I guess the place looks pretty different to you, huh? I've had some work done on it, and now Luc's been helping me out some."

Marnie nodded. "It looks good."

He motioned in the direction Marnie remembered led to the kitchen. "Either of you like something to drink?"

Marnie shook her head in unison with her mom. "Thanks, but I'm fine."

"All right." He turned toward the living room, where the sounds of a basketball game drifted from a large television set. "Let me just…"

He crossed to a brown leather recliner, fumbled around the cushion until he found the remote control, then hit the off button. The television immediately went blank. "Sorry about that, Corinne."

Mom smiled. After a moment, she glanced at the couch. "Maybe we should sit down?"

"Yeah, of course." He hurried forward, brushed nonexistent crumbs from the cushions, then gave the couch a pat and held out his hand. "Please."

They sat, Marnie next to her mom and George in the worn recliner, still clutching the remote. Mom pointed to it. "I hope we're not interrupting you."

"Oh no." He laid the remote on a side table and clasped his hands in his lap. "The Trail Blazers are playing. I got wrapped up in the game. That's why I didn't notice the fire."

Watching him, Marnie might have thought him nervous. But that was impossible, because George Graham could be described as loud, or belligerent, or grumpy, or any number of less-than-ideal adjectives—but nervous? That just wasn't one of them.

Her mom interrupted her thoughts. "Speaking of the fire, would you mind telling us what happened?"

The scowl returned to George's face, chasing away any sign of nerves. "Wish I knew. I was sitting here watching the game when a flash through the window caught my eye. Luckily, I keep a hose in the garage. Only took me a couple of seconds to put it out once I hooked that up."

"You put it out?" Marnie lifted her brows in surprise. "So who called the fire department?"

"One of the neighbors?" Mom suggested.

He grimaced. "Maybe, though it's just as likely one of them started the fire in the first place." He sighed and scrubbed his knuckles across his scalp. "I'm glad Luc wasn't here to see it."

"You won't be able to hide it from him," Mom said. "He'll hear about it eventually."

"I know." The lines around his mouth and across his brow deepened. "Someone sure is bent on chasing us off. Wish I knew who."

"What do you mean?" Marnie's gaze bounced from George to her mother. "The coat makes it look as though it was directed toward Luc. Why would you think it's also directed to you? And is one incident enough to draw that conclusion?"

"It's not just the coat," Mom said, looking at George. "Is it?"

He shook his head. "Earlier today, someone left a black envelope in the mailbox with a note inside saying Ilwaco would be better off without a Graham in it."

"Oh, George, I didn't know that," Mom said. "I was talking about what you told me yesterday."

"What happened?" Marnie asked.

He shrugged. "Luc got called out to help a couple of fishermen whose boat was in distress. One of them recognized him. Later, I heard folks talking down at the hotel restaurant about all the trouble he used to get into in high school."

Marnie had her own issues with Luc, but she bristled hearing that people had begun to gossip. "That was almost seven years ago."

A look of regret flashed over George's face. "Some people have long memories. I should know."

Unsure what to say to that, Marnie fell silent.

"What about the porch, George? Can we help you clean it up?" Mom asked.

His gaze swung to her, and Marnie thought she read genuine gratitude in his eyes. "I appreciate the offer, Corinne, but it's late, and the snow isn't supposed to let up until morning." He rose, and Marnie instinctively stood with him, followed by her mother. He crossed to her. "Besides, I'd feel better knowing you and Marnie got home safe."

To Marnie's surprise, Mom leaned forward to wrap George in a hug. "All right. I'll call you in the morning to see if there's anything you need. In the meantime, try and get some rest."

The whole conversation had taken a weird turn. George and Mom acted like old friends.

"So, tell me more about these chats you've been having with George," Marnie said once they were back in the car.

Mom glanced at her sideways. "What do you mean?"

"You two sure seem chummy," Marnie said. "How often do you talk?"

"Once or twice a week, I suppose." Mom shrugged. "Just whenever I run into him. It's like I said, Marnie, George isn't the man he used to be. I think more people would realize that if they gave him a chance."

Marnie pondered this as they drove home and woke up with it still in her thoughts the next morning as she walked into the office. Her mother was a big proponent of second chances. Growing up, Marnie had often heard the phrase "seventy times seven" on her lips in reference to forgiveness. She knew it was a Bible verse but couldn't remember the exact quote. She spent a moment looking it up.

"Whatcha workin' on?" Kate tapped the top of Marnie's laptop, jiggling the screen.

Marnie blinked and blew out a sigh. "I'm supposed to be answering email, but I got distracted thinking about the fire over at the Grahams' house last night."

Kate's eyes widened. "I heard about that. Was it bad? I heard the fire trucks were called out."

"Not bad. George seems to think it was a prank directed at Luc." She shrugged and clicked on the link to her email. "Anyway, I haven't got time to worry about it. Mayor Rudolf was supposed to message me this morning with her ideas for expanding the tourist trade. Have you talked to her?"

"Not me." Kate gestured toward Brandon's empty desk. "He may have. By the way, Brandon called and said he would be working from home today." Her eyebrows lifted, meaning Brandon was still stewing and Kate thought Marnie should do something about it.

"I'll talk to him."

Marnie dropped her gaze and refused to say more. Kate had been pushing Marnie and Brandon to date ever since he'd come to work for the agency. And while they had recently begun enjoying a few nice dinners together, Marnie had yet to experience that "spark" that said they would ever have anything more. She just hadn't told him that.

Eventually, Kate crossed to her own desk and booted up her computer. A few moments later, Marnie heard her typing and muttering under her breath when she had to keep correcting for sticky keys.

At least now Marnie could focus. She searched through her inbox until she found the mayor's message. It was good news, with the mayor approving most of her ideas, and even adding one of her own.

Marnie paused, her finger hovering over her wireless mouse as she reread the last lines.

What do you think of a boat parade, or maybe even a regatta later this summer? We can coordinate with the Coast Guard, maybe get them to show off some of their boats and specialized equipment. If need be, we can plan it during their station open house. It'll be good PR for them and the town. Anyway, we'll talk more later. Thanks again, Marnie.

It was signed, *Helen.*

Of course, Mayor Rudolf had no clue what she was asking. How could she? Marnie shuddered and rubbed her fingers over her eyes. A boat parade was a great idea, but that was exactly the problem.

Because it would mean working closely with someone from the Coast Guard. She couldn't exactly request that it *not* be Luc. After talking with George, it sounded like he had enough problems to deal with without her adding to them.

Then again, would she be okay seeing him every day? Even if she worked with another officer, she'd likely run into Luc at the station. Could she set aside their troubled past long enough to do as the mayor asked? She wasn't sure, but she had the sneaking suspicion she was about to find out.

Chapter Four

Marnie stood shivering beside her car outside the Coast Guard station early Monday morning, her feet buried in the snow that had fallen over the weekend. She had to go inside. Eventually, someone would notice her standing there and wonder what she was doing.

Her breath huffed out of her mouth in a white cloud. The station's commanding officer had left her name with security. Maybe he would meet with her. Better yet, maybe Luc would be off duty and she could avoid facing him altogether.

Armed with that hopeful thought, she crossed the parking lot and walked toward the white brick building. Above a row of windows, a life preserver ring sculpted from wood had been mounted, and two crossed oars on top of that, with the words Cape D on either side.

A life preserver is apt, Marnie thought, *seeing as I feel like I'm drowning.*

She shrugged the notion aside and scaled the cement steps leading to a set of glass double doors. Grasping the handle of one, she whispered, "Here goes," and stepped inside.

A uniformed coastie greeted her at the entrance. "Good morning. Can I help you?"

Not Luc. Marnie let out a relieved sigh and introduced herself, then got quickly to the point of her visit. "I'm supposed to meet with someone from the Coast Guard to discuss a joint PR project with the city. I believe your commanding officer was going to—"

"He did."

A shiver traveled Marnie's spine as Luc's low voice rumbled over her. Sucking in a breath, she turned to face him.

"I've got it from here, Matt." Luc nodded to the guardsman over her shoulder.

Marnie used the split second to quell a sudden bout of nerves. When Luc's attention returned to her, she lifted her chin and met his gaze head-on.

"So, I'll be working with you? What are the odds?" She tried inserting lightness in her tone but wasn't sure she succeeded.

"I volunteered," Luc said. Shocking her further, he leaned closer and lowered his voice. "I wasn't sure you'd talk to me otherwise."

Certain she hadn't heard right, she blinked and angled her head in confusion. "What?"

Luc motioned toward a door on his right. "Why don't we go in here?"

Yes. No!

"Okay." Had that word actually come out of her mouth? She turned on her heel and crossed the tiled carpet in the direction he pointed.

The room they entered was large, with two rows of long rectangular tables situated on one side. A dry-erase board on wheels dominated one wall, a TV screen the other. Above it, the black hands on a clock indicated the time.

As she took it in, panic twisted her belly. She was going to be alone…here…with Luc. At one time she'd have jumped at the chance, but now all she could think about was the sight of his broad back as he walked away from their chance of a future together and the sound of her heart shattering into a million pieces. Her breathing quickened. This was a bad idea.

She turned. "I'm sorry—"

Luc pushed a rubber stop under the door so it stood open to the hall, then grinned at her sheepishly. "Wouldn't want anyone to get the wrong idea."

Right. This was business. Nothing more. She yanked down the zipper on her coat then wriggled out of it and draped it over her arm. She could do this. "I should probably start by saying thank you. Tourism has been down the last few months, so putting an event together with the Coast Guard could be a big draw. We're grateful."

"I'll be sure to let my CO know."

She motioned to a chair. "Mind if I sit?"

"Of course not. Yeah. Please do."

A faint flush traveled up his neck, starting at the collar of his blue shirt and lodging in his cheeks. At least she knew he felt as uncomfortable as she did. Somehow, the knowledge helped ease her jitters. She slid into one of the chairs and pulled a tablet that she used to take notes from her backpack.

"I have a list of ideas I thought I would run by…well…you."

Her breath caught as he settled in the chair next to her. She licked her lips and touched the screen, bringing it to life. After several attempts, she found the file she was looking for and clicked it open.

"Sorry." She glanced at him. "I'm a little nervous. I thought I'd be working with someone else."

"I know. I shouldn't have sprung it on you. That wasn't fair."

His candor caught her off guard. Again. Would this new Luc never stop surprising her? She tore her gaze away from the amber flecks in his brown eyes to concentrate on the tablet. "So, first, I'd like your thoughts on a possible regatta. The mayor was thinking maybe this summer?"

"Are you talking Baker Bay?"

Hearing the doubt in his voice, she hesitated and fingered the rubber edge of her tablet. "Uh, well, yes."

Luc shook his head. "Won't work. The bay is too shallow for our boats."

This was something Marnie hadn't considered. "So, then a parade involving the Coast Guard would be out too?"

"Depends on the craft." He grinned and laced his fingers on the tabletop. "You could always host a 'build your own' kind of thing. On a smaller scale, of course."

Marnie brought her stylus to her lips, thinking. "Like a pinewood derby, only with boats?" She pointed the stylus at him. "Sailboats!"

"Exactly. We've done that kind of thing before. It was pretty popular with the local kids and their parents."

The gears in Marnie's head spun with ideas. "A family day. We could make the sailboat derby one of the events and tie it to the station open house. Do you think some of the guys here would be willing to help out?"

"I could ask." He stopped, a frown pulling at his lips. "But would a family day be the draw for tourists that you want?"

"It might be, if we get some of the local businesses and restaurants involved."

Luc seemed to catch her excitement as they listed a few of the establishments likely to participate. He leaned forward to tap the face of her tablet. "We could set up food tents along the boatyard."

Marnie snapped her fingers. "And call it 'A Taste of Ilwaco.' All the menus could focus on locally caught seafood."

"Yep. And we could ask some local artisans to spearhead a craft fair. Your mom would have connections, right?"

They looked at each other, and Marnie nodded.

"It could work," Luc said.

Marnie jotted several notes in her tablet. "I'll have to run all of this past the mayor, but it shouldn't be too hard to get her on board. She's really big on drawing families to Ilwaco."

"Good." Luc rubbed his hands together. "Now, besides lining up volunteers, what do you need from me?"

"Nothing yet, but if the mayor agrees it's a good idea, would you be up for helping me secure vendors?"

"Sure. Whatever you need."

"Okay." Their gazes locked. It was only a moment, but to Marnie it seemed to stretch on forever. Finally, she scooped up her tablet and stowed it in her backpack. "I should probably get going."

"Marnie, wait." He stretched out his hand on the table, not touching her but stopping her nonetheless. "Before you go, there's something else I'd like to talk to you about."

Her gaze slid to the door and back to him. "I'm not sure that's a good idea, Luc."

"Please. It'll only take a minute."

It went against her better judgment, but she nodded and let her backpack slide to the floor.

Luc let out a breath, then grasped the arms of his chair. "It's about my enlistment. If it's okay with you, I'd like to clear the air between us on a couple of things."

Her heart thumped painfully inside her chest. Because she couldn't look at him, she stared at her hands. "As I said before, Luc, you don't owe me an explanation."

"Maybe not. Maybe it won't make a bit of difference in the scheme of things." He cleared his throat, and then his voice dropped even lower. "Still, I'd like to think that if you understood—"

A knock on the door cut off what he was about to say, and the coast guardsman who'd been with Luc at the restaurant stuck his head through.

"Hey, man, sorry to interrupt."

"It's fine." Luc waved him in, then pushed up from the table. "Marnie, this is Chief Petty Officer Jeff Williamson. Jeff, this is Marnie Stewart, a friend of mine from high school."

Jeff stuck out his hand and shook hers firmly. "Just Jeff is fine. Nice to meet you."

Marnie's cheeks warmed under his appreciative gaze. "Nice to meet you too."

Letting go of her hand, he crossed his arms and rocked back on his heels. "So, you're the person Luc's going to be working with on this project, huh? No wonder he volunteered." He bumped Luc's shoulder with his. When Luc scowled, Jeff flashed a black envelope and grinned. "This just came for ya."

Luc took it, and Jeff angled his head at Marnie, his blue eyes glinting flirtatiously. "Marnie's a nice name. I'm surprised I've never heard of you. Are you from Ilwaco?"

Luc shifted so he stood slightly in front of her. "I appreciate you bringing me my mail. Was there anything else you needed?"

Jeff chuckled and raised both hands. "You know me…just trying to help." Peering around Luc's shoulder, he said, "See ya, Marnie."

Once he was gone, Luc glanced at her and slid a folded paper from the envelope. He opened it, and, as he read, Marnie saw his eyes narrow and his mouth turn hard. But when he looked up at her, his face was blank and he slipped the paper along with the envelope into his shirt pocket. "Sorry about that. Jeff's a nice guy, but he never misses an opportunity to flirt with a pretty woman."

The word "pretty" glanced off Marnie's brain, but her focus wasn't on that—it was on the black envelope in Luc's pocket. She swiveled in her chair and pointed at it. "What is that?"

He angled his gaze away and then back at her. "It's nothing. I'll take care of it later."

Unconvinced, she leaned closer. "It didn't look like nothing to me."

Luc gripped his chair, his jaw clenched stubbornly. "Right now, we have more important things to talk about, Marnie."

She matched the set of his jaw, just as stubbornly, and crossed her arms. "It's another anonymous note from your secret not-so-admirer, isn't it?"

His eyes narrowed. "My *what*?"

She waved her hand. "I know all about it. George told my mom the night of the fire. Someone's trying to force you out of town."

He mulled this a second, lips clamped. Finally, he nodded. "So?"

"So!" Marnie slapped both hands to her thighs. "What are you going to do about it?"

Luc's nostrils flared as he sucked in a deep breath and let it out slowly. Shoulders squared, he shook his head. "It's a note. Stupid, juvenile, but harmless."

"And the coat? That could have turned out much worse, Luc. Don't you want to know who's behind these things?"

His gaze hardened, growing into something dark and a touch menacing. "You think this is the first time stuff like this has happened?"

She drew back in surprise. "Isn't it?"

The sneer he gave in response might have sent her running had she not been sitting. As it was, she felt herself sinking into her chair as Luc straightened to loom over her, his dark brows bunching like clouds over the storm brewing in his eyes.

"The people in this town have hated my family since the day my great-grandfather robbed half of them of their money. Over the years, it's only gotten worse. So no, this isn't the first time someone has tried to rid Ilwaco of my family, Marnie."

His expression changed. Sorrow mixed with the weight of regret. Worst of all, she read resignation in the eyes that seconds ago flashed with fire.

His shoulders sagged, and he turned his head away. And though she couldn't see it, she felt the pain in his words, the hopelessness of which cut her to the core.

"And it won't be the last."

Chapter Five

Alone in the Coast Guard station conference room, Marnie fingered the metal zipper pull on her backpack and stared at the door Luc had disappeared through a few moments prior. She should leave. He'd made it painfully clear he didn't want her help. And yet…

Grabbing her coat, she slipped into the hall and cast around for sight of Jeff. She spied him in a kitchen alcove across from the main entrance, coaxing one last cup of coffee from an ancient coffeepot. Pasting a bright smile on her lips, she made her way toward him.

"Excuse me, Jeff?"

He glanced at her, his look of surprise changing to one of curiosity and interest. "Marnie. Hello again." He held up the empty pot. "Would you like some—?" He grimaced and replaced the pot in the coffee maker then smiled at her over his shoulder. "Oops. Sorry. I can brew another pot."

"No, no. Don't bother." She shifted the backpack to her other shoulder. "Have you got a second?"

"Of course." He set his cup down and turned. "What can I do for you?"

"Well, it's about that letter you brought to Luc. I was just wondering if you saw who delivered it."

He shrugged. "It was just some guy. I didn't ask his name."

A man. Marnie nodded. "Would you say he was older? Younger?"

"Younger, I guess. Maybe late twenties? He put the envelope on the counter, said it was for Luc, and left."

"Luc? Or Lucien?"

"Well, now that you mention it, yeah, he did say Lucien."

"By any chance, did you see what he was driving?" It would be too easy that the person would drive a distinctive vehicle, like a delivery van or a work truck with an emblem on the side, but she still had to ask.

Jeff shook his head. "Sorry. I didn't look."

"That's okay. Just one more question, if you don't mind?" Jeff nodded, and she forged on. "Do you happen to remember what he was wearing? Anything with a decal or logo that stood out to you?"

"No. He had on a plain blue coat. Black knit hat. Other than that, I didn't really pay attention. Matt was busy, so I offered to pass the note on to Luc." Jeff scratched his temple. "What's all this about?"

Marnie eased toward the door with a small smile. "Just being nosy. Anyway, thanks so much for your help."

"Anytime." She retreated another step. He followed. "Say, Marnie, I overheard Luc and the CO talking about your project. If I can be of any help, please, feel free to holler."

"Thank you. I'll do that." She waved, aware as she turned for the door that Jeff still watched her. She was flattered by his interest. He was tall and handsome, with sandy-blond hair, blue eyes, and a winsome smile most women would find attractive. But she preferred a more brooding look—

She drew up short as that thought struck, her fingers curled around the handle of her car door. She and Brandon were dating, but it was Luc's face she'd pictured just now. Luc's dark hair and brown eyes, instead of Brandon's hazel ones. Guilt pinched her cheeks and deepened when she pulled into the parking lot at the travel agency and saw Brandon's car.

Inside, Brandon sat behind his computer, steam rising from the battered steel coffee cup at his elbow. He rose when he caught sight of her, a hesitant smile on his lips. Marnie dropped her things on her desk and hurried over to him. Brandon probably wouldn't like that she would be working with Luc, but she wanted him to hear about it from her and not someone else.

"Hey." Instead of reaching out to her as she expected, he stuffed his hands in the pockets of his jeans. "I got your voice mails. Sorry I didn't call you back this weekend. It was immature of me."

She let her shoulders relax. "I was coming over here to apologize to *you*. I should have run by your place so we could talk. I just—"

"I know." He pulled out one hand to touch her arm. "I was jealous of your history with Luc. I should've known better—"

She held up her hand. "Before you finish…you should know that Luc and I are going to be working together on the mayor's project."

She didn't tell him Luc had volunteered.

A muscle knotted in Brandon's jaw, but he managed to force a smile. "Listen, my insecurities are my problem to deal with, not yours." His hand dropped, and his face grew somber. "Besides, we've never really talked about this thing between us. You know, if we're going to make it serious."

She did know, and for a split second, panic fluttered in her chest. But then the door swung open, and Kate sauntered in, sparing Marnie from a reply.

"Morning, all." She grabbed Marnie's arm with one hand and Brandon's with the other. "I see my two best friends are back on speaking terms."

"We were never *not* on speaking terms," Marnie clarified. "We just weren't...speaking."

Brandon's eyes widened comically as he peered at Marnie over the top of his glasses.

"Ha. Good answer." Kate swung toward the one-cup coffee maker tucked into a bureau that she and Marnie had converted into a coffee bar when they opened the agency. Plucking out the used pod, she held it up, shot a glare at Brandon, then tossed it into the trash and replaced it with a fresh one.

"Anyway, how's the project for the mayor going?" While her coffee brewed, Kate shrugged out of her coat and slung it across the back of her chair, then powered on her laptop. "Can I help you with anything?"

"Uh..." Marnie returned to her desk without looking at Brandon. "I think we're going in a different direction."

"What?" Kate straightened with a frown. "I thought Mayor Rudolf sent you some good ideas?"

"Turns out, they won't work for the Coast Guard vessels. Luc and I did come up with an alternative proposal for her though, something I think she'll like. I'm still working on the details, but I'll send you over what I have so far."

"Luc? You're working with him?"

Bowing her head, Marnie ignored the telling glance Kate shot in Brandon's direction and hit send on her email. "There. You should have it. Let me know if you have anything I can add before I meet with the mayor."

Kate's voice lowered a notch from her usual bubbly tone, a sure sign she wasn't happy. "I'll take a look."

"Thanks." Marnie cleared her throat. "In the meantime, don't forget it's your day to post on the blog."

"Already in the scheduler, if you want to check it for me before it goes live."

Marnie nodded. Though she and Kate were equal partners, they'd learned a long time ago to lean on each other for help with their weaknesses. Kate came up with the clever ideas, Marnie spell- and grammar-checked everything for a polished, professional post. The system worked.

By noon, Marnie had their proposal ready for the mayor to review. Sitting back in her chair, she stretched her arms over her head and tried not to yawn. "Okay, that's it. I'm gonna grab some lunch then head over to the mayor's office."

"Mind if I go with you?"

Brandon was already reaching for his coat and hat. Marnie shook her head. "I don't mind. Come on." She slipped her backpack over one shoulder and glanced at Kate. "Thanks for holding down the fort."

Kate shot her a pleased grin, which she made no effort to hide, and wiggled her fingers at them as they went out the door.

"Is Porter's okay with you?" Marnie pushed her hands into her coat pockets.

"Sounds good." Brandon hung back and let Marnie pass in front of him, then drew even with her as they hurried to beat traffic crossing the road.

Inside the café, several coasties clustered around tables or lounged in booths. The café was a favorite haunt of theirs, but that wasn't why Marnie had chosen it...was it? She avoided meeting Brandon's gaze as she settled in the booth.

No Luc. Had Brandon noticed?

He smiled at her as they sat. "Chilly."

"Yeah, it's pretty cold. I think it's supposed to warm up tomorrow though."

"No, I mean the special." Brandon tipped his head toward a chalkboard hanging above the cash register.

"Oh." Marnie plucked a menu from behind the napkin dispenser. "I thought you meant, well, you know."

Brandon didn't answer. The cold outside had made his glasses fog. He took them off and opened his own menu. When had things become so awkward between them? Marnie blew out a sigh, glad when their waitress arrived and then quickly returned with their drink orders. At least toying with the straw gave her something to do.

Brandon leaned forward to rest his arms on the table. "We didn't really get to finish what we were talking about earlier."

She dropped her gaze. This was it, then. The *talk*. "No, I guess not."

"Marnie, I don't think it's any secret how I feel about you. How I've always felt about you."

That was one thing she could definitely say about Brandon. He was open with his feelings. He didn't try to hide them or make apologies for them.

"Yeah, I know." She sucked in a breath and prayed for the right words. Careful words that wouldn't hurt so much. "Listen, Brandon—"

"It's probably not fair to put this on you right now, when you have so much on your plate." He shifted in his seat to peel off his coat. "I just...I don't want to make the mistake of not having made my intentions clear."

Watching him, Marnie felt a moment of panic. Surely, he wasn't going to propose? Because if he did, she'd have to tell him—

He reached up, took off his hat, and slapped it onto the table next to his drink.

"You're important to me, Marnie. I want to take our relationship to the next level. Maybe start thinking about the future. Is that what you want too?"

Marnie heard him talking but couldn't focus on what he said, because she was too busy staring at his hat. His *black* hat. And his blue coat. The same colors Jeff said the man was wearing who'd delivered the note to Luc at the station. Could it be? She didn't want to think so. Brandon had never seemed the type to go behind a person's back. If he had a problem with somebody, he told them outright.

But if not Brandon...then who?

Chapter Six

"Brandon, were you at the Coast Guard station?" The smells and sounds of the restaurant faded as Marnie peered across the table at him.

He blinked in confusion and dragged his fingers through the blond hair flopping over his forehead. "What?"

"Earlier today, did you go by the Coast Guard station?"

Brandon cleared his throat. "What are you talking about? No, I wasn't there. Is this your way of avoiding the subject?"

His lips curved in a small grin, but there was pain in his voice. Where it came from wasn't clear. Was it because she was confronting him about being at the station or the fact that she hadn't readily affirmed her desire to spend her future with him?

"I'm sorry. It's just"—she motioned to the table—"your hat. Someone wearing a black hat stopped by the station and left an ugly note for Luc while I was there."

"My hat." Brandon frowned and dragged it off the table. "Black is a pretty common color, Marnie."

"I know, but…they were also wearing a blue coat," she finished weakly. Saying the words out loud sounded way worse than they had sounded in her head. What was she accusing him of?

"What are you accusing me of?" Brandon's words echoed her thoughts.

She studied him a long moment, then shook her head. Leaving notes was one thing. Setting fires was something else. That, she couldn't accuse him of...not without proof. "Sorry. Forget I said anything."

"No, I don't think we should forget it, Marnie." The sadness in his voice cut her to the quick.

"Brandon—"

"We should order." He opened his menu with a snap and bowed his head over it.

This wasn't how she wanted to leave things, but hashing out their problems in a crowded restaurant wasn't ideal either. Marnie picked up her menu and stared, unseeing, at the list of blurred items.

"Sorry about the wait." Their harried waitress returned, her cheeks red. "Do you know what you'd like?"

Brandon closed his menu and slid it across the table. "Cheeseburger for me."

"And I'll take a chicken salad sandwich on rye, please." Marnie laid her menu on Brandon's. "Thank you."

The waitress finished scribbling on her notepad, collected the menus, and rushed off, the tails of her apron strings swinging.

"Hey, Betty!"

The waitress lifted her head to look for the voice.

"Where's my sandwich? I ordered it twenty minutes ago."

Samuel Peddycord. Marnie grimaced. She didn't care for the man. He was loud and pretentious and thought way too highly of his family name, but he did own a fancy art gallery downtown, and if the mayor approved Marnie's proposal, she would probably have to ask him to participate.

"It's coming right up, Samuel."

He shouted something else, but Betty merely went on her way. Poor girl.

He turned his head then, his gaze colliding with Marnie's. Caught staring, she had no choice but to acknowledge him. She nodded. He nodded back. She looked away.

Brandon clasped his hands and leaned over the table. "I heard Samuel's business isn't doing too well."

Marnie blinked and looked at him. "I thought the gallery was doing really well. I was just thinking about inviting him to be one of the vendors for the family day I'm proposing to the mayor. Isn't he getting enough business?"

Brandon shook his head. "Business isn't the problem, it's business *sense*. Apparently, he's been ordering expensive inventory, and people just aren't interested in paying the kind of prices he's asking. He also spent a pretty penny renovating the warehouse he bought to house his gallery, which means he's got high overhead. Instead of compensating, he just keeps buying more exotic stuff, hoping something will click."

"Oh no."

Brandon ducked his head lower. "What is this...his third try? First the charter business went under, then the gift shop, now this?" He ticked the items off on his fingers. "Where does he keep getting the money?"

That was a good question, and one Marnie didn't have an answer for. At one time, the Peddycord name had meant something in this town. Their wealth had helped to build local industry. Some bad investments, though, had brought all that to a halt.

Marnie tapped her finger against her lips. One investment in particular had almost ruined them. It involved Luc's great-grandfather and an insurance scam on some boat. Like many people in the town, Samuel's family had bought in and paid for it dearly. If anyone was likely to have a grudge against the Grahams, it was the Peddycords.

She shot a glance at the coat hanging on the back of Samuel's chair. It was blue. But then again, so were the coats on half a dozen chairs at half a dozen tables, all belonging to ordinary people just trying to grab some lunch and be about their workday.

"Brandon, will you excuse me for a minute?" She scooted out of the booth. "I need to talk to Samuel."

"Oh?" His eyebrows rose. "Is it agency business? Should I go with you?"

Brandon half-pushed to the edge of his seat before Marnie stopped him. "No, no. I can handle it. I'll be right back."

She patted his shoulder, then turned to look for Samuel. His food had still not arrived when she got to the table, and he didn't look a bit happy about it. He craned his neck toward the kitchen, but the only thing coming from there was the sizzle of the grill and the clatter of dishes.

"Samuel, I'm glad I ran into you."

He jerked around to nod at her. "Hey, Marnie. Do you see Betty anywhere?"

"I don't." Marnie laid her hand on a chair. "Do you mind if I sit for a second? I have an idea I'd like to run past you. It's about the gallery."

She had his attention now. He settled into his chair and squared to look at her. "Oh? What's going on?"

"Well, I suppose you've heard about the mayor's plans to revitalize the town? She's really working hard trying to come up with ideas to draw tourists to Ilwaco, and she asked me to help."

"Yeah, I heard something about that." He leaned back and crossed his arms over his chest. "How's it going?"

"Pretty good." Marnie summarized the proposal she'd be presenting to the mayor later that day, then shifted to rest her elbows on the table. "If the mayor agrees, I'm going to be working pretty closely with Luc Graham. He's back, you know. Stationed at Cape Disappointment."

"I heard." Frown lines formed around Samuel's mouth and eyes. "What I didn't know was that he'd be working with you."

"Basically, it was Luc's idea," Marnie said. "He's going to be helping me recruit vendors, but since I saw you here, I thought I'd get your perspective on the idea."

"You're asking what I think?" Samuel leaned forward, a scowl drawing his brows into a dark thundercloud. "I think you'd get further with the vendors around here if you weren't working with a Graham."

Was that true? Marnie bit her lip. "What do you mean?"

"I mean, a lot of businesses went under when the first Lucien Graham ran that insurance scheme a few years ago."

"It was more than a few," Marnie protested, trying hard to inject lightness into her tone.

"And then his son went to prison for embezzlement."

Luc's grandfather. She remembered hearing the whispers.

"To top it all off, his father is a hopeless drunk." A sneer curled Samuel's lip. "If you ask me, the whole family is rotten."

Marnie drew in a deep breath, dismayed to realize the restaurant had gone quiet. Too quiet. She felt the stares through her thick woolen sweater. Rising to her feet, she lifted her chin and looked Samuel in the eyes.

"Everything you just said is true, except for one thing—Luc had nothing to do with the stuff his family did before he was born." She held up her finger. "And you know what? Make that two things. George is no longer drinking. Maybe you'd know that if you gave him a chance."

She whirled. Betty stood beside her with her mouth hanging slightly open, Samuel's plate in her hands. Marnie grabbed it and set it on the table with a thunk.

"Enjoy your lunch, Samuel."

She might have relished the surprised look on his face if she hadn't realized in the same split second that he was looking past her at someone else.

She turned, expecting Brandon, thinking he'd heard the commotion and come to her rescue. Only it wasn't Brandon. It was Luc. And he didn't say a word when their gazes collided. He stared, lips pressed tightly together.

And then he spun and walked out the door.

Chapter Seven

"Luc!" Marnie slid on the icy sidewalk, recovered her footing, then sped after his retreating back. She had no coat. No gloves. She'd even left her backpack—and Brandon—in her rush to catch Luc when he walked out of the restaurant. Watching the letters USCG on the back of his coat grow smaller, she second-guessed that decision. "Luc, wait!"

Without warning, he whirled. Marnie stumbled to a standstill, then stood, shivering, her arms wrapped around herself in a futile effort to keep warm.

"For heaven's sake, Marnie." With his breath snorting from his nose in white plumes, Luc looked like an angry bull as he charged across the street toward her, unzipping his coat. A couple of feet shy of her, he stopped, tore off the coat, and tossed it around her shoulders. "You're gonna freeze to death."

"I w-wouldn't if you'd s-stopped sooner," she managed through chattering teeth.

Luc huffed a breath and grabbed her hand. "Come on."

She didn't ask where they were going—not that he gave her a chance. He led her to a battered white pickup truck—the same one he'd driven in high school—helped her in the passenger side, then circled around to climb into the driver's seat.

He set the heater to full blast, then twisted on the seat and reached for her. "Give me your hands."

She held them out hesitantly. "I'm fine, Luc."

He rubbed her hands between his, not looking up, not looking at her, just working on her cold fingers until she felt her skin tingle under his touch.

"You shouldn't have followed me." He stopped rubbing but didn't let go.

"Well, you shouldn't have walked out like you did. Not without giving me a chance to explain."

His gaze snapped to hers. "What is there to explain, Marnie? I heard what you said." He dropped her hands and shifted to grip the steering wheel. "I expected people to talk. I didn't think you would be one of them."

"What's that supposed to mean?" She leaned toward him. "Luc, I was defending you!"

"I don't need you to do that!" He took a deep breath and stared straight ahead through the windshield.

Marnie shook her head. "I don't think you understand. Samuel was in the restaurant, and I pretended like I needed to talk to him about the family day. I wanted to see what kind of reaction I got when I mentioned that I was working with you."

Luc closed his eyes. "Marnie."

"He knew you were in town, Luc. The Peddycords have always had a thing against your family. I wouldn't put it past Samuel to pull a prank like the notes or that coat someone set on fire on your dad's porch."

"Marnie!"

She fell silent at the genuine anger she heard in his voice.

"I said I didn't want your help, and I meant it. Snooping around trying to figure out who's doing this stuff is only going to make things worse. Best if I just ignore it and hope whoever is behind all this goes away or gets bored when I don't respond." He angled his head to peer into her face. "Do you hear what I'm saying? You're not helping things, Marnie. So stop. Just…stop."

Anger and hurt welled up to burn her cheeks. Across the street, she saw Brandon exit the restaurant, her coat and backpack clutched in one hand. Luc saw him too. He reached across her and jerked up on her door handle.

"You should go."

Marnie balled her hands into fists. She wanted to punch him. To call him all sorts of names. To tell him Kate was right, she should have stayed far away from him. Instead, she shrugged out from under his coat, dropped it on the seat, then climbed out of the truck and slammed the door hard behind her.

Stubborn man! So much for thinking he'd changed. He was just as pigheaded as he'd always been, and she was just as big a fool for letting herself get sucked into the drama that always seemed to swirl around his family.

"Are you okay?" Brandon looked past her at Luc's truck as Luc drove away. He slung her backpack over his shoulder and held out her coat. "Here, put this on. It's cold out here."

"Thanks, Brandon." He would have helped her, but Marnie didn't give him the chance. She took the coat, shoved her arms into the sleeves, then held out her hand for the backpack. "I'm so sorry about all that."

"Don't apologize. It's fine."

Marnie shook her head. "It's not fine." She rubbed her temples, where a dull headache was forming. "Look, we'll talk later, okay?

And I'll make lunch up to you. Right now, I just need to calm down a little before I talk to the mayor."

"Marnie." Brandon took hold of her shoulders, his hazel eyes warm and a smile twitching his lips. "You just do what you need to and don't worry about me. I'll call you tonight."

Marnie sagged with relief. It was true, there was no spark where Brandon was concerned, but there wasn't a blazing fire, either, which meant she wouldn't get burned. That wasn't such a bad thing.

"Thanks, Brandon."

He nodded, shot one more glance in the direction of Luc's truck, then backed away and turned for the restaurant.

For a long moment, Marnie watched him go, imagining what life with him could be like. Safe, for sure. And comfortable. But was that fair to him? Didn't he deserve someone who dreamed of him and him alone?

Her heart heavy, Marnie returned to the travel agency for her car, then made the short drive to the mayor's office across town. Fortunately, by the time she arrived, she'd managed to push aside all other thoughts and focus on the matter at hand.

Joan Anglund greeted her with a ready smile when she stepped inside. Aside from being a good friend of her mother's, Joan also took painting classes from Mom once a week. "Good morning, Marnie. The mayor is expecting you."

She waved Marnie close then poked her head into the office that adjoined hers. "Marnie Stewart is here to see you."

"Thanks, Joan. Please, show her in."

Joan smiled and held out her hand, then motioned toward the door. "Would you like me to close this?"

"No need." Helen Rudolf circled her desk and crossed to shake Marnie's hand. "Good to see you, Marnie. Thanks so much for coming."

"Thanks for making time for me." Marnie set her backpack down and removed her coat. She'd only been inside the mayor's office a handful of times, but she was always impressed with the tasteful decor, a reflection of Helen herself. Tall and slender, with immaculate hair, clothes, and jewelry, she exuded a confidence Marnie both admired and envied.

"So, I understand you have some ideas to run by me." Helen put on a pair of reading glasses and gestured toward a couple of leather club chairs. "Shall we sit?"

"That'd be great."

Marnie slid her tablet out of her backpack and quickly reviewed the proposal she'd spent all morning preparing. Then she came to the part about working with Luc. The mayor wasn't originally from Ilwaco, but she'd lived there long enough to know the stories. Surely, she wouldn't object.

"I'll be working closely with…" Marnie swallowed and resumed. "…Luc Graham, a member of the Coast Guard, assuming you like the idea," she finished carefully.

"I think it all sounds wonderful," Helen said, momentarily quelling Marnie's fears. "But about this coastie—I understand he's a local?"

Marnie bobbed her head. "That's correct." She tried to sound more confident than she felt and hoped she succeeded.

Helen removed her reading glasses and laced her fingers together slowly. "There's a bit of history there. Will that be a problem for you?"

"Not at all," Marnie replied quickly, meeting the mayor's gaze head-on.

"Glad to hear it. Because," she continued, "this event is about promoting Ilwaco. I can't stress enough the importance of staying focused and not allowing any unnecessary distractions to keep us from putting on the best possible experience for our people that we can."

"Of course. I understand completely," Marnie assured her. Still, deep down, a knot formed in her stomach. "You have nothing to worry about. I'll make sure everything goes according to plan."

"Good." Helen smiled and laid her hand on the arm of her chair. "I really can't thank you enough for your help with this project, Marnie. Will you keep me updated as things progress?"

"Absolutely. I'll be glad to."

"Great." She uncrossed her legs and stood. "And if there is anything you need from our office, just call. Joan has all the information, so don't hesitate to ask."

Marnie snagged her backpack and rose with her. "I'll do that."

"Okay. We'll talk again soon."

She gave Marnie's arm a light squeeze then ushered her to the outer office, where Joan pecked away at the computer keyboard on her desk.

"Bye, Marnie. Thanks again for coming in." Helen gave one last wave then directed her attention to Joan. "I'll be on a conference call for the next few minutes."

Joan looked up. "Got it."

Helen's office door closed her from view, leaving Marnie alone with Joan. Smiling, Marnie put on her coat then turned for the door. "Thanks, Joan. I'll talk to you later."

"Marnie, wait." She slid open a desk drawer. "In case you need anything," she said, holding out a business card.

"Awesome. Thank you." She tucked the card into the side pocket of her backpack.

"Um…" Joan fidgeted in her chair, the wheels creaking noisily under her. "I couldn't help but overhear." She motioned toward the door. "You're going to be working with Lucien Graham?"

Marnie's chest tightened. Another one? "Well, he goes by Luc now, but yes, I'll be working with him."

"Is that wise?" Joan's lips firmed into a line. "I mean, I know he's not his father, but—"

"No, he isn't his father. Or his grandfather." Reminded of Luc's anger earlier, Marnie bit her tongue. Better to change the subject. She forced a smile. "Are you coming by the house for your painting class tonight?"

"Yes, I'll be there."

"Okay. I'll let Mom know. Bye, Joan."

"See ya, Marnie."

She still looked hesitant, but Marnie hurried out before Joan could add anything else. Maybe taking on this whole revitalization thing for the city wasn't such a good idea. She could still back out, except tourism hadn't been so great lately, which meant business at the agency hadn't been good either. They couldn't afford to let this project go, not with last month's bills still pending and this month's looming around the corner.

No, somehow she'd have to make it work, even if it meant ignoring the jabs against Luc, and the Graham family in general.

Which was easy enough to say, Marnie thought, climbing into her car, but a lot harder to do when every word uttered felt like a stab in the heart.

Not a stab, she amended, and not her heart. She just didn't like seeing a person treated unfairly. That was it. Nothing more.

Except...it wasn't good to lie. No one ever gained a thing by lying to themselves.

But the truth was too hard to face.

She clutched the steering wheel, her breath adding to the frost building on her windshield. For now, she'd do as the mayor suggested and focus on her work. At least, she'd try. It would be difficult, because Luc was a lot of things, the *least* of which was a distraction.

Heaving a troubled sigh, she started the car and backed out onto the street, only instead of turning for the office, she headed for home. She couldn't face Brandon again, or even Kate. Right now, what she needed was some quiet time and a dose of her mother's wisdom.

And maybe a good cry. She sniffed as she felt her eyes burn. Yeah, a cry was good. Something to let out the emotions she'd kept pent up since learning of Luc's return. She'd feel better afterward and better able to tackle the pressure piling on her plate.

Or so she told herself. Except...it wasn't good to lie.

Chapter Eight

Marnie woke with a start Tuesday morning, her eyelids puffy and her head throbbing as though she'd been hit one too many times with a hammer.

What time was it?

Instead of the shadows she expected, sunlight streamed through her window. She flung back the covers and stared at her jean-clad legs. Except for her shoes, she was fully dressed, which meant her mother must've come in sometime during the night to cover her with a blanket. But that didn't explain why the alarm on her cell hadn't gone off.

Fumbling to retrieve her phone from her nightstand, she swiped across the screen then groaned. She'd silenced it when she got to the mayor's office and forgot to turn the volume back up. Her alarm had been ringing for almost thirty minutes.

Jumping out of bed, she hurried to the bathroom to wash up and change. Downstairs, her mom was smearing jam on toast.

"Morning, sweetheart. Are you hungry?"

"No time." Marnie grabbed a travel mug from the cupboard and sloshed in some coffee from the pot. "Why didn't you wake me?"

Mom took a bite of toast and shrugged. "You were up late. I figured you needed the rest."

"Mom. Kate is going to kill me," Marnie mumbled.

"No, she's not." She waved another slice of toast in the air. "I called her and told her you'd be late."

"Ugh." Giving in with a sigh, Marnie took the toast and shoved a healthy bite into her mouth. "I still wish you would've woken me up," she said around her mouthful. At the same time, she grabbed her shoes from the door where she'd left them and carried them to the table.

"Don't talk with your mouth full. You'll choke." Mom pushed the cream and sugar toward Marnie while she continued munching contentedly on her own breakfast.

Marnie hid a grin as she bent to shove her feet into the shoes. Then she doctored her coffee and snapped on the lid. She was a grown woman, but rolling her eyes would only earn her another scolding. "Gotta go. I'll talk to you this afternoon. Bye, Mom."

She pecked her mother's cheek, pausing when she felt Mom lean into the kiss. Instead of rushing off, she waited until Mom pulled back, because if there was one thing Marnie had learned since losing her stepfather, it was that moments weren't guaranteed.

"Love you, sweetheart," Mom said.

"Love you too. I'll call you later."

"Okay. Have a good day."

Marnie closed the door behind her, glad she'd lingered even for just a short while as she breathed in the scent of her mother's perfume still lingering on her clothes. Outside, a few rays of sunlight broke through the gray clouds to dapple the drifts that had blown up overnight. Fortunately, most of them had piled up lengthwise down the driveway, and she was able to back out onto the street without stopping to shovel.

Today, the plan was to head into the office, shoot a quick email to Luc letting him know what the mayor had said, then spend the day outlining activities and setting up some sort of schedule for the Taste of Ilwaco. Afterward, if she had time, she'd start working on a list of vendors. Of course, that meant checking in with Luc, but that was fine. The idea didn't seem as daunting as it had the night before. Maybe Mom was right. Maybe a good night's rest was all she'd needed.

Both Kate and Brandon were hard at work by the time she stepped into the office. Kate was her usual cheerful self. Brandon was reserved, but he brought her a cup of coffee and set it on the corner of her desk with a smile. A peace offering? Not that he needed it. As promised, he'd called after she got home last night, but, sensing her mood, he'd only stayed on the line long enough to let her know he was available if she needed anything. It was the best thing he could've done.

Brandon wrapped his fingers around his own cup and smiled at her over the rim. "You okay?"

"Better now." Marnie pulled her cup closer for a sip. "Mmm. Thank you so much for this."

"You're welcome." He tapped her desk. "Let me know if you need help with that project for the mayor."

"Will do. Thanks, Brandon."

As he walked away, Kate approached. Dragging a chair from her desk, she plopped down in front of Marnie's desk and crossed her arms. "So, Samuel Peddycord?"

"You heard?"

Kate nodded. "I'm pretty sure the whole town did."

Ugh. Marnie frowned and set down her cup. "What are they saying?"

Kate picked at the blotter on Marnie's desk. "It's not good. Most people agree with Samuel." She sighed and stared at Marnie. "It's not too late to listen to me. You can still stay away from him."

Why? What has he done to deserve being shunned by an entire town? The questions rose to Marnie's lips. She shot a glance across the office at Brandon and bit them back. "Really? You're gonna start with the 'I told you so's'?" she whispered, ducking behind her laptop.

Kate dropped her gaze.

Marnie straightened. "On another note, the mayor liked our proposal."

"I figured as much, though I'm surprised you didn't call."

"I know. I should have. I'm sorry."

Kate dismissed her apology with a wave. "What do you need from me?"

"Do you think you could go to the mayor's office and start lining up the permits we'll need? Getting them won't be a problem, but we don't want to miss anything."

"On it." She pushed up from her chair.

"Thanks, Kate."

At Kate's nod, Marnie opened her email, sent a message to Luc, then spent the next couple of hours absorbed in spreadsheets.

"Hey, you. Ready for a break?"

Marnie glanced up in surprise. Brandon stood at her desk, holding his coat. Kate was nowhere to be seen.

"A break already?" She glanced at the clock above her desk, blinked, then rubbed her eyes. "That can't be right. Is it noon already?"

"That's what happens when you sleep in," he teased. "The morning goes by in a blur."

"I guess so."

Brandon hitched his thumb toward the door. "I'm gonna grab some lunch. Wanna come?"

Her phone pinged, indicating a text. It was from Luc. Marnie turned her phone facedown and shook her head. "I need to catch up here. Thanks anyway."

"No problem." He slid his arms into his coat sleeves. "Do you want me to bring you something?"

"Don't bother." She grinned. "I had a late breakfast."

"Okay. I'll be back."

"See ya." She waited until he exited then opened the text. Luc's message was brief.

WE NEED TO TALK. CAN YOU MEET FOR LUNCH?

She blew out a breath, her thumbs hovering over the keyboard. NEED TO CATCH UP ON A FEW THINGS. MAYBE LATER?

She hit send then relaxed against the back of her chair to rub her eyes. Another ping had them flying open.

THIS AFTERNOON? 3:00?

Marnie tipped her head to stare at the watermarks on the ceiling. What was she waiting for? Hadn't she just told herself he'd done nothing to warrant her avoiding him? And in regard to the incident at lunch yesterday, she had no right to be angry with him. She was the one who'd been meddling. If anything, he should be angry at her. Unless…did he want to talk about the project?

SURE. WHERE? She typed the words and hit send before she could second-guess herself.

This time, she had to wait for his response. She drummed her fingers on the desk, waiting for the ping of an incoming message.

THE STATION. I'LL LET SECURITY KNOW YOU'RE COMING. DAD HAS THE TRUCK.

She wondered again about the old truck he was driving. Surely, he could afford to drive something else? She bit her lip, thinking, then startled at another ping.

ARE WE ON?

She tapped back a thumbs-up.

It nettled that now she kept one eye on her phone, waiting for another message, irritated when it didn't come. Fortunately, a couple planning a trip to Cozumel took up most of her time, and work on the project took up the rest.

By two thirty her stomach rumbled with hunger, but she didn't have time to grab something to eat before she met Luc. Brandon was at the copier plugging in a new ink cartridge. Kate's desk still sat empty.

Marnie packed up her computer then glanced at Brandon. "She's not back?"

He shrugged and closed the copier's front cover. "Maybe she had an errand to run."

"Huh. Okay, well, let her know I had to run by the Coast Guard station, will you?" She pulled on her coat and dug her gloves out of the pocket. "I'll see you both in the morning."

Brandon didn't look pleased by the news, but he didn't protest as she hurried out the door to make the short drive to the station.

Luc was waiting for her when she arrived and escorted her to the same conference room they'd used on her first visit. But, sliding her computer from her backpack, Marnie was surprised to realize she didn't feel the same discomfort.

"Thanks for coming." Luc gestured toward the kitchen. "Can I get you something to drink?"

He didn't look mad, or uncomfortable. In fact, gauging his mood would be just about impossible with the bland look on his face. Marnie rubbed a chill from her arms. "Coffee would be good. With a little cream and sugar, please."

"Coming right up."

While she waited for him to return, Marnie turned her attention to a bank of windows that spanned the length of one wall. Outside, heavy clouds threatened snow, and a sharp wind blowing off the bay formed whitecaps that crashed against the shore. Today the water definitely looked cold and uninviting, and she was just a teensy bit glad knowing Luc wasn't out fighting it.

"Here you go." He returned, a Styrofoam cup in each hand, one of which he placed in front of Marnie without looking at her. This time, there was no doubt. He was all business. And if he could do it, so could she.

"Thank you." She curled her fingers around the cup then motioned toward her computer. "I had a chance to work on the program schedule a little bit today. If you'll give me a second, I'll pull it up."

"Marnie, wait. Before we get started, I owe you an apology."

Marnie froze with her hand on her computer. Luc set his coffee on the table then sat next to her, his hands clasped and his elbows resting on his knees.

She cut in before he could speak. "Actually, if this is about yesterday, I'm the one who should be apologizing. I had no right to meddle."

He lifted his head. Meeting his gaze, Marnie's breath caught. This look…with one side of his mouth quirked like he could smile at any moment…this was the one she'd fallen in love with.

"Standing up for the underdog, eh, Marnie? It was one of the things I loved most about you."

Loved. Past tense?

She gave herself a shake. Of course it was past tense. They didn't have a future one, thanks to him.

"Then we're agreed. Apology accepted, and we move forward." She let go a long breath and opened her laptop. "Anyway, as I was saying, I worked out a tentative schedule for the day. I'll email you a copy so you can let me know what you think."

"That'll work."

"I also started putting together a list of vendors. Do you have a minute to look it over with me?"

He nodded and sipped his coffee. As they talked, Marnie felt herself relax. She even laughed at a couple of his jokes, which in itself was odd, because she never remembered him joking when they dated. By the time they finished, it was after four, and Marnie's stomach rumbled in annoyance.

"Sorry." She pressed her hand to her middle. "I was late getting to the office so I skipped lunch—"

"To catch up?" He grinned and tossed his empty cup into a trash can. "Yeah, you told me."

Finishing her sentences, just like the old days.

Marnie looked away to stow her laptop. "Anyway, I should get going."

"Or we could grab something to eat." When she looked at him, he shrugged. "That is, if you don't mind dropping me by the house after. Dad's—"

"Got the truck. Yeah, you told me."

His low chuckle made her smile. Marnie zipped her backpack closed and stood. "Sounds good, so long as I get to pick the place."

Luc crossed his arms. "Let me guess. Milano's?"

"It's not my fault their food is so good." She hiked her backpack over her shoulder and angled her head. "Ready?"

"I'll get my coat."

Milano's, like many of the restaurants in Ilwaco, was a small, family-owned business that had been around longer than Marnie had been alive. She breathed deeply of the savory scents of roasted chicken, garlic, and tomato as she and Luc wound their way to a table. As soon as their drink order arrived, she took a long sip of her Dr Pepper to quell the growling in her stomach.

"Could we get some bread?" Luc asked, motioning to their waitress. "You sound like you're about to starve," he said, smiling at Marnie.

"Ha. I'm a long way from starvation." She grimaced down at her hips, where she always seemed to carry five pounds more than she liked.

"You look perfect."

She jerked her head up. Luc watched her, his eyes twinkling as though he knew her thoughts. Nix that. He just knew her. She'd grumbled about dieting often enough.

Feeling heat rise to her face, Marnie scrambled to hide behind her menu. "Well, it's still early, but I'm starving. Ooh…" She paused and took her phone out of her pocket. "I should probably text Mom and let her know I won't be home for supper."

"I need to call Dad too." He wiggled his own phone. "He doesn't text."

Marnie chuckled, sent a message to her mother, then listened while Luc left a voice mail. "No answer?"

"No." He frowned.

She pulled a piece off one of the rolls the waitress had left. "Something wrong?"

Luc glanced at his watch. "He told me he needed the truck to run a few errands, but I expected him home by now."

"Speaking of the truck, I can't believe you're still driving it. How many miles does that thing have on it?"

He smiled and dropped his gaze. "A few."

"Don't you think it's time to trade it in?"

"Why? It still runs."

The waitress reappeared for their order, and then Marnie and Luc chatted like old friends until their food came.

Old friends.

Marnie swallowed the last bite of her pasta salad. The words didn't have such a bad ring. It was unlikely they would ever get back to what they once had, but maybe what they *could* have was okay too.

She pondered that as they left the restaurant to head to Luc's house. By now, the sun had set, and though it wasn't quite dark, she was surprised by the absence of light streaming from the windows. His truck was also absent, the drifts across the driveway indicating George had been gone some time.

"He's not back." Marnie put her car in park. "Do you want to try calling him again?"

"That's a good idea." He dialed, but in the quiet of the car, Marnie heard the call go immediately to voice mail.

"Could be his phone died." She motioned toward the house. "Maybe he left a note. Do you want to check? I can wait."

Luc shook his head and reached for the door handle. "Don't worry about it. I'm sure he's fine. Besides, you probably want to get home."

"It'll take two seconds, Luc." She motioned him on. "Go. I'll wait."

He grimaced but didn't argue. Illuminated by the headlights, she watched him jog across the driveway in front of her and disappear into the house. He returned a few moments later with something clutched in his hand.

She rolled down the window. "Well?"

"No note, but I found this." He held up a phone. "He's always going off without it."

Tiny lines of worry creased his brow. Seeing them, Marnie felt an anxious knot twist inside her belly. "Where do you think he is? Did he say where he was going?"

He shoved the phone into his coat pocket and gripped the door. "Nope. Just errands."

"Well, then maybe we should look for him." The fact that he didn't immediately argue set off alarm bells in her head. "Get in. We'll drive around a bit."

Luc nodded and got back in the car. "Start with the community center," he said as he buckled in and she backed out of the driveway. "He goes there sometimes to walk."

"Mom told me. And speaking of Mom..." She clicked the phone button on her steering wheel and told the computer to call her mom. After a couple of rings, the call connected.

"Hey, Mom. I'm in the car with Luc, and you're on speaker. Have you by any chance seen George today?"

"George?" Her mother sounded puzzled. "No, I'm afraid not. Doesn't Luc know where he is?"

"Well, he was supposed to be running errands," Marnie explained, "but we just went by the house and he's not there. Also, he left his phone, so we got a little worried."

"I see. I'm so sorry, Luc," Mom said. "Do you want me to make a few phone calls?"

"Maybe let us check a couple of places first," Luc said. He didn't explain why and didn't have to. The last thing he wanted was to stir up gossip about his father.

"I understand," Mom said. "Please call me back when you've found him."

"Will do. Thanks, Mom."

Marnie disconnected then glanced sideways at Luc. His jaw was squared, his gaze fastened on the road ahead. What was he thinking? She didn't dare ask. All she could do was pray for him. Pray they found George.

At the community center, only a handful of people had braved the cold weather, and none of them had seen George. Marnie suggested he might have gone to eat, but a sweep of his favorite haunts revealed nothing. With each stop, Luc grew quieter, the tension in his body more palpable. Though she hated to think it, Marnie knew there was still one possibility they hadn't discussed.

She gripped the steering wheel. "What about a bar, Luc?"

When he didn't answer, she risked a peek. He nodded. There were several establishments in town, but everyone knew George Graham's preference was a tavern on the outskirts. Marnie headed there.

For a Tuesday night, there were quite a few cars parked in the lot. Marnie was relieved to see Luc's truck wasn't among them. Next to her, Luc's long breath said he felt the same.

Her heart ached for him. George's drinking had been devastating to a boy who'd spent too many afternoons waiting to be picked up at school by a father who never came. She pulled to a stop at the end of the drive and shifted to look at him. "Where to? Should we try another place?"

Luc thought a second, then shook his head. "No, let's try the Cape Disappointment Lighthouse." At her puzzled frown, he added, "Dad used to go there after Mom left. He said he liked the view. But it was usually to drink."

Marnie wasn't fooled by his wry grin. That was the look he had when he didn't want anyone to know he was hurting. Or angry. At this moment, she couldn't tell which.

She pulled out onto the street. The road to the lighthouse was long and winding, and they made their way there in silence.

"The Lewis and Clark Interpretive Center," Luc said, pointing out her turn as they neared. "The trails to the lighthouse are closed now, so if this is where he came, he would have parked there."

Marnie followed his directions, sucking in a breath when her headlights brought Luc's truck into view. George *was* here. She breathed a prayer of thanksgiving then pulled to a stop next to the truck, anger mingling with the relief building in her chest. How could he have let his son worry so? And to go back to drinking now, when Luc had requested a transfer specifically to care for him, was simply mind-boggling.

"Wait here," Luc said grimly.

Marnie nodded. He knew better than anyone what he'd find if his father had been drinking. He was trying to protect her.

Luc climbed out to check the truck, but instead of finding George inside, the cab was empty.

Fighting panic, Marnie clambered out to join Luc. George could have wandered off, gotten lost, any number of things. And with the temperature dropping, not finding him could be fatal.

Luc crossed to the front of the truck and laid his hand on the hood. "Still warm." He scanned the parking lot.

"Where do you think he's gone?" Marnie asked.

"No idea—" He broke off and lifted his nose to sniff the air.

"What are you doing?"

"I keep smelling gas." He circled toward the driver's side where the gas cap was located, then dropped to his haunches to drag his fingers across the wet pavement. "It is gas. A lot of it."

"A leak?"

He peered up at her, his gaze somber. After activating the flashlight on his phone, he rolled onto his back and shoved under the truck. He reemerged a short while later and pushed to his feet, his dark eyes wide with worry.

"What is it, Luc? What did you find?" She frowned, knowing what he would say before he said it.

"It's not a leak, Marnie," he said, confirming the fear building in her belly. "Someone cut the gas line."

Chapter Nine

Marnie's breath knotted in her chest. "Luc, are you sure? Maybe it was rotted, or damaged by accident."

He opened the driver's door and grabbed an old towel from under the seat to wipe his hands. "Clean cut. It wasn't an accident, Marnie."

He tossed the towel into the truck bed then wound to the passenger side to retrieve a flashlight from the glove box.

"What are you doing?"

"I'm gonna check the trails. The parking lot was plowed, but the trails aren't. With all this snow, it should be easy to see if he took one of them."

"I'll come with you." Marnie took her phone out of her pocket, but Luc's flashlight was powerful enough she didn't need to use it. It was obvious the fresh snow on the trails was undisturbed.

Marnie pressed closer to Luc's side. With darkness closing in earnest, and only the sound of the wind rustling through the trees, she was more than a touch creeped out. "Maybe he didn't wander off, Luc. Maybe he started back to town when the truck wouldn't start."

Luc growled his frustration and swung the flashlight beam through the surrounding trees. "We'd have passed him on the road."

"Not if he was headed for the Cape D Café' on Fort Canby. He might have been going there to call for help."

Luc thought a moment, then straightened. "You're right. We should check."

Their steps were more hurried as they headed back toward the car. Twice, Marnie slipped, sending snow into the sides of her shoes. The second time, Luc drew her close to steady her.

"Sorry," Marnie said, huffing to keep pace with him. "I don't have my boots."

"To be fair, you didn't know I'd be dragging you down hiking trails through the snow."

She laughed a little, the sound cut short when the beam of Luc's flashlight caught the yellowish glow of a woodland animal's eyes.

Luc's arm tightened around her shoulders. "Just a racoon."

"Right." She forced herself to relax until they reached the car. Once inside, they drove the half mile to the café, Marnie's thoughts whirling like a typhoon in her head. What if George wasn't there? Should they have called the police when they found the truck? More importantly, who had cut the gas line and why?

The "why" part she could guess...it was to drive Luc—and now maybe his father—away. Fresh anger swelled inside her chest until she felt like she'd explode. How dare someone—anyone—be so arrogant and cruel?

"There he is!"

Marnie startled at the barked words. "Where?"

Luc pointed, and she cut the wheel to her left where a dark figure had turned toward them. It *was* George. His coat was zipped to his chin, and he had his hood over his head against the wind, but in the light cast by her high beams, she could make out his face. Marnie's eyes instantly burned with relief.

"Thank goodness." She drove over to him. Barely had the car stopped when Luc jumped out, leaving the door gaping open.

"Pop!"

George lifted one hand to shade his eyes from the glare of the headlights. "Luc?"

Marnie cut the beams so only the parking lights glowed.

George dropped his hand. "What are you doing here? Who've you got with you?"

"Marnie. We're out looking for you."

He didn't act like he'd been drinking. In fact, George looked and sounded completely sober.

"I don't understand," he said. "How did you know about the truck?"

"We didn't, Pop. You left your phone. When you weren't home, I got worried."

His face crumpled with dismay. "I'm sorry, Son. You've told me a thousand times…"

"We'll talk about it later." Luc put his hand on his dad's shoulder. "Let's get you someplace warm."

"And the truck?"

"I'll take care of it tomorrow."

George let Luc lead him around to the passenger side, where Luc directed him to get into the front seat before climbing into the back himself. Marnie bumped up the heat and turned the vents so they blew in George's direction.

George held his hands up to the vent in front of him. "Marnie, I can't tell you how much I appreciate you coming to look for me. I was sitting there with the truck idling, enjoying the view. Somehow,

I ran out of gas. I have no idea how it happened. I had over half a tank when I left the house."

Marnie exchanged a quick glance in the rearview mirror with Luc. So, George didn't realize what had happened? Luc gave a slight shake of his head.

"It's no problem, George," Marnie said, switching the headlights back on. "I'm just glad you're okay."

"I'm fine." He chuckled as he stretched his seat belt across his chest. "'Course, it was taking me a little longer than it used to, to walk to the café. I was starting to think I made a mistake heading out in the dark."

His laugh was good to hear. The cough that followed it was not.

"We should get you home." Marnie dropped the car into gear and set off down the road. Once they reached the house and were inside, she called her mother, who was not at all pleased to hear about what had happened.

"Mom's on her way," Marnie said, after she ended the call. "She's bringing George some soup."

"I appreciate it," Luc said.

George was still coughing, so Luc walked over to bump the thermostat up, then draped a blanket over his shoulders. "Here you go, Pop."

"Thanks." George shook his head. "I tell ya, the wind was blowing off the bay something awful. I didn't realize it until I'd gone a ways down the road." His effort to talk set off another fit of coughing.

"I'll get you some water," Marnie said, and turned for the kitchen. Luc followed her in.

Once out of George's earshot, she whirled to him. "Okay, I know you said you didn't need my help, but meddling or not, this is getting serious, Luc. You dad could have really been hurt tonight."

"I know."

"I'm glad, because I don't think sitting around and hoping whoever is behind this gets bored, or goes away, or…whatever it was you said, is going to work."

He turned to lean against the counter, his arms crossed over his chest. "You're right."

She drew back and stared. "I'm what?"

"You're right, Marnie. I shouldn't have let this go so long. If something had happened to Pop tonight, it would have been my fault."

"I wasn't saying that."

"You didn't have to."

It took her a moment to realize the anger she heard in his voice was directed at himself—which made the anger *she* felt vanish. She moved closer to rest her hand on his arm. "It was a couple of notes and a small fire. You couldn't have known it would escalate like this."

He dragged his gaze to hers. "Actually, it might have been more."

She pulled her hand away, apprehension simmering inside her. "What do you mean?"

He hauled in a deep breath. "This morning I found a bunch of trash in the yard. I blew it off. Figured it was a random act by some thoughtless kid."

"Okay," she said, cautiously.

"That's not the only thing. The day after I got here I went to the hardware store downtown to pick up some stuff for the house. When I came out, someone had busted out my taillight."

"This doesn't sound good," Marnie said.

He nodded. "Maybe whoever's doing this stuff figured we weren't taking the hint."

"They're not hinting anymore." She blew out a breath. "We have to find whoever's behind this."

"We?" He shifted closer.

Did she dare think he sounded hopeful? With only a hand's breadth separating them, Marnie could feel the warmth rolling off him. See the amber flecks in his eyes. Smell his cologne.

His cologne. It was the same one he'd worn when they were dating. She closed her eyes and leaned into him, breathing it in.

"I need you, Marnie."

Her eyes snapped open.

He stared at her, his gaze dark and penetrating. "I need your help figuring out what's been going on."

The words were strangled, as though he'd had a hard time forcing them out.

"Oh." She let out a shaky breath and nodded. "Good."

"Good?"

"We're agreed then."

He puffed out a curt laugh, the sound cut short by the ringing of the doorbell.

Marnie glanced toward the hall then up at Luc. "That would be Mom."

He retreated a step. "I'll go let her in."

Was that regret that flashed across his face? It shocked her how much she wanted to think so. "Thanks. I'll get your dad's water."

He strode off. Alone in the kitchen, Marnie rubbed her hands over her face. What was happening to her? It was like she and Luc were back in high school, only this time, she knew the outcome.

Knew...and didn't care.

Her hands shook as she searched the cupboards for a glass then filled it with water.

This was dangerous ground she was treading. The problem was, she'd traveled it before. Had she learned nothing from his leaving?

Then again, could she ignore what was happening to him and walk away?

No.

The answer came without hesitation. Turning toward the door, she paused with the glass clutched in her hand and lifted her gaze to the ceiling.

"Help me, God. Please. Don't let him break my heart again."

It was a feeble prayer, and if she was honest, she'd probably voiced it too late. Because her heart was already in Luc's hands.

What he did with it was completely up to him.

Chapter Ten

Mom sat at the kitchen table waiting for her when Marnie got up Wednesday morning. Mom's Bible was open in front of her and a pair of reading glasses dangled from her fingers. Judging by the bags under her eyes, she'd slept as fitfully as Marnie.

Marnie shuffled to the coffeepot and poured a cup. "Morning, Mom."

"Good morning, sweetheart." She angled her head toward the counter. "I heard you get up. There's a bagel in the toaster for you."

"Thanks." Marnie snagged it and carried it with her coffee to the table. "Any word from Luc or George?" she asked as she sat.

"Not yet." Mom braced her elbows on the table. "Marnie, what is going on?"

"I wish I knew." Marnie sighed and pushed the bagel away, choosing instead to nurse the coffee. "I'm worried, Mom. This is getting much more dangerous than a coat on fire in a can."

"I agree." She fingered her bottom lip nervously. "Thank goodness Luc is off the next few days so he can get the truck fixed."

Marnie raised her eyebrows. "I didn't know he was off."

Mom pulled her own cup closer. "He's taking George to his doctor's appointment in Astoria."

"Why's he going to Astoria? Why not here?"

"There's a liver specialist there Luc wants him to see." She set her reading glasses aside then pressed her palms together. "Marnie, there's something I haven't told you about because I know your feelings where Luc and George are concerned, and I've tried to respect them. But I think it's time we talked."

Marnie brought her hand to her neck. "Okay."

Mom blew out a breath. "A couple of years ago, George was diagnosed with cirrhosis. He'd already been sober quite a while by then, but the damage was irreversible. His doctor recommended a liver transplant. Luc was a match."

Marnie blinked, processing the information.

"George refused to let Luc be a donor. He was afraid it would impact his career. Ruin his health." She shook her head. "Honestly, he came up with all kinds of excuses. I think the truth is he regrets not being there for Luc when he was growing up and just didn't want to take anything else away from his son."

"I had no idea."

Her mother stretched out to cover Marnie's hand with her own. "I know you think Luc came back to take care of George, but that's only part of the reason. George says Luc's been trying to talk him into changing his mind about the transplant."

Of course he'd try. She would do the same.

"There's one more thing." Mom pulled her hand away to cradle her cup. "Luc sold his car so he could pay for some repairs to his dad's house. He wants to open things up to make it easier for George to get around."

"That's why he's driving the truck?"

She nodded. "Honey, what happens between you and Luc is your business. But he has reasons for the things he does. I'm telling you this because I'm hoping you'll listen to what he has to say about why he enlisted. Maybe it'll make a difference."

Lips pressed tightly, Marnie gazed deep into her mother's eyes. "You know why he left, don't you?"

She lowered her head, her shoulders sagging. "He never told me, or George, but…I have an idea." She grasped Marnie's fingers and squeezed. "Promise you'll listen?"

Marnie squeezed back and lifted her chin. "I'll try. Later. Right now, my only concern is figuring out who cut the gas line on Luc's truck before they do something else."

"Okay." Mom straightened her shoulders. "What can I do?"

"Keep George company when Luc can't be there? I think it would be good if he wasn't alone right now."

"Of course. I'll put a casserole in the oven and take it over there this afternoon after they get home from the doctor."

"Good idea." She slipped out of the chair. "While you're doing that, I'm going to run by the office and talk to Kate. She's definitely not one of Luc's fans, but maybe she can help me figure out what's been going on."

"But first"—Mom grabbed the plate with Marnie's bagel and slid it across the table to her—"you eat."

Laughing at the scowl her mother shot at her, Marnie reached for the bagel. "Fine. Eating." She pressed a kiss to her cheek. "Love you, Mom."

"Love you too."

Taking an obedient bite of the bagel, Marnie angled a teasing smile at her mom then walked out of the kitchen. An hour later, she headed to the office, realizing as she drove that she hadn't asked how Luc was getting George to Astoria with his truck not running. The minute she parked, she shot him a quick text. He responded with a brief message.

Borrowed Jeff's car. With the doctor now.

So, he couldn't talk. Marnie slid her phone into her pocket and climbed out of her car.

The office door was already unlocked, which meant either Brandon or Kate had gotten there before her. Odd, because unless Marnie was running late, she was usually the first to arrive. Kate's voice drifted to her as Marnie stepped through the door.

Kate paced as she talked. She treaded a path from the filing cabinets to the watercooler. "I understand. I'll run by as soon as I get off work. Thanks, Lyle." Catching sight of Marnie, she grimaced and held up her phone. "Mom's attorney. We're still working through some of the stuff with Dad's will."

"Ugh. I'm so sorry." Marnie pulled the backpack off her shoulder and let it drop to her desk. "Anything I can do to help?"

"No, but I might have to skip out a little early this afternoon."

"No problem. But before you go, can I get your help with something?"

Kate set her phone down and tucked her hair behind her ear. "Sure. Is it the family day?"

"Actually..." Marnie dragged a chair close to her desk and patted the seat. "You're gonna wanna sit for this."

Marnie told her everything that had happened after she left the office the day before. As she explained about the truck, Kate frowned. "That's Luc's truck. What was George doing driving it, and why was he all the way out at the Interp Center?"

"Luc said he used to go there a lot after his mother left," Marnie said.

Kate rubbed her fingers over her forehead. "The weather's been bad, Marnie. He's so lucky he wasn't hurt."

"I know. And that's why I need your help figuring out what's been happening so we can put a stop to it."

Kate bit her lip, hesitation building in her eyes. "Okay, you know I love you, and I'll do whatever you ask, but…what did Luc have to say about this? Is he okay with you stepping in?"

"He agrees it's time to do more than just ignore this person," Marnie answered.

"Well, that's good." Kate clasped her hands in her lap. "Has he called the police?"

"You know, I'm not sure." Marnie pinched her bottom lip, thinking. "Last night, our only thought was getting George home and warm. But you're right, we should probably let the police know what happened."

She reached for her phone, but Kate held out her hand to stop her. "Hold on now, that's a call you should probably leave to Luc, assuming he wants to."

"But he said—"

Kate shook her head. "If it's taken him this long to ask for your help, imagine how upset he'd be if you didn't talk to him before involving the authorities."

Marnie replaced her phone in her pocket and slouched in her chair. "You're right. So, I guess there's really not a whole lot I can do until he and George get back from Astoria, which won't be until this afternoon."

"Astoria? I thought you said his truck wasn't running."

"It's not. He borrowed a car from a friend while his is in the shop."

Kate nodded. "So, tell me about the other stuff. You said several things have happened?"

Marnie listed them then frowned. "They're getting progressively worse, which has me worried."

"I would be too." Kate locked gazes with Marnie. "Okay, now hear me out."

"Um…that's not a good start."

"I know. But I was just thinking—have Luc and George considered stepping away for a bit?"

Marnie stiffened. "And by 'stepping away,' you mean…?"

"I don't mean leaving permanently. I'm just saying, what if they let things cool down a little?"

"Kate, that's not an answer. Besides, even if they wanted to leave, they couldn't. George is pretty sick."

"Well, I know his health isn't good."

Marnie shook her head. "No, I mean, he's *sick*. He has cirrhosis of the liver. That's why they had to go to Astoria, so George could see a specialist."

Kate leaned back in her chair. "I had no idea."

Marnie squeezed her friend's arm. "I didn't either. But you see what I mean about them staying here."

Kate cleared her throat. "All right. I don't have any clients until this afternoon. What do you need me to do?"

"Like I said, I'll talk to Luc about calling the police when he gets back. In the meantime, would you mind asking about his truck around town? See if anyone saw something suspicious—like a person hanging around, or watching Luc as he went about his business."

"Yeah, sure, I can do that."

She rose as the doorbell chimed, and Brandon walked in. Seeing him, Marnie felt her own moment of hesitation. Brandon had certainly seen her get out of Luc's truck. Her heart skipped a beat. What if…

"Morning, Kate. Marnie." He lifted a brightly colored box. "Hope you haven't eaten breakfast. I brought donuts."

"Donuts!" Kate groaned but grabbed one on her way out the door.

"Marnie?" Brandon lifted the box lid, releasing a warm, yeasty cloud of cinnamon and sugar. "I got you a bear claw. Your favorite."

Fumbling for her coat and backpack, Marnie shook her head. "Thanks, but I'll have to get it some other time. Do you think you can hold down the fort this morning?"

"Sure, but where—?"

"Can't stop now. See you later, Brandon."

Hustling to the door, Marnie waved and let herself out. Seeing Brandon had made her realize something. What if the person wasn't targeting both George and Luc as they'd come to believe? What if they were just targeting Luc? What if they'd cut the gas line expecting Luc to be driving? Did that make her feel better…or worse? She wasn't sure, but suddenly, one thing was certain.

She needed to talk to Luc.

Chapter Eleven

Marnie paced the distance from her car to George's front door so many times, she expected to see wear in the sidewalk. Where was Luc? He and George were supposed to be back from Astoria over an hour ago. Finally, the rumble of an engine sounded, and she whirled to see Luc's truck rounding the corner.

When they'd parked and climbed out, she said, "There you are. I've been waiting for you."

"Sorry." Luc hitched his thumb over his shoulder. "We swung over to the service station to get the truck so I could drop off Jeff's car." He leaned in close to whisper. "I told Pop it was a rotted fuel line."

"Right. Sorry."

"Come in out of the cold, Marnie." George motioned her toward the house. As he passed, she noticed he looked a little gray around the edges, as though the trip had sapped him of strength. Or hope.

She sucked in a breath, everything else forgotten, and followed him up the steps. Inside, she wriggled out of her coat and gave it to Luc. "How did the doctor's visit go?"

"Same as always." George chuckled and peeled off his hat, his thinning hair crackling with static and standing on end. "More doom and gloom."

Marnie caught Luc's eye over his shoulder. He shrugged. "They're still recommending a transplant, and Dad is still refusing to consider it."

"Now, Son, we've talked about this." George laid his hat on top of the coats in Luc's arms then smiled at Marnie. "Don't let him worry you. My liver function is fine for now."

But was it?

Marnie waited impatiently while Luc stowed the coats in the closet. Finished, he gestured toward the kitchen. "Can I get you something to drink?"

She rubbed her hands over her arms. "Coffee?"

"Coming up. Pop?"

"Just water for me," George said, and then added, "and maybe something for a headache. I got it hanging around with this guy." He nodded at Luc. "Who knew he'd hover so much?"

"I'll get it," Marnie offered. "Bathroom medicine cabinet?"

"Yes," Luc said. "Anything with acetaminophen." He turned to George. "And I don't hover."

Marnie fetched the pain reliever and pressed it into George's hand. "He's definitely hovering," she whispered, smiling when the comment drew a wink. "Will you be all right for a bit? I have something I'd like to talk over with Luc."

"I'll be fine." He shooed them away.

Marnie led Luc to the living room, out of earshot of the kitchen but still close enough they could hear if George called.

"Everything okay?" Luc asked, handing Marnie her coffee.

"I'm not sure." She explained what she thought about the gas line, half expecting Luc to dismiss the idea and surprised when he didn't.

"It would make sense that it was meant for me," he said. "Since the second envelope was delivered directly to me and it was my taillight that was targeted."

Marnie moved to the sofa and set her mug on the coffee table. After a moment, Luc joined her.

"Let's think this through. Who knows you're driving that truck?"

He shook his head. "Too broad. Anyone in town could know that."

"Okay, then let's look at the other things. The coat? It was Coast Guard issue."

"Still too broad," Luc said. "It might have been lost or stolen, purchased off the internet, taken from an auxiliary member." He shook his head. "There's just too many possibilities."

Auxiliary? She hadn't considered them. She tucked the thought away to ponder later. "Okay, what about the notes? What did they say?"

He looked away, his lip curling in disgust. "Just your typical idiotic nonsense."

"Luc, that's not helpful. Was there anything about the messages that stood out to you?"

"Besides the typos?" He sneered and shook his head. "Nothing."

"Anything special about the paper?"

"No."

"The handwriting?"

"They were typed."

She frowned. The person knew enough not to want their handwriting recognized but couldn't use spellchecker. "All right, so our culprit isn't the brightest crayon in the box."

He snorted.

"Can I see the notes?"

"You could, but they're at the station. I left them in my locker."

"All right, last thing—"

He held up his hand. "Before you ask, no. There was nothing special about the trash."

So where did that leave them? She dragged her gaze to the darkening sky outside the windows. Someone out there wanted Luc gone. How far would they go? And what if she couldn't stop them?

"Hey."

His strong fingers closed around her hand, pulling her attention back to him.

"Stop worrying. It'll be all right."

"*Humph.* You're more confident about that than I am."

The glint in his eyes turned mischievous. "It's nice that you care though."

"Very funny." Suddenly, his teasing was infectious. She lifted her chin. "It's George I'm worried about."

"Oh, really?" He moved closer to touch the skin between her eyes. "'Cause you're doing the thing you do when something is really important to you."

Her breath caught at his nearness. "Wh-what thing?"

"Pinching your eyebrows together to make these little wrinkles."

Suddenly, he wasn't teasing. He shifted to run his thumb down the side of her face, his gaze locked to hers, his lips slightly parted. He leaned in. Like he wanted to kiss her. Like he'd been thinking about it for a while.

The glare of headlights flashed across the windows. Marnie let go a shallow breath. "That's my mom. She said she was bringing over a casserole."

He swallowed hard and dropped his hand. Both hands. She hadn't realized he was still holding on to her with the other. "Okay."

She rose when he did, but unlike him, had to wipe her palms on her pant legs the second he turned his back to open the door for her mother. Soon, Mom's cheerful voice filled the hall.

"I hope you all like bacon and cheddar, because this dish is one of Marnie's and my favorites. Oh, hi, sweetheart." She drifted into the living room. Behind her, Luc held the casserole dish.

"I'll take this to the kitchen."

"Thanks, Luc."

Mom turned to Marnie. "Everything okay?"

"Good. I'm good."

Which wasn't exactly true, because she *did* have a hard time keeping her thoughts away from that "almost" kiss and she *was* sneaking glances at Luc during supper when she thought no one was looking.

Was Mom right? Should she give him another chance to explain why he'd left so suddenly?

Watching him laugh with Mom and George as they washed the dishes after they ate, and seeing how easily he shared about how life in the Coast Guard had taught him to rely on people other than himself, she thought so. But then the conversation changed. While her mother made coffee, Luc talked about his decision to become a Christian and how that one choice had led him back to Cape Disappointment.

"It brought me home, gave me a chance to work things out with Dad. And my mom. That one was a little tougher, but it was time," he finished. Looking across the table at his father, Luc's eyes shimmered with unshed tears—tears he quickly blinked away, but not before the last vestige of reserve fell from Marnie's heart.

Luc was not the same man he'd been when he left Ilwaco. Granted, he was still stoic, and proud, and too stubborn for his own good, but he was also sweet and protective. And seeing him like this reminded her of all the reasons she'd missed him.

It also made her certain that everything would be all right. Because if she could see the change in Luc, it wouldn't be long before others did too. And then everyone would forget about the things those other Graham men had done that had hurt so many people.

From the other room, a phone rang. Luc went to answer. Marnie used the chance to pull her mother aside.

"You're right, Mom," she whispered. She glanced over her shoulder at George, who was busy scraping the last of the casserole into a storage container and paying them no attention. "I'm going to talk to Luc. I'm going to let him explain why he left."

"I'm so glad, sweetheart," her mother whispered back. "It's the right thing, I'm sure of it."

So was Marnie, and she could hardly wait to tell Luc so. Except, when he walked back into the kitchen a few minutes later, the smile he'd worn when he left the room was gone. And he was angry. Really angry. His jaw looked like it had been chiseled from stone, and his eyes were so dark they were almost black.

in Cape Disappointment, Washington

He laid the phone on the counter carefully, but the way he kept his other hand bunched into a fist, Marnie suspected it was to keep from throwing it across the room.

"That was Jeff."

"From the station?" George closed the door on the refrigerator and straightened.

Luc nodded. "He was calling to let me know that one of the museums in town was broken into this afternoon and several items were stolen."

Marnie glanced from him to her mother and back in confusion. "I don't understand. What does that have to do with you?"

"He called because they found the missing stuff," Luc said. His gaze slid to George. "It was in the trunk of Jeff's car."

Chapter Twelve

"Surely Jeff doesn't think we took that stuff?"

"Which museum?"

"When did this happen?"

All three of them were talking and firing questions at once. Luc held up his hand.

"It was the free museum next to the library," he said, then turned to George. "And no, he doesn't think we took the stuff. But someone reported seeing it in Jeff's trunk."

Rage expanded Marnie's chest. "Someone, who?"

Luc grimaced. "Anonymous tip. Jeff called to give me a heads-up. It's likely the police will call us in for questioning."

"The police?" Her mother's eyes widened. "Is the historical society pressing charges?"

Marnie pressed her fingertips to her eyelids and blew out a sigh. "The police. I meant to talk to you about reporting the cut gas line."

"Reporting...what?" George looked at Luc.

Realizing her mistake, Marnie slapped her hand over her mouth.

For the second time, Luc held up his hand. "Okay, let's all move to the table so we can talk."

Once there, Marnie told George and her mom her theory about the notes and incidents targeting only Luc instead of both Grahams. Then Luc told his dad the truth about the gas line. "I'm sorry I lied,

Pop. I just didn't want you worrying about it today with your doctor's appointment and all."

George shook his head. "Son, you're the one who shouldn't be worrying. I keep telling you, I'm stronger than you think." He looked at Marnie. "So, the truck was another attempt to force Luc out of Ilwaco?"

"I'm afraid so, George," Marnie said. "And probably the stuff from the museum too. What I don't understand is why."

"Or who," Marnie's mother added. She reached out to cover George's hand, lines of sympathy creasing her brow. "Just like last time."

"Mom?" Marnie's brows rose.

Her mother kept her lips pressed into a thin line. Luc looked as confused as Marnie felt. She turned to George.

"What is she talking about?"

George sighed heavily. "She's talking about when Luc's mother left Ilwaco."

Luc leaned forward over the table. "What about her?"

"The same thing happened then." George's eyes reddened, and he ran his hand over his face. "Now, before I say another word, let me make it clear that your mother and I have put the past behind us. Though it took some doing, we've forgiven each other for the mistakes we made and we've moved on."

Luc nodded, and George continued.

"Your mother loved us, Luc, but she was never a strong woman. When we were first married, she acted like she didn't mind the gossip about our family, but then things started happening, and she got scared. I was drinking pretty heavily by then, leaving her here alone with you to face the talk and the critics. She was sad and scared, and I just couldn't see it."

"What happened years ago was not your fault, Pop."

Regret carved lines across his brow. "No, but I blame myself for the way I handled her leaving. Or *didn't* handle, I should say." He clasped Luc's shoulder, his face twisting in agony. "I did the same thing to you that I did to her. I left you alone to deal with your pain while I tried to drown mine."

A look passed between them that Marnie could only describe as commiseration—shared grief. Shared regret.

She cleared her throat. "So, what kinds of things did Jeff say were in his car?"

Luc blew out a breath then turned to look at her. "A bell. Life preserver. Some cutlery. All from the same shipwreck."

"The *Pacific Star*?" The look on her mom's face said she hoped she was wrong, but Marnie knew what Luc would say before he said it.

"Yeah. There were also a few photos missing, but they weren't in Jeff's car."

"Which means they'll probably show up in your stuff later," Marnie muttered, fighting a fresh swell of anger.

"More than likely." Luc combed his fingers through his hair and expelled a heavy sigh. "I should call my CO, give him my side of the story before he hears it from the police."

He rose and left the table. Marnie followed him into the hall until they were away from her mother and George.

Lowering her voice, she said, "You don't think this will affect your career, do you?"

Luc glanced past her toward the kitchen, then met her gaze somberly. "It could, if I'm accused of stealing."

She stepped closer. "But that's not fair. You didn't take anything."

He matched her motion and moved in, cutting the distance between them in half. "That's not the problem. *Proving* it wasn't me is."

"Well, then, that's what we'll do. It'll be easy enough."

A spark of hope lit Luc's eyes. "What do you mean?"

"Depending on when the stuff went missing—which I'm assuming was sometime yesterday or today since we're just now hearing about it—you have an alibi." She held up one finger. "First, you were with me when we were out looking for your dad, and then with your dad this morning in Astoria. You weren't alone, Luc, and that will be easy enough to prove."

His shoulders relaxed, and he nodded. "You're right. I guess it'll depend on when the museum was broken into."

"Not just the time." She lifted her chin adamantly. "Your CO has got to know what type of man you are by now. When we explain what's been happening, he'll know this isn't you."

Luc clamped his lips together, the muscles in his jaw working. "You…" He swallowed and started again. "You really think so?"

"I do." This time, she didn't stop herself from reaching out to him. She pressed her palm against his cheek, holding her breath when he laid his hand on hers to hold her there.

"Thank you, Marnie. For believing in me."

"I should have never stopped." The words slipped out before she could catch them. She dropped her gaze and pulled her hand away. "I should let you make your call."

"Before you go…" He fisted his hands at his sides. "I'd like to tell you why I left."

She looked back at him. "You don't need to." This time, she really meant the words. Whatever had driven him to go, he had good reasons.

He held her gaze steadily. "But I'd like to."

She nodded, holding her breath.

"I loved you, Marnie. There was no doubt in my mind that I wanted to spend the rest of my life with you. But I wanted…because of my family's history, I needed to make sure I went about things the right way. So I talked to your stepfather."

Her heart rate sped. "You…when?"

"Right after you graduated high school."

She pressed her hand to her head, trying to think back. "I never knew."

"I didn't tell you."

Suspicion sparked in Marnie's heart. "What did he say?"

Luc's jaw worked as he mulled the words. "Nothing that wasn't true." When he looked up, his gaze was calm. "He said that I needed to make my own life right before I brought another person into it. He told me to examine my choices. Think about what I wanted to do with my life. And he asked me to be honest with myself about why I wanted to be with you."

"I don't understand."

"He said if it was because I wanted you to save me, then he couldn't give his blessing, because only Jesus could do that."

Tears flooded Marnie's eyes. "That sounds like him."

"I was angry at first, but he was right. When I finally came to terms with it, when I admitted he wasn't pushing me away because of my name, I knew I couldn't stay."

"That's when you enlisted?"

"Yes."

Marnie paused to swipe the tears from her eyes. "Why didn't you tell me?"

He smoothed a stray lock of hair from her face and tucked it gently behind her ear. "I spent years hating my father. I didn't want to be the cause of that same kind of rift between the two of you."

She opened her mouth to argue...and stopped. He was right. While she might not have hated her stepfather, she likely would've shifted blame to him. And that would've robbed them both of the last years of his life.

Blinking rapidly to ward off the tears, she nodded. In that moment, it was all she could manage. She needed time to think over everything he'd just told her. "You need to make your call."

She spun and walked back to the kitchen. It was important now more than ever that they find the person trying to drive Luc away and stop them.

Their hope for a future together depended on it.

Chapter Thirteen

Marnie took out her tablet and opened a page to take notes. "Okay, George, let's start with the car. What time did you pick it up?"

He scratched his chin, thinking. "Well, it was early. Must've been around seven thirty, I guess."

"And you went by Jeff's place? Where is that?"

"An apartment over by the hospital."

"Was there anyone around?" Marnie pressed. "Did you notice anything or see anyone?"

George wrung his hands in agitation. "Not that I remember, no."

Mom touched Marnie's wrist, the look in her eyes stressing restraint. Marnie drew in a slow breath.

"Okay, so once you got to Astoria, you went right to the hospital?" At his nod, she continued. "Did you go anywhere else after you left?"

"Straight home, well, except a stop to fill Jeff's car up with gas before we swung into the service station to get Luc's truck."

The service station. Could that have been when the items from the museum were hidden in the trunk?

"George, did you stay in the car or go inside with Luc when you stopped to pick up the truck?"

He shrugged. "I went inside, but we weren't there long. Luc paid for the repairs, collected the keys, and we left. All told, it was maybe ten minutes."

Plenty of time to drop something in the trunk. And then another thought struck. "George, the service station—was it the one over on First Avenue?"

"Carter's. Yeah. They do a good job."

"Do the employees still wear those blue coats?"

"Maybe. I mean the guy we talked to wasn't wearing one, but we were inside."

"What are you thinking, Marnie?" Mom asked.

"Just that the person who delivered the note to the Coast Guard station was wearing a blue coat."

"But don't they also have a patch with their name on the front?"

Marnie bit her lip. "True, though Jeff said he wasn't paying a lot of attention. Do you think he just missed that?"

"It's possible," Mom said. George agreed.

"He also had on a black knit hat," Marnie continued, "but—"

"Those are pretty common," Mom finished.

"Exactly."

"It's still worth checking out," George said.

Luc walked into the kitchen, the phone in his hand. "What's worth checking out?"

Marnie filled him in, and then added one more thought. "I would also like to swing by the museum and talk to the curator, see if we can find out who the person was who broke in and what time."

"I'll go with you." Luc looked at his watch. "It's too late today. First thing tomorrow? I can pick you up."

"You know what? I'm thinking I should drive. Your truck apparently has a target on it."

It wasn't funny, but they still laughed. Afterward, Mom collected their coats and gloves, told George goodbye, then joined Marnie at the door.

She shot a glance at Luc then winked at Marnie. "I'll wait for you outside."

"Okay."

She slipped out, an awkward silence lingering after she left.

Wriggling her fingers into her gloves, Marnie risked a peek up at Luc. "So, I guess I'll see you in the morning."

"Yeah."

He moved closer. She expected him to open the door. He didn't.

"Marnie?"

She swallowed hard. "Yeah?"

His voice dropped to a husky whisper that sent shivers running down her spine. "I really want to kiss you."

So why didn't he?

He shifted to shove his hands into his pockets. "But I won't. Not until we get this mess sorted out."

Her heart sank a little, but she nodded. "Okay."

She let herself out the door, fast. *Okay*? She groaned and rolled her eyes heavenward. A handsome coastie told her he was waiting to kiss her, and the only word that came to her lips was *okay*?

If her mother sensed that something had happened between her and Luc, she didn't show it, not even the next morning when Marnie rushed out of bed an hour earlier than usual to wash, dress, and grab a bite of breakfast.

Seeing the ever-present Bible open on the table, Marnie slowed to sit across from her mother.

"He talked to Dad before he enlisted." She didn't have to say who. Mom knew. "Did Dad tell you?"

She slid her reading glasses off and laid them on the table. "Only that Luc had asked to meet." She stretched out her hand to Marnie. "Sweetheart, you know your stepfather only wanted the best for you."

"I know." She smiled and squeezed her mother's fingers. "It worked out the way it was supposed to, Mom."

"This will too. Eventually." She kissed the back of Marnie's hand and let her go. "I'll be praying for you both. Text me and let me know what you find out."

"Will do."

She headed out. A few minutes later, she pulled into George's drive, where Luc was already waiting. This time, when he climbed in, Marnie appreciated how much smaller her car felt with him inside it.

"Where to first?"

"The service station?" He pulled the seat belt across his chest and fastened himself in. "It's on the way, and it'll be open earlier than the museum."

Made sense, and they could grab coffee, because after a restless night spent replaying the words, *I really want to kiss you* on an endless loop in her head, she knew she'd need the caffeine.

Outside the service station, several employees walked around in blue coats. A couple even wore black hats.

Luc moved to climb out. Marnie grabbed his arm. "Maybe we should start by asking if anybody saw someone hanging around Jeff's car."

"Why?"

"Because the other option is to ask if they know of anyone who likes passing nasty notes."

A chuckle rumbled from his throat. "Right. Okay."

Inside the service station, Luc pointed out the man who'd helped him and George. He hadn't noticed anything unusual and neither had the other employees they talked to.

"Well, it wasn't a complete waste of time," Marnie said, taking a sip from her cup once they got back to the car. "The coffee's good."

"Only because it's early and the coffee hasn't had a chance to sit on the burner all day. Hopefully we'll have better luck at the museum."

Not discouraged by his pessimism, Marnie took another sip then offered him the cup. "Want some?"

He stared at her a second, his mouth quirked in that almost smile she loved. "Yeah."

"Yeah?"

He grabbed the coffee from her and took a long sip, but instead of returning it to her, he braced the cup on his knee.

"Hey," she protested.

"Hey, what?" He nodded to the road ahead. "Both hands on the wheel."

Marnie hid a smile as she backed onto the street and headed toward the museum. As a kid, she'd come here often with her class. She still remembered listening in fascination as the tour guide walked them through the many dangers found at the mouth of the Columbia River, specifically the area known as the Graveyard of the Pacific. What she didn't remember was the museum being so small. Or cramped.

Shelves crammed with maritime artifacts lined every inch of wall space inside the museum. Piled on the floor were anchors, stacks of coiled rope, even an old dinghy from one of the vessels that had capsized crossing the shoals.

"Careful." Luc grabbed Marnie's arm and pulled her away from a skewed photo that was hanging precariously from one nail. The glass across the picture was already cracked, as though it had been knocked from its spot one too many times.

"I'll be right with you," a voice called from the rear of the museum.

A little while later, a short woman with graying curls bustled toward them, a stack of magazines balanced in her arms. "Sorry about that. I was sorting through inventory."

She dropped the magazines on a stool, and the resulting cloud of dust sent her into a fit of sneezing.

"Are you all right?" Marnie asked. "Can I get you some water or something?"

"No need." She pulled a tissue from the pocket of her sweater vest and blew her nose. "Stupid allergies. Anyway, how can I help you?"

"Well, we were hoping to speak to the museum curator if he or she is available," Marnie said.

The woman shook her head and shoved the tissue back into her pocket. "No curator here, hon. This museum is run by the Coast Guard Auxiliary. We're all strictly volunteers."

Marnie glanced at Luc. "I see. Well then, maybe you can help us."

"I'll try. Whatcha need?"

Marnie mulled her words carefully. The woman did not appear to recognize Luc, which was helpful. She motioned to him. "My friend and I heard there was a break-in here recently."

The woman nodded. "Night before last."

"I'm so sorry to hear that. Was there a lot taken?"

LOVE'S A MYSTERY

"Not really." The woman scratched her head. "That's what was so strange about it. I mean, if you're going to break in and steal a bunch of stuff, why not make it worthwhile?"

"So, the missing items weren't valuable."

"Only to a history buff like me," the woman said. Her gaze shifted to focus on Luc. "Don't I know you?"

"I don't think so."

"Tell me more about the break-in," Marnie continued quickly. "Did anyone see anything unusual?"

"Unfortunately, no. It took place after hours."

"What time does the museum close?" Luc asked.

"Five o'clock." She squinted at him. "You look very familiar."

Luc chuckled. "I get that a lot."

"I guess." The woman pulled her gaze away from Luc slowly. "Anyway, most of the items stolen were from the wreck of the *Pacific Star*."

"Most?"

"There were also a few photos missing from the same time period. Oddly enough, it's the photos that are still missing. Everything else has been returned."

"Photos." Luc frowned. "Do you know what they were of?"

"People. The town. Stuff like that." She paused to push a wayward curl behind her ear. "I didn't learn about the break-in until I came in yesterday morning."

"So you were the one who reported it?" Marnie asked.

"That's right."

"I don't suppose you have any security cameras?" Luc scanned the ceiling and along the walls.

260

"Never had any need for them before now," she said. "Besides, we're a free museum. We operate on donations from local families and volunteers. There's just not a lot of money for stuff like that."

"I see." Marnie bit her lip, thinking. "Just one last question, if you don't mind?"

"Sure, hon." She motioned her on.

"Who locked up the night the museum was broken into? If possible, I'd like to talk to them, maybe ask them a few questions."

She held up one finger. "Hold on. I have a schedule." She scrolled through her phone, then had to take a pair of glasses from her pocket to see it. "That would have been Joan Anglund who was on duty."

"Joan." Marnie glanced at Luc and back. "The mayor's assistant?"

"You know Joan?" The woman smiled in delight. "She's a dear, isn't she?"

"But I thought you had to be a veteran of the Coast Guard to be a member of the auxiliary."

"Oh no, hon. Coast Guard veterans are welcome, of course, but anyone honorably discharged from any military branch of service can apply, so long as they're US citizens. We've got a few members who are currently active duty too, and one reservist." She chuckled and slid her phone into her pocket. "As you can see, we're a varied bunch."

"I guess I didn't realize," Marnie said.

She smiled warmly. "Most people don't. Anyway, if I can be of any more help, don't hesitate to ask. And feel free to look around while you're here."

"We'll do that. Thank you." Marnie waved as the woman disappeared the way she'd come then dropped her hand and turned to face Luc. "Well? What do you think?"

"I think whoever broke in here had a pretty easy time of it." He strode over to the door. "Did you see this?"

"Lock and key?" Marnie asked, puzzled.

"Not even a deadbolt. The thief literally could have used a credit card to open it."

"Maybe they didn't even have to do that." Marnie gestured toward the back. "If a different person locks up every night…"

Luc's eyebrows rose. "Multiple keys, multiple suspects?"

"That's what I'm thinking." Marnie checked her phone. "It's a little past eleven. Do you have time to make one more stop?"

He snorted. "Until this gets resolved, I have plenty of time." At her stare, he shook his head. "I'm on administrative leave, Marnie. While the theft is being investigated, I won't report to the station."

Chapter Fourteen

A stone formed in Marnie's stomach. "That's not fair. Obviously, we can prove that you were nowhere near the museum when it was robbed."

"Can we?" He shrugged. "And anyway, my CO is still gonna want to investigate for himself." He leaned closer and tucked his finger under her chin. "Stop worrying. It'll be okay."

How he could be so certain, Marnie didn't know, but she didn't want to take away his confidence by asking questions. "We should head over to the mayor's office before Joan leaves for lunch."

Fortunately, it wasn't far. They pulled up just as Joan was approaching her car.

"There she is." Marnie threw open her door and stuck her hand in the air. "Joan, hold up. Could we talk to you for a minute?"

Joan looked curious to see Marnie, until Luc joined her on the sidewalk. Suddenly, she couldn't stop fidgeting with the zipper on her coat. "Marnie, hello. Are you here to see the mayor? We really need to get moving on those permits."

"Actually, it's you we came to see." She held out her hand. "This is—"

"Lucien Graham. I'm aware." She shifted her purse into her other hand and reached for the door handle on her car. "I need to go, Marnie. I was just leaving for lunch."

"I know, and I'm so sorry, but this will only take a minute."

Joan crossed her arms. "All right. What can I do for you?"

"We understand you were working at the free museum the night it was robbed," Luc said.

Joan's gaze slid to him. "Yes, that's right."

"Did you happen to see anything unusual?" Marnie asked. "Maybe notice someone lingering about?"

Her agitation growing, Joan shuffled her feet. "I didn't see anyone. You know, I already talked to the police about this."

"We stopped by the museum just a few minutes ago." Playing a hunch, Marnie leaned closer. "The lady said a few artifacts from the *Pacific Star* were the only things missing."

Joan swallowed hard and lifted her chin. "Yes, that's correct."

"Actually, I believe she also said there were some photos missing," Luc interrupted, his eyes narrowing to fix on Joan.

"Oh…" Her hand fluttered up to touch her cheek. "Yes…I forgot. It's all been so upsetting." She gestured to her car. "I'm really sorry, but I only have thirty minutes for lunch. I need to get back."

She scooted into her car without waiting for an answer and drove away, snow swirling up from the road to block her taillights from view.

Marnie glanced up at Luc. "Is it just me, or was she acting very guilty?"

"But why?" Luc let out a growl of frustration. "And why lie about the items that were stolen? I barely know her. What does she have against me?"

"I suspect the answer is in those pictures."

"Which doesn't help us much, since they're still missing."

"The originals maybe, but I think I might know where we can find copies."

Interest gleamed in Luc's eyes as he squared to face her. "Where?"

Marnie circled back to the car. "Get in. I'll show you."

The warehouse that housed Samuel Peddycord's art gallery was actually two buildings, connected together to form one giant open space. The alley between the buildings had been roofed in glass and now served as an atrium for patrons to sip coffee while they waited for their purchases to be wrapped.

Luc's eyebrows rose as he looked around. "Nice place."

"Mm-hmm." Marnie pointed. "There's Samuel." She glanced up at Luc. After two lukewarm receptions, he might not want to deal with a third. "Do you want to wait here or…?"

He shot her a wry look.

"Right. Let's go then."

Samuel looked up from the computer he was working on as they approached. "Marnie, this is a surprise." He angled his head at Luc. "Graham."

"Peddycord."

With the greetings out of the way, Marnie dove into the purpose of their visit. She told Samuel about their visit to the museum and the photos that were still missing.

Samuel stuffed his hands into the pockets of his expensive trousers. "I heard about the break-in. From what I understand, the missing items were found in the trunk of some guy's car."

He let the words dangle meaningfully.

Marnie bit back a sigh of exasperation. "Obviously you're aware that Luc drove the vehicle the items were found in," she said.

Samuel's lips curled in a sneer. "I'm aware, and I can't say I'm surprised."

He was baiting, but thankfully, Luc wasn't biting. His posture remained casual, his hands hanging loosely at his sides.

Marnie frowned. "Look, Samuel, we just want to know about the missing photos. Apparently, they are the only things that weren't directly related to the *Pacific Star*."

"And?"

"Your family donated a lot of the items in the museum, right? I was hoping maybe you could get us copies of the missing photos."

"How am I supposed to do that if I don't know which ones were taken?"

"The woman at the museum said they were all from the same time period as the *Pacific Star*," Marnie said.

Samuel took a long moment to size up Luc. Unphased, Luc matched his gaze with a hard one of his own. Finally, Marnie stepped between them to end the stare down.

"Well, Samuel? Can you help or not?"

Samuel crossed his arms over his chest, the grin on his face evoking images of a certain Cheshire cat. "I might be able to help, though, to be honest, I'm not sure why I should."

"Then let me make it clear." Marnie matched his posture. "The mayor's project I'm working on could bring a lot of traffic through your place, but only if you're on the approved vendor list."

She wouldn't—and likely couldn't—do that, but she needed to hit someplace where she knew Samuel was vulnerable. Money.

After a long moment, he sighed. "Fine. Do you know where Harbor Light Books is? Go in there and ask for Marge. A couple of

in Cape Disappointment, Washington

years ago, my family put together a history of the area. You'll find copies of the missing pictures in there."

"Thank you, Samuel." She meant it. Luc too seemed grateful. He stuck out his hand. Even more surprising, Samuel took it.

It didn't take long for Marge to find the book Samuel mentioned. In the section on the *Pacific Star*, Marnie and Luc perused page after page of pictures. Marnie only recognized the people in a few.

"I'm not sure this is going to help," she said after a few moments.

"Maybe Pop can help. We should take the book to him. Let him look through the pictures."

Marnie agreed, Luc paid for the book, and they left. Marnie tapped the book with her finger. "You know, I'm still thinking about the way Joan acted when she saw you. But what possible tie could she have to these pictures?"

"Hopefully, Pop will shed some light on that too."

When they got to the house, Marnie pulled out her phone. "Hold on one second, will you? I need to call the office and let Kate and Brandon know where I am."

Kate answered on the second ring. Marnie explained she was with Luc, then, remembering something Joan had said, she asked, "Have you had a chance to file the permits for the family day?"

"I...uh...sorry, Marnie. It slipped my mind. I'll take care of it this afternoon."

"No problem. Thanks, Kate. I'll talk to you later."

"Everything okay?" Luc asked as she walked back into the living room. At some point, he'd made coffee, and the aroma of roasted beans filled the air. He handed her a mug.

"Fine. Just need to make sure we stay on track with the mayor's project." She motioned to George sitting on the couch with the book open on his lap. "See anything interesting?"

"A lot of history in these pages. Unfortunately, our family plays a big part, and not in a good way."

Compassion swelling her chest, Marnie went to sit next to George. "What about Joan Anglund? Is there anything in there that might involve her family?"

"Oh no. Joan didn't move to Ilwaco until she was in her twenties, about thirty years ago. She was stationed here with the Coast Guard."

"She must've really liked it here." Luc sat in a chair opposite them. "Doesn't she have family somewhere?"

"None to speak of." George cleared his throat and lowered his gaze.

Luc and Marnie exchanged a look.

"Pop?" Luc leaned forward to rest his elbows on his knees. "Is there something you're not telling us?"

He looked uncomfortable, but he nodded. "Joan…well, she may have had a thing for me when she first moved here."

Marnie shot a glance at Luc to see how he was taking the news. As always, he appeared unperturbed.

"And?"

George rubbed his thumb across his eyelid. After a long moment, he spoke. "Remember when I told you last night that things started happening because of the gossip in town? Your mother went through a lot of the same things you have, Son. Anonymous notes, ugly pranks. I always thought…maybe…Joan was involved." He held up his hand. "I can't prove any of that, now, and it doesn't explain why she would take the photos."

Excitement built in Marnie's chest. "But she was acting strangely, and she lied about the photos being missing. Doesn't that point to her being guilty?"

"Guilty, or ashamed?" Luc said quietly. "She couldn't look me in the eye. Oftentimes, when a person does that, it's because they're embarrassed by something they've done."

"Exactly. Like trying to run you out of town," Marnie insisted.

Luc shook his head. "I don't know, Marnie. I'm not convinced she's our culprit. Call it a gut feeling."

Marnie's shoulders slumped, and she turned back to George. "Okay, what else is in there? Anything that can help?"

"Well, there are a couple of photos of my grandfather." He turned the book for Marnie and Luc to see and tapped the page. "Right there. That's the first Lucien Graham."

Luc grimaced. "The one who stirred up so much trouble for the rest of us."

"Oh, I think we stirred plenty of our own troubles," George said with a wry chuckle. His gaze turned somber as he looked at his son. "Did I ever tell you why I chose to name you after your great-grandfather?"

Marnie jerked her head up. Luc shook his head.

A sad smile curved George's lips. "The Graham name hasn't been worth much since Lucien Graham did what he did. Don't get me wrong, we all made our own choices. Still, I sort of hoped that by naming you after him…well, maybe you could change all that, if anyone could."

Luc bent closer to the page to study the picture. In it, four men in shirtsleeves and ties stood side by side, the Ilwaco shipyard in the background. "That's Lucien," he said quietly, pointing. "Who are the other three?"

George slipped on his glasses to look. "That one there is John Baker. His family left Ilwaco after the shipwreck." He frowned and tapped the third figure in the photo. "Don't rightly know who that fellow is, but the one next to him is Robert Winther."

"Winther? Kate's great-grandfather?" Marnie squinted to see him.

"You know, I think I saw him in another picture." George flipped back a couple of pages and pointed. "There he is."

Once again, he stood alongside Lucien.

Marnie frowned. "George, do you remember anything about him? Was he partners with Lucien?"

"Partners? No." George scratched his head. "Though I do remember there being questions about Robert's involvement with that whole shipwreck business."

"What kind of questions?" Luc asked.

"Well, it seemed some folks thought maybe he was in deeper cahoots with Lucien than he would admit. It never was proven though, and most people just didn't want to believe a man as upstanding as Robert would have any part in what happened."

Marnie rose to pace, a seedling of an idea taking root in her head. "Luc, do you remember what Joan said earlier today? She said we needed to get moving on the permits for the family day."

He nodded, his gaze fixed to her as she moved from the couch to the window and back. "I remember."

Marnie stopped and turned to him. "I asked Kate about them when I called the office. She said it had slipped her mind."

Luc glanced at George, who looked as puzzled as he. "We're not following, Marnie."

"A couple of days ago, she asked if there was anything she could do, and I said she could take care of the permits. She left the office. If she didn't go to the mayor's office, where did she go?"

"Maybe she ran an errand?" George offered.

"She did say something about running by to see her mom's attorney, something about working out the details of her father's will." She angled her head, thinking. "Do either of you know an attorney named Lyle?"

Both Luc and George shook their heads. The feeling of dread that had been growing in Marnie's stomach moved up into her chest. Luc stood and crossed to her.

"What's wrong?"

"Do you think we could swing over to the service station where you got your truck fixed?"

"Sure. Do you want to go now?"

Marnie reached for her coat. "I think so. I'm sorry, George. I'll explain when we get back." She looked at Luc. "Ready?"

Marnie didn't look at Luc as they made the drive to the service station. How could she? If her hunch was right, her best friend and business partner—

She left the thought unfinished. It couldn't be. Not Kate. What reason could she have? The possibilities nearly brought her to tears.

After pulling into the station, Marnie sniffed and reached for the door handle. "Let's go."

"Hold on." Luc caught her hand. "Marnie, look at me."

She blinked past a sheen of tears. Finally, drawing a steadying breath, she turned.

"What's going on? Why are we here?"

Marnie glanced through the windshield at the service station. "The blue coats. Whoever dropped off the note to you was wearing one. I heard Kate talking to someone named Lyle. She said he was an attorney."

"But you think he works here?"

Marnie nodded miserably. "I think she may have hired him to do it for her. And maybe she hired him to do other things too."

"I see." He sucked in a breath. "We don't have to do this. I don't care what people think, you know."

"Your career?" she whispered.

He dropped his gaze, then dragged it back up again, the misery in his gaze matching hers.

Marnie grasped his hand. "We have to find out, Luc. If I'm right, and Kate is behind this, it's not fair to you, or George, to let her get away with it."

His jaw hardened, and then he nodded.

They climbed from the car and made their way inside to the counter, where Marnie asked to speak to Lyle.

"Yeah, he's here. Hold on a minute and I'll find him for you," the attendant said.

Soon, a man in a blue coat walked in from outside. On his head was a black knit hat.

"No nametag," Marnie said, elbowing Luc in the side.

When the man saw them, he hesitated near the door. Marnie crossed to him. "Are you Lyle?"

"Yeah," he said warily.

Marnie stuck out her hand. "I'm Marnie Stewart."

He shook it. "Nice to meet ya."

"And this is my friend, Luc Graham. Lucien," she corrected, remembering the name the person making the delivery had given.

Lyle's eyes widened. Glancing around the station, he motioned toward a break room off the main area. "Let's go in there."

Marnie followed him in, trailed by Luc. Though it pained her to ask, Marnie knew the best way to get answers was just to spit it out. She drew a bracing breath and lifted her chin. "Lyle, do you know Kate Winther?"

Lyle's gaze slid from her to Luc and back. "Maybe."

"Did she hire you to deliver a note to the Coast Guard station?"

He swiped the hat from his head and scratched above his ear. "I have no idea what you're talking about."

Marnie's heart leapt. Could she be wrong about Kate?

"What about the artifacts from the museum?" Luc pointed to the security cameras mounted on the walls near the exits. "Did she ask you to plant them in the trunk of the car I was driving?"

Lyle's breathing changed, became shallow. "Look, I had no idea what was in that bag she gave me. She told me to put it in the trunk and forget about it. That's what I did."

With each word, Marnie's heart sank lower. "So, you did leave the note?"

He growled nervously. "Yeah, I left it. She paid me a hundred bucks. Am I going to get in trouble for this?"

That was all he was worried about? Filled with anger, Marnie stepped toward him. Luc blocked her path.

"Don't. It's not worth it," he said, lowering his voice. "It wasn't him, Marnie," he continued when she strained against his hold.

Their eyes met, and he shook his head.

How could he be so calm when she felt so outraged? Gradually, she relaxed. "You're right." She peered around him at Lyle. "Luc's commanding officer may be calling you. I assume you'll tell him the same thing you told us?"

"Yeah, sure." Lyle looked around, clearly anxious to be anywhere but here. "I gotta get back to work."

At Marnie's nod, he skittered out the door. Weary to her marrow, she rubbed her hands over her face, dreading what was coming, knowing she had no choice but to tackle it head-on.

"We need to confront Kate."

"Not *confront*, Marnie. Maybe…we just ask her why."

"I…" She shook her head helplessly. "I don't understand how you can be so calm about this. Do you realize what she was trying to do?"

Luc's sigh was heavy. "I guess it's because I've spent most of my life fighting what people think of me. Wishing someone would give me a chance. I don't know why Kate did this, *if* she did this. I do know, before we do anything else, that I want to give her a chance to explain."

Marnie's heart melted at the peace she read in his eyes. By all rights, he should be furious, but he wasn't. He just looked sad.

in Cape Disappointment, Washington

She laid her hand on his arm. "We'll go by the office. We can talk there."

"Will Brandon be there?"

Surprised, she nodded.

"I'd rather wait until we can speak to her alone."

Once again, his answer melted her heart. "Okay." She looked at her watch. "The office doesn't close for a couple of hours yet, but I can text her and ask her to meet me after work."

He agreed, and a few minutes later, Marnie had set up a meeting at the Winther house. Though Marnie would have preferred someplace a little more neutral, Kate insisted, saying she didn't like to leave her mother by herself. Reasoning it out, Marnie thought it might be best to meet in a place where Kate wouldn't feel threatened.

Since they hadn't eaten, they grabbed something to eat at a local restaurant, the meal sliding tastelessly down Marnie's throat. What would she do if Kate turned out to be guilty? Could their friendship survive such a blow?

She reached for her napkin and blew her nose. At Luc's questioning look, she said, "I was just thinking about all the times Kate stayed over at my house, or me at hers. She was always such a good friend, Luc. I can hardly believe…"

More hot tears threatened.

"Wait. Just wait until we've had a chance to hear her side," he said quietly. "It may not change anything, but maybe it will. Okay?"

She nodded, and after another cup of coffee, they left to head for Kate's house.

One of the oldest homes in Ilwaco, the Winther home was a two-story brick structure, with a porch that wrapped around the front and two sides, and two columns flanking the front door.

Marnie's hand shook as she approached to knock. As many times as she'd been in this house, this was the first time she'd dreaded it.

Kate opened the door, a smile on her face. "Hey, Marnie." Her gaze slid to Luc over Marnie's shoulder, and her smile fled. "What... uh...what's going on?"

Marnie shook her head sadly. "We need to talk, Kate. Can we come in?"

Her shoulders sagging, Kate pushed the door wider.

"Who is it, Kate?" Mrs. Winther's voice drifted from the kitchen.

"It's Marnie, Mom."

"Oh." There was a rattling of dishes, and then Mrs. Winther walked out, an apron tied around her waist. "I was just making dinner. Can you stay—?"

She cut short as she caught sight of Luc and switched her gaze to Kate. Swinging between them, Kate cut her from view.

"Marnie and I need to talk. Will you excuse us for a minute, Mom?"

Mrs. Winther still looked hesitant as she moved back down the hall, casting glances over her shoulder.

Kate motioned to the study off the main hall. "Let's go in here."

Moving to sit behind her father's desk, Kate looked cool and in control as she met Marnie's gaze. "What is this about?"

"Kate," Marnie whispered, pleading.

For a split second, the controlled mask slipped. But only for a second. It was replaced by anger, and something else Marnie couldn't quite put her finger on.

She glared at Luc. "Why did you come back here? Why couldn't you just stay away?"

"I told you why," Marnie interrupted. "His dad is sick."

"A sickness he brought on himself," Kate spat.

Shocked, Marnie let her mouth fall open. "You don't mean that."

Kate propped her elbows on the desk and brought her clasped hands to her lips.

Marnie eased into a chair across from her. Luc did the same. Kate didn't look at either of them.

"You can't prove I did anything wrong," she said, shocking Marnie further. "There are no security cameras at the museum."

"We talked to Lyle," Luc said. "He told us you paid him."

"So?" She swung her gaze to him. "He was an errand boy, nothing more. As far as you know, he could have been delivering groceries."

"That won't hold up, and you know it," Marnie said, starting to feel angry now. "There are security cameras at the service station. As soon as Lyle figures out that the thefts could be pinned on him, he'll point to you. What I don't understand is why, Kate. What would drive you to do this? What do you have against Luc?"

She slumped back in her chair. "I don't have anything against him."

"Then who?" Marnie insisted. "And why?"

"I know." All heads swung toward the door as Mrs. Winther stepped into the room, a worn leather Bible in her hands.

Kate immediately rose, knocking her chair against a tall bookshelf. "Mom."

Her voice cut sharply through the silence. Mrs. Winther ignored her and walked straight to Luc.

"Before you read this, I hope you'll believe that we...Kate and I...had no idea."

"You don't have to show him that." Desperation rose in Kate's voice. "I can figure this out, Mom."

She looked sadly at her daughter and then at Luc. "I don't know what all Kate has done, but I do believe whatever it was, she did it to protect me."

She held the Bible out to him. When Luc took it, Kate let out a small gasp.

"Read the inside front cover," Mrs. Winther said gently. She reached out, squeezed Luc's shoulder, then went to stand next to her daughter.

For several long seconds, Luc read silently to himself. When he finished, he hung his head, sorrow carving lines across his brow.

"I'm so sorry." He looked up at Mrs. Winther. "I didn't know."

"No one did."

Mrs. Winther's knees gave, and Kate slipped her arm around her mother's waist. Leaping to his feet, Luc helped her into the chair he'd vacated. Mrs. Winther sniffed, pulled a tattered napkin from her pocket, and pressed it to her eyes.

"That is the Winther family Bible." She nodded to the corner of the desk where Luc had laid it. "I always knew of its existence, but Kate's father would never let me see it. He kept it in the safe until the day he died. I think he wanted to protect me." She reached up to press her hand to Kate's cheek. "Like you."

Kate sighed and straightened to look at Marnie. "My great-grandfather, Robert Winther, knew about the scheme to wreck the *Pacific Star*. Right before the incident, he took out an insurance policy on the ship that made him a lot of money. Though it looked bad, no one believed he could've done something so wrong, and he never admitted otherwise. He just stood back and let Lucien Graham take the blame for what happened alone. In the end, he couldn't stand the guilt he'd lived with all those years. He wrote his confession in the family Bible and passed it on to his son before he died." Her lips trembled. "I couldn't let the truth get out."

Marnie shook her head, disbelief making her stutter. "But why Luc, Kate? You just heard him say he didn't know anything about your great-grandfather's guilt."

Kate rounded on her. "Because I heard Luc's father talking to your mother about a month ago at the café. They were in the booth behind mine and obviously didn't know I was there. Mr. Graham told your mom that he'd always wondered if my great-grandfather was as good a man as everyone said he was. He said he didn't think that one man alone could do what Lucien Graham had done."

Marnie raised her hands. "But, Kate, that still doesn't make sense. Why did you wait until Luc came home to do all this? When it was his dad you were afraid of?"

Kate shrugged. "I wasn't afraid of Luc's dad. Who was going to believe him? Everyone would just think his brain was affected by all the alcohol he'd drunk over the years." She glared at Luc. "But then Luc came back...and I knew that even though people wouldn't listen to

Luc the troublemaker, they might listen to Luc the coast guardsman." She sniffed and frowned at Marnie. "Even you thought he'd changed."

"B-but how does that...why would you..." She swallowed and began again. "That's why you did this? Almost ruin Luc's career because you didn't want the truth to get out?" She threw up her hands in exasperation.

Luc grunted softly. "She was afraid her family would receive the same backlash mine did."

Mrs. Winther grabbed Marnie's hand. "She was afraid of what it would do to me."

Unable to meet Mrs. Winther's gaze, Marnie looked at her lifelong friend. "Kate."

It was then that Kate's resolve crumbled. She dropped to her knees next to her mother and hugged her. "I'm so sorry, Mom."

"I know, sweetheart," Mrs. Winther said, tears flowing down her own cheeks as she stroked Kate's hair.

Catching Marnie's eye, Luc tipped his head toward the door. "Let's give them some time."

Outside, despair washed over Marnie in waves. Her best friend. Her confidant. Unable to control the emotion gushing out of her, she pressed her face into Luc's chest and let him lead her to the car.

"Keys." He held out his hand.

Marnie looked at the house in panic. "We can't leave. What if she...?"

"She's not going to leave, Marnie. In fact, I think her mom will insist she go to the authorities and my CO to explain what happened."

"But the gas line...what if your dad had been hurt?"

"You said it yourself, Marnie. It wasn't about my dad. I was supposed to be driving that truck. At most, Kate probably figured it'd be an inconvenience. She never meant to hurt me or Pop."

He looked at his hand and back at her. Sighing, Marnie pulled her keys from her pocket and laid them in his palm, then let him help her into the car. Closing her eyes, she laid her head against the seat as he drove. And drove. Finally, they pulled to a stop outside the Cape Disappointment Lighthouse.

He smiled sheepishly at her. "I needed a minute to think."

Marnie joined him in staring at the whitecaps rolling off the bay. "I can see why your dad likes coming here."

"Me too." Luc glanced sideways at her then twisted on the seat to take her hand. "Marnie, I can understand why Kate was so afraid. Think about the rumors that would have been stirred, the gossip. She didn't want her mother to go through what mine did."

"The *Pacific Star* went down years ago, Luc. People aren't going to react now the way they did then."

"For Kate and her mother, the *Pacific Star* went down the day Mr. Winther died and they discovered the truth about their family."

Marnie shook her head at him in disbelief. "You aren't the same man you were when you left here, Luc Graham."

He smiled and lifted her hand to his lips. "I hope not. I hope today I'd be the kind of man your stepfather could approve of and accept." His gaze changed, deepened. "That you could accept."

Looking at him, at the way his hand shook holding hers, her chest tightened.

"Marnie, I've wanted for so long to tell you how I feel. How I've always felt."

She pulled her hand away. "Luc, wait."

"I can't, Marnie. I've waited too long already." His voice lowered to a whisper. "I love you. I always have. Marnie, will you marry me?"

The hope in his eyes nearly crushed her. Robbed her of breath. Letting go a shuddering cry, she said, "I'm sorry, Luc. I can't. Not yet. There's just…something I have to do first."

Chapter Fifteen

Later that night, Luc eyed Marnie warily as she stood on his porch, her mother smiling and chatting over her shoulder.

"I can't tell you how relieved I am to have all this nasty business behind us," she said, pushing past Luc to go into the house. "Where's George? I want to talk to him."

"Kitchen." Luc hitched his thumb over his shoulder, but his gaze was still on Marnie. "I didn't expect to see you back here tonight."

"I know, and I'm so sorry." Her heart felt lighter than it had in days. Freer. She held out her hand. "Can we talk?"

Luc hesitated a moment, then reached behind the door for his coat and shrugged it on. "What's going on, Marnie?"

His words cut sharply. He was hurt and angry, and of course he would be, under the circumstances. She motioned toward the sidewalk. "Let's go for a walk."

At his pause, Marnie felt a moment of panic. She hadn't stopped to consider what she would do if he refused to listen…the way she had.

"I promise, I can explain," she leaned in to say.

He relented with a nod.

"I went to see Brandon," Marnie said, matching her strides to his longer ones, her breath mingling with his on the frosty air. "After we left the lighthouse. I owed it to him to tell him that there would never be anything between us. There can't be. I'm in love with someone else."

Luc drew to a halt and swung to look at her, his eyes narrowed against the sun. At the look of hope that crossed his face, she smiled and lifted her palm to his cheek. "I wasn't free to say yes to your proposal until I'd cleared things between me and him. I've done that now."

Puffing out a breath, he covered her hand and dragged it down to his chest. "Are you saying…?"

"Ask me again," Marnie whispered. "Will you? Ask me one more time. I promise, it will be the last time you ever need to."

Dropping to his knee, her hand still clasped in his, Luc stared up at her. He swallowed, his Adam's apple showing just how nervous he was. "Marnie, will you—"

That was all he got out.

"Yes!" She squealed and threw herself into his arms. "Yes, Luc, I'll marry you. I love you. I always have. And from this moment on, I don't care who knows it."

Feeling his tears wet on her cheeks, Marnie knew their future was bright. It wouldn't be easy, but the best things in life never were. The only thing that mattered, now and forever, was that they would walk through what came together.

Rising to his feet, Luc swiped a tear from her lashes. "Marnie, are you sure? You don't have to answer now, you know. I won't pressure you—"

"I'm sure, Luc. I've never been more sure of anything in my life." She hesitated and bit her lip. He gently rubbed his thumb over it.

"What's wrong?"

"I was just thinking about what your dad said about your mom...and Joan. If she was the person who tried to drive your mother away, wouldn't you want to know for sure?"

Luc thought for a long moment, and then shook his head. "I made my peace with all of that a long time ago. Pops too. We're okay leaving it in the past where it belongs."

He smiled at her and then glanced back at the house. "We should probably tell your mother we're getting married."

"Oh, I think she already knows." She pointed at the window where there was some hasty movement, and laughed. "I think they both do."

Luc smiled and pulled her close. "And you think they approve?"

"I do." Her breath caught at the promise she would soon make. "But we'll talk to them later. Right now, there's something else I would rather do."

He leaned in closer to rest his forehead against hers. "And what is that?" he asked, his voice husky.

"I'd rather kiss you."

His lips quirked in that precious, dear smile. "I'm happy to oblige."

And then his lips closed over hers, as sweet as she remembered but different too. Because he was different. There was no desperation this time. No hurt or angst. His kiss was tender, and passionate, and full of promise.

It was all she could have hoped for.

Dear Reader,

Three things made writing *Love's A Mystery in Cape Disappointment, Washington, Love's Beacon* a joy for me!

1). Spending time on Cape Disappointment. Only two hours from my home in Portland, Oregon, Cape Disappointment is a magical place. I spent hours exploring! It's one of the most majestic landscapes I've ever seen. The views of the Pacific Ocean, the Columbia River, and both the rocky and sandy beaches to the north and south are truly magnificent, and the old-growth trees, the mossy trails, and the scent of the forest add an earthy comfort to the rugged terrain. The setting is unlike anywhere else I've ever written about!

2). Delving into the past of the area. The history of Cape Disappointment is layered with intrigue, from the original Chinook people to the early explorers, from the first European settlers to the over two thousand ships that have wrecked in the Graveyard of the Pacific. As a history major, researching the area was a thrill!

3). Working with author Lisa Ludwig. The life of a writer can be solitary, so I cherish all collaborative projects that come my way! Before Lisa and I chatted about the contemporary and historical threads, we'd separately come up with parallel ideas for our stories. Once we emailed and talked and then emailed some more, we marveled at how our original ideas had already connected the two stories. As we researched, it was fun to share sources and photos, both from the past and present, and also share the excitement of writing about such a beautiful and fascinating area.

I hope you enjoyed reading these stories as much as we enjoyed writing them!

Signed,
Leslie

Dear Reader,

Someone once told me life is full of disappointments. While that is certainly true, I have also found life to be full of promise and excitement, joy and victories. It is these periods of blessing that carry me through the darker days and remind me of God's goodness, even when the challenges ahead seem bitter. Without my even realizing it, that message seeped onto the page!

It was an honor to be able to write such a story for Luc and Marnie. Luc especially touched my heart. With each word, I wanted to pay tribute to the men and women in our armed forces who daily choose the difficult task of defending our great nation. While Luc was far from perfect, his willingness to accept his past and move forward in the confidence of his salvation and forgiveness was a message for us all. I pray this story is a blessing to you, dear reader. May you also go forward in the peace that is found in a relationship with the Lord.

Sincerely,
Elizabeth Ludwig

About the Authors

Leslie Gould

Leslie Gould is the #1 bestselling and Christy-Award-winning author of over forty novels. She's also won two Faith, Hope, and Love Readers' Choice Awards and has been a finalist for the Carol Award. She and her husband, Peter, live in Portland, Oregon, and enjoy hiking, traveling, and spending time with their adult children and grandbaby. Visit Leslie at LeslieGould.com and follow her on Facebook and Instagram to learn more about her books and writing journey.

Elizabeth Ludwig

Elizabeth Ludwig is a *USA Today* bestselling author whose work has been featured on Novel Rocket, More to Life Magazine, and Christian Fiction Online Magazine. She is an accomplished speaker and teacher, often attending conferences and seminars where she lectures on editing for fiction writers, crafting effective novel proposals, and conducting successful editor/agent interviews. Her first novel, *Where the Truth Lies*, which she co-authored with Janelle Mowery, earned her the IWA Writer of the Year Award. Her second novel, *Died in the Wool*, also co-authored with Janelle Mowery, was nominated for a Carol Award.

In 2012, her Edge of Freedom series released from Bethany House Publishers. Books one and two, *No Safe Harbor* and *Dark Road Home*, respectively, earned 4 Stars from RT Book Reviews. Book three in the series, *Tide and Tempest*, received top honors with 4½ Stars and was named a finalist for the Gayle Wilson Award of Excellence.

Elizabeth was also honored to be awarded a HOLT Medallion in 2018 for her book, *A Tempting Taste of Mystery*, part of the Sugarcreek Amish Mysteries series from Guideposts. She was named a dual-finalist in the 2020 Selah Awards for her novella *In Hot Water*, part of the bestselling collection, *The Coffee Club Mysteries* from Barbour Publishing and *Garage Sale Secret*, part of the Mysteries of Lancaster County series from Guideposts. Her latest release *Christmas in Galway*, part of the *Christmas Lights and Romance* collection from Winged Publications, was a finalist for the 2021 Carol Award.

Along with her husband and children, Elizabeth makes her home in the great state of Texas. To learn more, sign up for her newsletter at ElizabethLudwig.com or visit her on Facebook.

Story Behind the Name

Cape Disappointment, Washington

Cape Disappointment overlooks both the Pacific Ocean and the Columbia River in the very southwestern corner of Washington State, on the Long Beach Peninsula. In 1788, British trader John Mears named it "Cape Disappointment" because, while looking for the elusive Northwest Passage, he only found what he thought was a bay. His disappointment led to the name.

Four years later, American Captain Robert Gray sailed over the bar and discovered the body of water wasn't a bay as Mears had claimed—but a mighty river. Captain Gray named it the Columbia, after his ship the *Columbia Rediviva*.

But by then the name Cape Disappointment had already stuck.

The cape was no disappointment to the Chinook People, the original inhabitants of the area. They called the cape "Kah'eese." It is also not a disappointment to the thousands of people each year who visit Cape Disappointment, which is preserved as a Washington State Park. Two historic lighthouses, military fortifications from the Civil War era and World War II, the Lewis and Clark Interpretive Center, camping sites, and miles of trails make the cape a fascinating vacation spot. The next-door town of Ilwaco offers restaurants, shops, lodging, a waterfront area, a marina, and the Columbia Pacific Heritage Museum.

If you have a chance to visit, DO! You won't be disappointed by Cape Disappointment either!

Enjoy this Taste of Ilwaco!

Salmon Cioppino

Cioppino can be made using a variety of fresh fish and shellfish. The key is to use only the freshest seafood. Additional shellfish that may be used include calamari, ocean prawns, lobster, scallops, or Alaskan king crab.

Ingredients for sauce (make this first):

- 2 tablespoons olive oil
- 1 cup minced onion
- 1 tablespoon minced garlic
- 2 tablespoons minced parsley
- pinch of coarsely ground black pepper
- ¼ cup fresh basil, chopped
- 2 tablespoons fresh marjoram, chopped
- ½ tablespoon ground fennel seeds
- 20 ounces diced sweet plum tomatoes
- 6 ounces tomato paste
- ½ gallon clam juice
- 12 ounces cooking wine

Directions:

Sauté onions and garlic in olive oil over low heat until they become soft. Add parsley and seasonings. Cook for one minute. Add tomatoes, tomato paste, clam juice and white wine. Let simmer for 45 minutes then set aside.

Ingredients:

- 2 tablespoons olive oil
- 1 teaspoon of minced garlic
- 3 quarts Cioppino Sauce (recipe above)
- 8 pieces or ¾ lb. firm white fish (halibut or lingcod), cut in pieces
- ½ lb. fresh king salmon, cut in pieces
- 1½ pounds (approx. 3 per serving) mussels
- 1½ pounds (approx. 3 per serving) Manila clams
- 1 whole cracked Dungeness crab
- ¼ lb. small spot prawns

Directions:

Sauté white fish and salmon in olive oil and garlic. Add all shellfish and Cioppino Sauce. Cover and steam until fish is cooked (clams and mussels should be open) but do not boil. Arrange in bowl and serve.

Read on for a sneak peek of another exciting book in the Love's a Mystery series!

Love's a Mystery *in* Cut and Shoot, Texas
by Janice Thompson & Ruth Logan Herne

Love Pieced Together
By Janice Thompson

Cut and Shoot, Texas
Saturday, December 14, 1912

"Why didn't you tell me Gilbert Sutton was coming home for Christmas?"

Patience Cochran ducked behind a mercantile shelf filled with lanterns and peered out from behind them. Across the room, she caught a glimpse of Gilbert. Her Gilbert.

Well, not hers anymore, though years of childhood friendship had led everyone in the town of Cut and Shoot to believe they would one day marry. Of course, that was before the big uproar last summer. These days, she wouldn't be caught dead speaking to him, for fear of what folks would say.

"What are you doing, Patience?" Her cousin Adeline planted her hands on her hips and shot a glance her way. "Why are you hiding back there behind those shelves?"

"Shh!" Patience put her finger over her lips and reached out to pull her cousin closer. "You know perfectly well. The Cochrans and Suttons haven't spoken since that awful day last summer. I can't let Gil see me."

"Well, that's just plain silly." Adeline brushed a loose blond hair from her face. "You and Gil have been best friends since you were little. You can't let a little thing like a town feud come between you."

Patience adjusted her position so that she could see between a couple of the beveled glass hurricane lanterns. She observed Gil chatting with a handsome young man with dark, wavy hair.

She turned back to face her cousin. "Easy for you to say. You don't live here anymore. You have no idea how bad things have been. The whole town is split right down the middle. And Gil has been living and working in Conroe, so I've barely seen him." Until now.

With a wave of her hand, Adeline appeared to dismiss any concerns. "It's just stuff and nonsense. And I refuse to have my Christmas visit spoiled by childish squabbling. I've come all the way from Houston to be with my cousins for the holidays, and I won't have something as silly as a misunderstanding ruin my visit."

"It was a bit more than a misunderstanding, Adeline," Patience said. "There were knives and guns involved."

"Pooh. No one got hurt, right?"

"Not physically. But my little brother was traumatized."

Adeline batted those big brown eyes of hers and reached for Patience's hand. "Ernest will be fine. Now come on out of there, and let's say hello. That's the proper thing to do when you run into an old friend in a public setting, is it not?"

Patience swallowed hard and summoned the courage to face Gilbert. She took that first step, but then someone else caught her eye, and she ducked behind the lanterns once again. "Oh, no! He's with his grandmother." She peered across the store at Florence Sutton and noticed how frail the elderly woman looked. "This is dreadful! I knew we were taking a risk, coming into town on a Saturday."

"For pity's sake." Adeline reached for a tiny perfume bottle and gave it a closer look. "That's ridiculous. A person should be able to come to town whenever they like without having to worry about what anyone else thinks of it." She placed the bottle back on the shelf. "Now, come on out, or I'll drag you out. And I assure you, that would not be pretty."

"But you know me, Adeline," Patience said. "I can't abide feuding. No doubt any encounter between the Cochrans and Suttons would end poorly. I can't risk that."

Adeline seemed perplexed by this statement. "But you've always loved Florence Sutton. She's Granny's best friend, after all."

"Not anymore. They don't speak."

Adeline's eyes widened. "I don't believe you! I thought you were just exaggerating in those letters you sent last summer."

"I wasn't exaggerating, trust me." Patience took hold of her cousin's arm and pulled her a little closer as Florence and Gilbert filled a basket with items for purchase. Her heart thumped in her ears as Gil's jovial voice rang out just a few feet away from her. She ducked down a bit lower and tried to make herself invisible.

That's when she heard a little girl singing. The youngster trilled a familiar Christmas carol. Patience peeked out once more and saw that Gil's younger sister Violet had arrived. The whole family must be here. Violet made her way to the candy counter, where Florence—ever the doting grandmother—offered to purchase licorice sticks. Then Florence turned her attention to a shelf with homemade preserves. A shelf that happened to be just a few feet away from where Patience now stood.

She had no choice but to plan an escape, to get out of the mercantile while the gettin' was good, as Granny Cochran was prone to say. Patience took a couple of steps in the direction of the door, tiptoeing across the creaky, wood-planked floor. Unfortunately, she was so busy making sure Gilbert didn't see her that she bumped into a bin that was balanced precariously on the edge of a table. It came crashing down, creating quite the stir. Potatoes rolled across the floor and under the shelves. In her attempt to fetch them, she tripped and fell head-first into a stack of flour sacks, breaking one open.

Patience sprang up as quickly as she could and brushed the white powder from her hair and skirt, doing her best not to groan aloud.

"That's one way to hide from your enemies." Adeline giggled and faced Gilbert, who was rushing their way. She greeted him with a smile and a friendly, "Hello, stranger!"

He responded with a rushed, "Hello," then turned his gaze to Patience.

"I had no idea we were expecting snow." A smile tipped up the edges of Gilbert's lips. "That's a first for these parts."

"Very funny." Patience straightened her skirts as she stepped across the busted flour bag, then did her best to brush the white powder from her blouse. She must look absolutely ridiculous.

He brushed flour from her cheek. "I won't ask how this happened."

"Thank you."

"But were you here all along? I didn't see you when we came in."

"Well, I—"

"Were you hiding, by chance?"

"Who, me? Hiding? Now why would I need to do that?" She turned her attention to a display of baking powder on a nearby shelf. "I was just giving the baking supplies a closer look."

"Since when have you had an interest in baking? Your granny tried to teach you to make biscuits a dozen times, and you were a sensational flop."

"I was no such thing. It just so happens I excel at biscuit-making. Ask anyone in town."

"I would if I could, but half the town isn't speaking to me." He gave her a knowing look. But did he have to be handsome while doing it? Did those bright blue eyes of his have to twinkle with such merriment? They captivated her, just as they always had. And his honey-blond hair still fell fetchingly over his forehead.

How could she avoid staring? And how could she get past those old feelings that threatened to creep up, even now?

"Only half the town?" Adeline chuckled as she rested her hand on Gil's arm, a move that rankled Patience. "I'd think you would have more enemies than that, Gilbert Sutton. As I recall, your antics turned nearly every townsperson against you, back in the day."

"I've grown up since then." He smiled. "And I can't remember the last time I pulled a prank on anyone."

Patience wasn't so sure about that. The lawsuit he had helped the Suttons file against her family came off as the worst prank ever. Only, it happened to be real. Very, very real.

Suddenly he didn't look so handsome anymore. He was the enemy, after all, as were all the Suttons and their crew.

"Well, I'm glad to hear those days are behind you." Adeline leaned in a little too close to him. Was she flirting?

On the other side of the store, the handsome stranger with the dark wavy hair was asking Mr. Pepperdine about the grocery items he wanted to purchase. Adeline must've decided she was the perfect person to answer his questions, because she strolled in his direction and engaged him in conversation.

In her nervous state Patience began to finger the products on the shelf, finally grabbing hold of a book.

"What's this?" Gil quirked a brow. "You're reading dime novels now?"

"I am?" She glanced down, and heat rose to her cheeks when she saw the title. *Knickerbocker's Sixpenny Tales.* "No, no. This is for Granny Cochran. A Christmas gift."

"I see." He took the book and flipped it over, skimming the back cover copy. "Your granny is now reading salacious tales of intrigue and romance?"

"Yes, well, she might enjoy it."

Violet was now singing "O Little Town of Bethlehem." This afforded Patience the perfect opportunity to change the subject.

"I hear the children are caroling tonight."

"Violet has asked me to transport several of the carolers in my motorcar. Are you coming?"

"Heavens, no." She shook her head. "There's no telling who will be there, and I can't risk—"

"Singing? You can't risk singing the praises of God with your fellow men? And women? And children?"

"No, I can't," she responded.

"That's just silly." Adeline reappeared, just in time to interject her thoughts on the matter.

"I agree." Gilbert gave her a pensive look. "After all, the town that sings together, stays together."

"This, from the man who helped the Suttons file a lawsuit against the Cochrans?" She didn't mean to mention that, but the words were out now, and she couldn't unsay them.

His smile immediately faded. "Patience, you know I had no choice. My uncle's law firm took the case. He put me on it. I had to—"

"Had to hurt the very people you'd spent most of your life claiming to care about." She shoved the dime novel back onto the shelf. Knickerbocker could wait.

"*Claiming* to care about?" The pain in those beautiful blue eyes was undeniable.

"I heard you were working with a big law firm over in Conroe," Adeline crooned. "I'm so proud of you."

"Proud of him?" Patience could hardly believe her cousin's response. "He represents the people who sued us after the feud." She still couldn't believe he had betrayed her family in such a way. Was nothing sacred anymore, even a friendship that went back twenty years?

"Well, not your family specifically," he said. "And to be fair—"

"There was nothing fair about it." She planted her hands on her hips and glared at him, determined to lower her voice so as not to draw attention. "And we shouldn't even be speaking about such things, especially in public. If you came around more often, you would know that. But you don't come around anymore, do you?"

"What are you saying, Patience?" His eyes narrowed, and she could read the concern in his expression. "That we're supposed to be sworn enemies just because our people aren't speaking?"

"Our *people*?" She shook her head, agitation setting in. "Don't you mean our *families*?"

"Well, yes, but the lawsuit involves a lot more people than just your family."

"And yet, you took it on, knowing my pa would be named in it. And my grandmother. How could you, Gil?"

"I told you, I didn't have a choice. My uncle—"

"Pulls the strings and you snap to attention." She paused as heat filled her cheeks. "Yes, I know. He's the most important attorney in the county, and you're proud to be working for him."

"Well, I—"

Heat washed over her cheeks as embarrassment set in. "I'm sorry, Gil. I didn't mean that. This whole thing has me very—"

"Worked up. I know. I feel the same."

An awkward silence grew up between them.

Violet stopped singing, and Patience saw her lift her hand in a friendly wave. She wasn't sure how to respond. These days, even the simplest gesture could be misconstrued. She offered a hint of a smile and a tiny wave...until Florence noticed her. Then she turned back to her cousin. "I think we should go now, Adeline. Let's pay for Granny's baking supplies and get out of here."

"If you say so." Her cousin's gaze was firmly planted on the handsome stranger, who wrapped up payment for his goods.

Patience tugged at her sleeve. "Granny wanted my help with dinner tonight, and I promised. Besides, I need to check on Goldie. She's due to have her puppies any day now, and I want to make sure she's comfortable in the barn. So let's pay for our items and go. Please."

Adeline sighed. "Sure."

"Great to see you," Gil said. "If you change your mind about the caroling—"

"I won't." She turned and headed toward the counter, where she paid for the items they had placed there earlier. Then they gathered their baskets to leave.

When they reached the door, the handsome stranger approached. In true gentlemanly fashion, he held the door open for them and tipped his hat as they walked by.

"Who is that?" Adeline asked as soon as they were outside. "Is he new to town?"

"No idea." Patience glanced back over her shoulder and noticed the man was peering at them through the paned glass in the mercantile door.

"I tried to strike up a conversation with him." Adeline reached into her basket and came out with a stick of candy. She took a bite of it.

"More than *tried*, I'd say."

Adeline offered an exaggerated pout. "Now, don't be like that. I was just being hospitable. He's mighty handsome, wouldn't you say?" She took another bite of the candy.

"Is he?" Patience cleared her throat. "I hadn't noticed."

"Sure you hadn't." Adeline laughed. "I very nearly lost control of my senses when I laid eyes on him. I cannot be held responsible for what happens when I'm under the spell of a handsome young man like that. Can you?"

"It's not something I think about."

"Then why did your cheeks turn such a delightful shade of pink when Gilbert Sutton walked up?"

"They did no such thing."

"Mm-hmm. Sure they didn't. And you weren't glued to his baby blues, either."

"I...well..."

"As I said." Adeline paused and glanced down the street, looking a bit perplexed. "I meant to ask you this earlier, but why is only one side of the street decorated for Christmas?"

"The Suttons couldn't seem to get in the Christmas spirit, I suppose you could say. We Cochrans did our part." Patience shifted the basket to her other arm and kept walking.

"Oh, I see." Adeline gave the decor a closer look. "Well, that's sad. Why didn't you just decorate the whole thing, then?"

"Pa said we should give them the benefit of the doubt. He thought if we did half, they might do the other."

"But they didn't."

"No, but that's life in Cut and Shoot for you, at least these days."

"I still can't get over the name you all have given this once fair town." Adeline shook her head. "'Cut and Shoot'? Sounds ominous."

"Well, after what we've been through, it's fitting. But the name was actually just an expression from Ernest on the day of the big feud."

Adeline looked intrigued by this idea. "Are you telling me your eight-year-old brother named the town by accident?"

"Yes. In his haste to leave the terrifying scene going on at the church, he said he was going to cut around the corner and shoot through the bushes in a minute."

"My goodness. And such a silly little phrase stuck?"

"Yes. Though, to be honest, I've heard more outsiders use it than locals. I don't think folks here want to be remembered for the one day that drove us apart."

"Understandable." Adeline reached into her bag for a handkerchief, which she used to cover her nose as dust from the road blew into their faces. She pulled the handkerchief away and said, "I simply don't understand people who kick up a fuss and then refuse to forgive one another."

"It's more complicated than that, Adeline."

"But doesn't the Bible say we should offer forgiveness?"

How could she explain that some situations required more time and effort to get there?

They passed a man with a matted, shaggy beard and dirty, long hair. His clothes were in need of a good washing, and his boots were worn almost through. Patience's heart twisted as their eyes met. He coughed and kept moving, diverting his gaze to the far side of the street.

Adeline clutched Patience's arm and whispered, "Who is that man? Do you know him?"

"No." She shook her head. "But I heard there was a drifter in town. Jeb, the foreman at the mill, said he's been stealing from folks. Jeb said we should watch out for him."

"That's terrible! What has that awful man stolen?"

"One of Granny's pies, for one thing."

"What?" Adeline tightened her grip on Patience's arm. "Are you saying he's been on the family's property?"

Patience's gaze shifted back to the man, who shuffled down the road, moving toward the meetinghouse. "We think so. Granny set her pies out for the sawmill workers yesterday afternoon and one of them went missing before they got there. Jeb is sure it was the drifter. He was on our property earlier."

"Why?"

"Who knows. Maybe hoping for a job?"

"What kind of pie did he steal?"

"Apple."

Adeline sighed. "That's my favorite."

"It's everyone's favorite. No one tops Granny Cochran when it comes to apple pie." Patience lowered her voice as she watched Gil, Violet, and Florence leave the mercantile, headed toward his car. She turned back to face her cousin. "But don't tell the Suttons. There's an ongoing feud between Florence and our grandmother over that."

"I've never tasted one of Florence's pies, but I can't imagine anyone would come close," Adeline said. "It's a shame that awful man took off with the pie before the workers could eat it."

"Agreed." Her gaze traveled behind them once again to the man, who hobbled, hunched over, down the road. She only hoped he would hop on board the next train and leave Cut and Shoot once and for all, before something even worse happened.

Gilbert watched as Patience and Adeline walked down the street in the direction of her family's home, just a few blocks away. Should he offer them a ride? No doubt Patience would turn him down. She seemed very out of sorts today. Not that he blamed her, of course. The lawsuit had driven an even larger wedge between the townspeople, and he was at the very center of that, though he had little to do with the feud.

"Gil, can you help, please?" He looked back to see his grandmother trying to juggle her basket while attempting to open the passenger door of his Model T.

"Coming, Grandma. Sorry." He raced to her side of the car and opened the door, then took the basket from her and put it in the rear.

He diverted his gaze to the Cadillac Touring Car that buzzed by with Daniel Jennings behind the wheel. He knew the man from Conroe and didn't trust him as far as he could throw him. Daniel's over-the-top articles for the *Tribune* were nearly as salacious as those dime novels Patience seemed to be interested in.

"Was that a Cadillac?" his grandmother asked from her spot in the passenger seat.

"Yes, ma'am."

"My goodness, I've heard such stories about them." She pulled her coat a bit tighter to ward off the cold. "They don't require a crank to start?"

"No, ma'am." Which served as his cue to move to the front of his vehicle to crank his Model T into motion. Seconds later the Walkaround's engine sprang to life.

Violet climbed into the rumble seat, and Gilbert climbed into the driver's seat. They were soon on the road, headed to the family's property on the south side of town.

"I feel so special, tooling down the street in a Walkaround. No one else in town has one." Violet giggled as she waved at a friend standing in front of the post office with her mother. She let out a gasp. "Gil, slow down! I want Margaret to see me. She'll be green with envy."

"Is that the goal here?" he asked. "To make people green with envy?"

"Of course. Honk the horn, please!"

He obliged, grabbing hold of the rubber ball and giving it a squeeze until a honk rang out.

Violet leaned out of the open window and hollered, "See you tonight, Margaret!"

Violet's friend turned to face them, her mouth falling open at the sight of the car moving down the road. Violet made quite the production out of greeting everyone who happened by, but Gilbert shifted his gaze back to the road, his thoughts still in a whirl after his run-in with Patience. Clearly, she was angry with him. That much was evident. And he didn't blame her. Not really. Besides, what could he do this late in the game? Nothing would change the past, so why even bother?

A Note from the Editors

We hope you enjoyed another exciting volume in the Love's a Mystery series, published by Guideposts. For over seventy-five years Guideposts, a nonprofit organization, has been driven by a vision of a world filled with hope. We aspire to be the voice of a trusted friend, a friend who makes you feel more hopeful and connected.

By making a purchase from Guideposts, you join our community in touching millions of lives, inspiring them to believe that all things are possible through faith, hope, and prayer. Your continued support allows us to provide uplifting resources to those in need. Whether through our online communities, websites, apps, or publications, we strive to inspire our audiences, bring them together, comfort, uplift, entertain, and guide them.

To learn more, please go to guideposts.org.

Find more inspiring stories in these best-loved Guideposts fiction series!

Mysteries of Lancaster County
Follow the Classen sisters as they unravel clues and uncover hidden secrets in Mysteries of Lancaster County. As you get to know these women and their friends, you'll see how God brings each of them together for a fresh start in life.

Secrets of Wayfarers Inn
Retired schoolteachers find themselves owners of an old warehouse-turned-inn that is filled with hidden passages, buried secrets, and stunning surprises that will set them on a course to puzzling mysteries from the Underground Railroad.

Tearoom Mysteries Series
Mix one stately Victorian home, a charming lakeside town in Maine, and two adventurous cousins with a passion for tea and hospitality. Add a large scoop of intriguing mystery, and sprinkle generously with faith, family, and friends, and you have the recipe for *Tearoom Mysteries*.

Ordinary Women of the Bible
Richly imagined stories—based on facts from the Bible—have all the plot twists and suspense of a great mystery, while bringing you fascinating insights on what it was like to be a woman living in the ancient world.

To learn more about these books, visit Guideposts.org/Shop